THE FIRE OF TONGUES

The Fire of Tongues

ANTÓNIO VIEIRA AND THE MISSIONARY
CHURCH IN BRAZIL AND PORTUGAL

Thomas M. Cohen

Stanford University Press
Stanford, California

Stanford University Press
Stanford, California
©1998 by the Board of Trustees of the
Leland Stanford Junior University
Printed in the United States of America
CIP data appear at the end of the book

Published with the support of
the Camões Institute, Portugal

For Lisa

Acknowledgments

My most lasting debt is to the late Frederick Bowser, a great teacher and friend who advised me throughout my work on this book.

Stanley Rabinowitz shared with me his love of learning and of language when I was a college freshman. For twenty years, he has been as generous a friend as he was a mentor. I owe special thanks to Richard Morse for his inspired intuitions about Ibero-American culture and for guiding me toward many of the themes addressed in this book.

My thanks to John Wirth and George Collier for their careful reading of my dissertation on Vieira at Stanford University, and to Dauril Alden, the late José van den Besselaar, Dain Borges, Sabine MacCormack, Adma Muhana, and José Carlos Sebe bom Meihy for their comments on the manuscript. At Stanford University Press it has been a pleasure to work with John Feneron, Pamela Holway, and Eleanor Lahn, whom I thank for their wise criticism and advice. The University of Wisconsin Press and the Jesuit Historical Institute kindly granted permission to reprint two articles in different form: "Millenarian Themes in the Writings of António Vieira," *Luso-Brazilian Review* 28:1 (1991): 23–46; and "'Who is my neighbor?' The Missionary Ideals of Manuel da Nóbrega," in Joseph A. Gagliano and Charles R. Ronan, S.J., eds., *Jesuit Encounters in the New World: Jesuit Chroniclers, Geographers, Educators, and Missionaries in the Americas, 1549–1767* (Rome: Institutum Historicum Societatis Iesu, 1997), 209–28.

It has been a privilege to write this book at the Oliveira Lima Library, the Luso-Brazilian collection at the Catholic University of America. I warmly thank Elena Bacmeister, Blanche Ebeling-Koning, and María Angela Leal for their many contributions to the library. Thanks also to my colleagues Adele Chwalek, Nelson Minnich, Jerry Muller, Larry Poos, James Riley, Jon Wakelyn, and John Wippel.

The love of my parents, Amy Cohen and the late Saul Z. Cohen, and of my brothers and sisters, Helen, Daniel, Gail, David, and Carolyn, has sustained me through the years. For welcoming me into their families, I am grateful to María Luisa Muñoz-Ledo de Fuentes and the late Valentín Fuentes Lima, and to Andrew Arkin, Mara Linden Cohen, Valentín Fuentes Muñoz-Ledo, Valentina Fuentes Muñoz-Ledo, and Jonathan Schorsch.

My wife, Lisa, and our children, Ricardo, Michaela, Hannah Luisa, and Raphael Avishai, fill my life with their love and teach me the things that matter most.

T.M.C.

Contents

THE FIRE OF TONGUES

Introduction

LOOKING BACK in old age on his life in the Brazilian missions, António Vieira summed up the Jesuit vocation with a striking inversion of biblical imagery. Instead of possessing the tongues of fire with which the Holy Spirit infused the Apostles at Pentecost, he argued, the Society of Jesus possessed the fire of tongues, which Ignatius of Loyola had ignited and his successors had sustained by learning languages to convert the non-Christian peoples of the New World.[1]

Vieira's representation of the Jesuit vocation in terms of the fire of tongues was part of a broader meditation on the relationship between Portugal and its empire. Early in his career, Vieira had recognized a fundamental truth: traditional European distinctions between the metropolitan center and the colonial periphery were an impediment to the imperial enterprise as well as to the missionary one. The subtitle of this book, *The Missionary Church in Brazil and Portugal*, underlines Vieira's effort to create a unified Luso-Brazilian church animated by the New World missions. Brazil presented religious and social problems that were entirely new, particularly the problem of the Indians and their place in colonial society. These problems could not be addressed with any readily accessible European vocabulary. Drawing on Scripture and his own experience, Vieira intuited such a vocabulary for the Portuguese. He then reshaped his theology to accommodate this insight,

---

[1] "And there appeared to them tongues as of fire, distributed and resting on each one of them" (Acts 2.3). Vieira presented his thoughts in a sermon preached in 1688 as a formal exhortation to the Jesuit novices of Bahia on the eve of Pentecost (Vieira, *Sermões*, 8: 514–33). All biblical citations are from the *New Oxford Annotated Bible with the Apocrypha. Revised Standard Version* (New York: Oxford University Press, 1977).

which called for a rethinking of the diffusion of Portuguese power and its exercise but not for any concomitant reevaluation of the imperial enterprise itself.[2] Vieira was effective both as a missionary and as a social thinker because he shared the crown's purposes even as he advanced a wide-ranging critique of secular and religious authority throughout the Portuguese world.

Vieira's criticisms of Portuguese imperial and ecclesiastical institutions were deeply rooted in the pastoral thought of the Society of Jesus in general and of Manuel da Nóbrega, the founder of the Jesuit missions in Brazil, in particular. Under Nóbrega's leadership in the mid-sixteenth century, the Jesuits established a network of missions along the length of the Brazilian coastline; they also developed the missionary theory and practice that shaped the work of their successors until the Society's expulsion from Brazil in 1758. In his letters and treatises, Nóbrega produced a critical analysis of colonial society that included an emotional defense of Indian rights and placed increasing emphasis on the church's mission to the Indians. The development of Vieira's social thought in many respects paralleled that of Nóbrega. Nóbrega defined the debate in Lisbon and Bahia about the nature of the Jesuit enterprise in Brazil, and the basic terms of that debate were still in place when Vieira rose to prominence nearly one hundred years later.

Vieira's life reflects the same reversal of European perceptions of center and periphery that he advocated in his sermons and prophetic

---

[2] Vieira's project was of a piece with the project of accommodation as discussed by Funkenstein in his analysis of interpretations of progressive revelation. See *Theology and the Scientific Imagination*, especially chap. 4, "Divine Providence and the Course of History." See also MacCormack, *Religion in the Andes*. Analyzing the Spanish Jesuit José de Acosta's understanding of the term, MacCormack defines *accommodation* as "a method of expounding Scripture by extending its meaning to topics the scriptural author did not mention and could not have known about. Thus, the vision of devastation and the sun going down at noon that God showed to the prophet Amos referred in a literal sense both to the death of Jesus and to the sack of Jerusalem by the Romans. But by accommodation, the same words could be extended to signify the devastation of Catholic churches during the wars of religion in Europe, even though the prophet did not have these events in mind" (262). The project of accommodation was central to the pastoral and prophetic thought of many of the important exegetes of the Iberian world in the sixteenth and seventeenth centuries. Besselaar refers to this method of interpretation as "discovery exegesis" and "the new exegesis." See Vieira, *Livro anteprimeiro da história do futuro*, ed. Besselaar, vol. 2, *Comentário*, XII, 586–87, 1240; and Thompson, *Strife of Tongues*.

writings. Born in Lisbon in 1608, he moved at the age of six with his family to Bahia, where his father became a clerk in the high court. At fifteen he ran away from home to live in the Jesuit college in Bahia, from which his family tried unsuccessfully to remove him. He entered the novitiate but proved a poor student until he experienced a revelation (*estalo*) during prayer. (Indeed, the term *estalo de Vieira* has passed into the Portuguese language to suggest a sudden, transforming illumination.[3])

The intellectual confidence that sustained Vieira throughout his career dates to this period, as do his literary talents, which his superiors formally recognized when they called on him to write the Jesuits' annual letter to Lisbon in 1626.[4] It was also during his novitiate that Vieira embraced the missionary vocation that would guide him throughout his life. The Jesuits sent him to an Indian village, where he dedicated himself to learning Tupi-Guarani. The special vocation of all Jesuits (particularly the novices) to learn the languages of non-Christian peoples was a duty that Vieira affirmed throughout his writings and mission work.[5]

Despite his early resolve to spend his life in the Brazilian backlands, Vieira was sent at the age of seventeen to teach rhetoric at the Jesuit college in Olinda, Pernambuco. Three years later he was ordered back to Bahia to continue his studies in philosophy and theology rather than proceed to the mission field as he had hoped. The tension between thought and action, between intellectual life and mission work that developed from this time on provided much of the impetus for Vieira's effort to integrate the New World into European consciousness as he moved back and forth between Brazil and Portugal. Both in his

---

[3] Vieira "felt as if something had exploded in his brain. . . . His mind underwent a transformation of which he was conscious" (Azevedo, *História de António Vieira* [hereafter *HAV*], 1: 12). He attributed the revelation to Mary, and his writings (particularly his sermons) reflect his continuing devotion to the Virgin.

[4] Vieira, *Cartas do Padre António Vieira*, ed. Azevedo, 1: 3–74.

[5] Tupi-Guarani, which became known as the *língua geral* in Brazil, was used as commonly as Latin in the Jesuit houses. Azevedo states that Vieira studied the dialects of the African slaves during his novitiate but offers no evidence for this claim (*HAV*, 1: 15). Vieira spoke of *gentios* (gentiles) as the first Christians spoke of *gentes*. He used the word to refer to the non-Christian peoples of America, Asia, and Africa. In the Iberian empires as in late antiquity, pagans and barbarians were considered culturally inferior, while gentiles were culturally other. In his writings that emphasized the primitiveness of the Brazilian Indians, Vieira spoke in cultural rather than strictly religious terms, referring to the Indians as *barbaros*.

work among the Indians and in his sermons in Europe and the colony, Vieira sought to renew the missionary vows he had first made as a novice and to enlist his own personal experience in the service of the imperial enterprise.

Vieira spent most of the decade leading up to the Restoration in 1640 (ending sixty years of Spanish rule) as a missionary in Bahia.[6] Preaching to Portuguese settlers in the city and to black slaves and Indians in the sugar mills and aldeias (Indian settlements established by the Jesuits), he established his reputation as the colony's most gifted orator.[7] Throughout this period, Vieira's pastoral work focused on Brazilian issues, such as slavery and the strengthening of the Jesuit mission system. Despite a certain sympathy for Sebastianism (the popular Portuguese belief that D. Sebastião was the hidden king who would return to restore the nation's independence), Vieira's concerns were local.[8]

Only in 1641, returning to Portugal for the first time since early childhood, did Vieira make the transition from provincial figure to national one. When news of Portugal's independence from Spain reached Bahia, he and his fellow Jesuit Simão de Vasconcelos were selected to convey to D. João IV the loyalty of his Brazilian subjects.[9] This loyalty could not be taken for granted; many people in Portugal questioned the legitimacy of the Bragança family's claim to the throne and continued to await the return of D. Sebastião. In this uncertain political climate, Vieira emerged as one of the foremost exponents of the view

[6] The period between 1627, when Vieira returned to Bahia to continue his studies, and 1635, when he was ordained, remains the most shadowy part of his career. Vieira's surviving writings from this period are limited to five sermons preached between 1633 and 1635 (see ibid., 32).

[7] If Vieira's god was a "god of battles," as Boxer has suggested, he was also a god of mercy, and it is fitting that Vieira's first public sermon was preached to a brotherhood of black slaves at a sugar mill outside the city. See *Sermão XIV do Rosário*, in *Sermões*, 5: 484; Boxer, *A Great Luso-Brazilian Figure*, 12.

[8] Azevedo notes that while in Brazil Vieira displayed little of the "Portuguese feeling" that would characterize his writings of the 1640s.

[9] Simão de Vasconcelos (1597–1671), who shared certain of Vieira's visionary inclinations, would later write the first history of the Brazilian Jesuits, *Crônica da Companhia de Jesus* (1663). Vieira was sharply critical of the book; see Francisco Rodrigues, who defends Vasconcelos (*História da Companhia de Jesus na assistencia de Portugal*, 3, pt. 1, 156).

that Gonçalo Bandarra's prophecies about a hidden king applied not to D. Sebastião but to D. João.[10]

Within two years of his arrival in Lisbon, Vieira had become not only the court preacher but a trusted political and economic adviser to the new king. In the latter capacity, he undertook a series of diplomatic missions throughout Europe that made a lasting impression on him. In 1648, an eight-month sojourn in Amsterdam brought Vieira into contact with the city's Jewish community. His long discussions with the Portuguese-born rabbi Menasseh ben Israel challenged him to develop his nascent views on the relationship between Christianity and Judaism. Menasseh in 1650 would publish a prophetic treatise titled *The Hope of Israel*; Vieira's ideas would fully emerge in 1659 in his own work, *The Hopes of Portugal* (*Esperanças de Portugal*). These ideas were characterized by what the Dutch critic José van den Besselaar calls a "Lusocentric millenarianism" that was distinctly Vieira's own.[11] Vieira continued to refine this millenarian thinking, with an increasing emphasis on its Brazilian element, in his sermons and especially his prophetic writings of the 1660s.

This book takes up Vieira's story in 1653, when he began to link his ideas about Christianity and the conversion of the Jews to the larger problem of the conversion of non-Christian peoples throughout the New World. That year, Vieira was named Superior of the Jesuit missions in the Amazon. The cosmopolitan outlook he took back with him to Brazil has led most writers to conclude that he was never again at home in the circumscribed world of the colony.[12] This study, by contrast, argues that Vieira remained rooted throughout his career in his vocation as a Brazilian missionary. Vieira's view of his vocation was transformed, however, by the failure of the Jesuits' attempts to coexist with the Portuguese settlers of the Amazon.

[10] The Jesuit João de Vasconcelos, writing under the pen name Gregorio de Almeida, was the author of the most famous early defense of the Restoration. See *Restauração de Portugal prodigiosa*, ed. Peres.

[11] Besselaar, "Erudição, espírito crítico e acribia na *História do futuro* de António Vieira," 47. See Vieira, *Esperanças de Portugal* (1659), in *Obras escolhidas*, 6: 1–66; see also Chapter 4.

[12] Azevedo interprets Vieira's return to Brazil as a victory for Vieira's many enemies in Portugal, who had long wanted to remove him from the court (*HAV*, 195). Leite takes the opposite view, albeit while acknowledging Vieira's Portuguese opposition. See *História da Companhia de Jesus no Brasil* [hereafter *HCJB*], 4: 32.

The Society of Jesus was in conflict with Brazil's European settlers for two centuries. The Portuguese rulers frequently called on the Jesuits to administer the system for distributing Indian workers among the Portuguese. Because the control of indigenous labor represented the principal means of accumulating wealth in Brazil before African slaves were introduced, the power granted to the Jesuits transformed them, in the popular imagination, into hated representatives of royal authority.[13] In the Amazon, Vieira was also responsible for bringing under Jesuit control the notorious slaving expeditions the Portuguese were conducting in the backlands, by which the settlers captured Indians for forced labor. The Jesuits under Vieira converted as many as two hundred thousand Indians in the Amazon region, but they could not protect the Indians from a community of settlers that faced a perpetual shortage of labor. After nine years of combating the illegal slave trade and the mistreatment of Indian workers, Vieira and his fellow missionaries were expelled from Maranhão and sent back to Lisbon in 1661. While he did not abandon his pastoral work among the Portuguese, the violent conclusion of his years in the Amazon led Vieira to recast his missionary strategy for Brazil in general and for the Amazon in particular.[14]

[13] African slavery was not widely introduced into the Brazilian Amazon until the mid-eighteenth century. Stuart Schwartz has observed that the settlers' sustained opposition to the Jesuits' secular authority played a central role in the development of a Brazilian colonial identity. Citing the Amazon conflict in which Vieira was involved and other disputes farther south, Schwartz concludes, "It was not only in the military struggle against the Indians but in the political conflict with the Jesuits over control of Indian labor that colonists defined themselves and took their first concerted actions. . . . I would suggest that the localism, independence, isolation, and 'Indianness' of the peripheral colonies were the earliest manifestations of a distinct colonial mentality." See "Formation of a Colonial Identity in Brazil," 27, 32.

[14] Vieira's pastoral agenda in the context of the debate over Indian slavery is described well by Azevedo (*HAV* 1, especially 228). Although he rarely singles out Vieira's missionary vocation as the driving force in Vieira's career, here Azevedo gives it the attention it deserves. In doing so, however, he slights Vieira's ministry to the Portuguese and focuses almost exclusively on his work among the Indians. As a result, Azevedo collapses the time frame of Vieira's mission in the Amazon and makes it appear as if Vieira's missionary strategy did not change over the course of the mission. His analysis of Vieira's ideas during the years in Maranhão suggests that if Vieira shifted his emphasis during this period, he did not fundamentally shift his intent. Azevedo argues that Vieira was at best conditionally willing to compromise with the settlers, and that even this limited compromise was possible only during his first two years in the colony.

Although the conflict between the Jesuit missionaries and the Portuguese settlers over slavery grew increasingly bitter during the second half of the seventeenth century, it did not express any fundamental divergence of the assumptions guiding the two groups.[15] As both his prophetic writings and his pastoral work demonstrate, Vieira never derided or underestimated the importance of the economic forces that drove the empire. Instead, he sought to convince the Portuguese that their economic well-being depended on conducting themselves as Christians, and that only if they treated the Indians as fellow Christians would Brazil prosper.

Like the problem of Vieira's ministry to the settlers, the problem of Indian slavery has not been adequately addressed in studies of Vieira's career. Azevedo's tendency to obscure the developmental stages in Vieira's ministry during the Amazon mission is shared by Luís Palacin, who argues that Vieira recognized as early as 1639 the "impossibility of a good and just colonial government," and believed throughout his career that the colonial system "necessarily corrupts the governors." Palacin notes that the institution of slavery posed a painful dilemma for Vieira, and concludes that ultimately Vieira failed to face the issue squarely, opting instead to preach that divine providence would bring justice to the enslaved. The slavery dilemma, however, permitted a greater diversity of responses than this analysis suggests. Vieira's ideas about slavery changed throughout his career; the argument from divine providence was his first, and he did not systematically sustain it over the long term. Furthermore, Vieira used this argument only with reference to black slavery, and was always more critical of the enslavement of the Indians. Palacin writes nevertheless that "caught between the necessity and the incongruity of slavery and unable either to go against the established order (that is, the rational and moral justification of society itself) or to find a coherent explanation for the existence of slavery, Vieira put off the solution to the life to come" (*Vieira e a visão trágica do barroco,* 20–21, 109).

[15] J. S. da Silva Dias focuses on the partnership between the Jesuits and the crown and suggests that the two partners' purposes were not necessarily shared by the Portuguese settlers. "With regard to Brazil, it is well known that the Jesuits were in accord, at least in principle, with the administrations of Tomé de Sousa (1549–53), D. Duarte da Costa (1553–57), Mem de Sá (1557–72), and their successors until the end of the century. That there was a pact with the governors does not mean, however, that there was a pact with the settlers and those who protected and defended them in the metropolis" (*Os descobrimentos e a problematica cultural do século XVI,* 266–67). The final, elliptical reference to the settlers suggests a divergence between the colonists and the missionaries that Vieira did not accept until late in his career. Silva Dias's characterization of the partnership is sound, however, and may be extended to cover most of the colonial period. The most serious strains in the partnership did not begin to develop until the seventeenth century, partly because the close collaboration between missionaries and governors that characterized the settlement of the Amazon produced problems that did not arise during the colonization of the south.

After the expulsion, Vieira placed ever greater emphasis on what he called the "second effects" by which divine providence allows the negative consequences of human actions to occur while yet guiding the overall outcome of those actions. Vieira developed a missionary strategy and an exegetical style that did not merely accommodate reversals in human history but actually required such reversals to advance the work of conversion.

Two years before the expulsion, Vieira wrote *The Hopes of Portugal*, the prophetic treatise that had begun to take shape in Amsterdam. The work circulated in Lisbon and served as the pretext for his arrest by the Inquisition when he returned to Portugal. During the period he spent under house arrest and in prison (1663–67), he further developed the ideas from *The Hopes of Portugal* in his unfinished millenarian treatise, *The History of the Future* (*História do futuro*). Vieira also produced a learned defense against the charges of the Inquisition in which he reinterpreted traditional Jewish messianism, as well as apocalyptic folk beliefs current in Portugal during the sixteenth and seventeenth centuries.

Vieira's prophetic writings challenged the authority of Lisbon's ecclesiastical hierarchy by placing the missionary enterprise at the heart of the Luso-Brazilian church. Vieira sought to recast the traditional relationship between metropolis and colony by identifying Brazil as the precise place where the words of the Hebrew prophets would be fulfilled, and by arguing that for his Portuguese contemporaries—particularly Portuguese religious—the only ministry that had any value was ministry in the New World.

Following his release from prison, Vieira went into self-imposed exile in Rome, returning in 1681 to Bahia, where he remained until his death in 1697. It was during this period that he preached his Pentecost exhortation on the fire of tongues. Vieira no longer sought to enlist all Portuguese society in the church militant. Instead of working toward the proximate creation of a society of apostles in Brazil, he returned in his later writings to the two entities he believed could still successfully advance the missionary enterprise: the Jesuits and the Portuguese crown.

Vieira's writings can be divided into three general categories: state papers and letters, sermons, and prophetic texts. Critics and historians have focused on his state papers, his letters, and a handful of his most famous sermons. João Lúcio de Azevedo has written the classic biography, as well as many other works that have earned him a central place in Luso-Brazilian historiography.[16] Azevedo seeks a balanced portrait of his subject: while he admires Vieira's courage and honesty, he sees Vieira as an intellectual tyrant whose arrogance was typical of the Portuguese Jesuits. Azevedo, moreover, is more interested in Vieira the politician and publicist than in Vieira the missionary and social thinker. His studies focus on the state papers and letters; only in his introduction to the *História do futuro* and in his work on Sebastianism does he devote any sustained attention to the prophetic writings.[17]

Azevedo provides a dramatic narrative of a career in which Vieira was alternately welcomed into the palace inner circle and hounded out of Lisbon. But the forces that swayed this shifting balance were more complex and less predictable over time than Azevedo's rigid periodization of Vieira's rise and fall can suggest. Thus Azevedo provides a brilliant but limited portrait in which Vieira's interpretation of the New World and its place in Scripture figures merely as one of his many failed projects.

José van den Besselaar has written a series of books and articles focusing on the millenarian and apostolic elements of Vieira's thought that Azevedo ignored or misrepresented. Besselaar's critical edition of the *Livro anteprimeiro da história do futuro* offers the most insightful treatment to date of Vieira's prophetic writings.[18] Hernani Cidade and

---

[16] Azevedo, *HAV*. The only other important biography is that of the eighteenth-century Jesuit André de Barros, *Vida do padre António Vieira* (1746). Although written in the manner of a hagiography, it remains valuable for its emphasis on the missionary orientation of Vieira's career. Barros also collected several of Vieira's previously unpublished texts in the fifteenth volume of the first edition of the *Sermões* (1748).

In a fine summation of Vieira's career, Boxer writes that Vieira was "certainly the most remarkable man in the seventeenth-century Luso-Brazilian world" and expresses regret that English is not among the many languages into which his writings have been translated (*A Great Luso-Brazilian Figure*, 3–4, 29). In a similar vein, A. J. R. Russell-Wood has noted, "It is nothing short of incredible that there is no full-length study in English of António Vieira" or of the other great Brazilian Jesuits, Anchieta and Nóbrega ("United States Scholarly Contributions to the Historiography of Colonial Brazil," 715–16).

[17] These discussions reflect his belief that these writings were an unfortunate "aberration of an elevated spirit." See *História do futuro*, ed. Azevedo, 115.

[18] Vieira, *Livro anteprimeiro da história do futuro*, ed. Besselaar. Among Besselaar's other studies of Vieira and his world are *António Vieira: o homen, a obra, as ideias* (1981) and *O sebastianismo—história sumária* (1982).

António Sérgio analyze several of these texts in their introductions to the *Obras escolhidas*, and Cidade's long biographical introduction to Vieira's sermons on Brazil takes up some of the central elements of Vieira's social thought and its reception by his contemporaries.[19] More recently, Adma Muhana has published important critical editions of unpublished documents from Vieira's Inquisition trial, and Margarida Vieira Mendes has analyzed the full range of Vieira's sermons and prophetic writings.[20]

Vieira has also been well served by a succession of accomplished Jesuit historians.[21] The comprehensive histories of the Jesuits in Brazil and Portugal by Serafim Leite and Francisco Rodrigues are milestones in the historiography of the Society and of the Portuguese Empire. Both writers provide detailed treatments of Vieira's career that draw heavily on Jesuit archival materials. Rather than analyzing individual texts, however, Leite and Rodrigues wrote narratives that underlined Vieira's importance in the Jesuit order and European society as a whole. Their most original research on Vieira, moreover, was published apart from the histories, in articles that prepared the ground for further work on the prophetic writings.[22]

Few of the major interpretations of Vieira's life and writings come

---

The *História do futuro* proper, which comprises the fragments of text that follow the *Livro anteprimeiro*, has received little critical attention except for the edition by Maria Leonor Carvalhão Buescu (1982). For a survey of the critical literature on both parts of the text, see Chap. 4. The literature on Vieira's other prophetic writings is smaller; several years after publishing the *Livro anteprimeiro*, Besselaar noted that a full treatment of the Inquisition defense remained to be written (*António Vieira: o homen*, 137).

[19] Vieira, *Obras escolhidas*, ed. Cidade and Sérgio; Cidade, ed., *Padre António Vieira*, 1: 3–187.

[20] Both of Muhana's edited volumes appeared after this book was completed. See Vieira, *Apologia das coisas profetizadas*; *Os autos do processo*; and Vieira Mendes, *A oratória barroca de António Vieira*, "Vieira no Cabo de Não," and "Comportamento profético."

[21] Among Vieira's Jesuit contemporaries, the most important historians of the Society in Brazil were Vasconcelos (on the founders of the missions) and João Felipe Betendorf (ca. 1628–ca. 1724), a Belgian who served in the Amazon missions after Vieira's expulsion in 1661. His *Chronica da missão dos padres da Companhia de Jesus* remains a standard source on the history of the Amazon in the seventeenth century. See Betendorf, *Chronica*.

[22] Leite, *HCJB*; idem, "O Pe. António Vieira e as ciências sacras no Brasil"; Francisco Rodrigues, *História da Companhia de Jesus na assistencia de Portugal*; idem, "O P. António Vieira: contradicções e applausos."

from Brazil. Instead, the critical literature has been shaped by the concerns of European critics, who emphasize Vieira's cosmopolitan aspect at the expense of his colonial focus. The best-known Brazilian work on Vieira is the polemical attack by the nineteenth-century Maranhense historian João Francisco Lisboa.[23] In recent years, historians and critics such as Sérgio Buarque de Holanda and José Guilherme Merquior have touched on Vieira's work in their studies of Brazilian culture, but only Alcir Pécora, Ivan Lins, Luiz Felipe Baêta Neves, and Luís Palacin have produced monographs.[24]

The primary contribution of these Brazilian scholars (with the exception of Pécora, who focuses on Vieira and the Christian tradition) has been to call attention to the importance of the colonial experience in shaping Vieira's life and writings—a theme that is fundamental to the present study. Throughout his career, Vieira incorporated his Brazilian experience into his interpretation of the missionary church and its progress in the New World. In analyzing the development of Vieira's social thought, therefore, this study emphasizes the dynamism of both his pastoral thought and his view of colonial society. Vieira articulated a vision of apostleship that challenged the Portuguese to live according to a high standard of Christian conduct and, at the same time, responded to the mitigating contingencies of colonial life. Drawing on his experience in Brazil as his most important extrabiblical authority, Vieira argued that the far reaches of the empire were as important as the metropolis itself in realizing the role of the Portuguese: they were to be the successors of the Israelites in completing the universal church.

This study follows a chronological outline. The gradual transforma-

[23] João Francisco Lisboa, *Jornal de Timon e vida do padre António Vieira* (1858).
[24] See especially Pécora's superb analysis of Vieira's sermons, and the brief treatments of Vieira in Buarque's study of colonial images of Brazil and Merquior's survey of Brazilian literature (Pécora, *Teatro do sacramento: a unidade teológico-retórico-política dos sermões de António Vieira*; Buarque, *Visão do paraíso*; Merquior, *De Anchieta a Euclides (breve história da literatura brasileira)—1*). Ivan Lins's study *Aspectos do Padre António Vieira* offers few insights into Vieira's texts; he sees Vieira as a precursor of nineteenth-century liberalism. Palacin (*Vieira e a visão trágica*) offers a suggestive analysis of Vieira's social thought concerning the Brazilian colony, although, like Azevedo, he devotes little attention to the apostolic orientation of Vieira's work. Luiz Felipe Baêta Neves Flores provides useful readings of several sermons of the 1650s, particularly the *Sermão da sexagésima*. See *Imaginação social jesuítica e instituição pedagógica*; and "Palavra, mito e história no *Sermão dos Sermões* do Padre António Vieira."

tion of Vieira's missionary strategy resulted not only from the external constraints of the Jesuits' relationship with the crown and the settlers, but also from the internal logic of the church's progress throughout the New World as the Society completed 150 years of evangelization. Thus, after situating Vieira within the Jesuit tradition in general and Nóbrega's pastoral project in particular, the study analyzes three distinct periods of Vieira's career—his mission in the Amazon, his Inquisition trial, and his last years in Brazil—in an attempt to link the European sojourner to the Brazilian provincial, the imperial strategist to the village priest.

Vieira's biographers and critics tend to focus on his political goals in isolation from his apostolic ones, and thereby allow the reader to forget that Vieira was first and always a priest. Vieira wrote in a religious idiom regardless of the subject. In a body of sermons and other writings accessible to a wide audience, he challenged his contemporaries to draw on Scripture and their own experience to revitalize their belief in the role of the Portuguese nation in postbiblical history. Vieira was both an exemplary exponent of Portuguese social thought and a visionary continuously at odds with the people he sought to enlist in his effort to create a society of apostles. This book attempts to explain Vieira's thought and action in the light of the social and religious values of his day, underscoring the conflict Vieira faced between the ideal of Christian conduct and the improbability of its universal realization.

CHAPTER ONE

Manuel da Nóbrega and the First Jesuits in Brazil

W HEN SIMÃO DE VASCONCELOS set out in the 1650s to write the first history of the Society of Jesus in Brazil, the missionary enterprise in Brazil was already a century old. By recounting the accomplishments of the first generation of missionaries, in particular, Vasconcelos hoped to establish a documentary foundation for the Jesuits' claim to primacy in the Brazilian missions. In the mid-seventeenth century, the crown and many religious still accepted these claims (as D. João III did at the time the Society was founded). The opening words of Vasconcelos's narrative succinctly express both the self-consciousness and the sense of drama that characterized Jesuit writings about the New World.

> I shall write of the heroic mission that the Sons of the Society embraced in order to overcome the power of hell which had ruled the vast Empire of Brazilian Paganism for more than six thousand years. I shall recount the great deeds of these Religious, the regions that they discovered, the backlands they traversed, the enterprises they undertook, the victories they gained, and the nations they subjected, and I shall speak of the fame that was won by the spiritual arms of the Portuese of the Squadron, or Company, of Jesus.[1]

The heroic imagery of this opening passage and the proprietary view of Brazilian history suggest the central theme of the Jesuit missionary enterprise. From the time they arrived, in 1549, the Jesuits claimed not only Brazil but the rest of the non-Christian world as their mission field. For most of the colonial period, moreover, the Portu-

---

[1] Vasconcelos, *Crônica*, 1: 49. Vasconcelos's account ends with the death of Manuel da Nóbrega in 1570.

guese crown supported them in this claim. Four months after settling in Brazil, the Superior of the first group of missionaries, Manuel da Nóbrega, wrote to Simão Rodrigues, the Provincial in Lisbon, "This land is our enterprise, as are the rest of the gentiles of the world."[2] That Nóbrega drew no distinction between the lands of the New World and the non-Christians who inhabited them was characteristic of Jesuit missionary discourse.

Despite the support from their royal benefactors, the Jesuits' relationship with the crown was often strained. The history of the Jesuits in Brazil may best be understood as shaped by efforts on both sides to address the persistent tensions between the missionary enterprise and the imperial one. From the beginning, the Jesuits were influential in shaping crown policy on both religious and civil affairs. The crown relied on the Jesuits to help establish its presence in Brazil, particularly in the Amazon and the southern backlands. By the late seventeenth century, however, the Portuguese empire was in crisis, and the Jesuits were vilified not only in Brazil but also in Asia.[3] The longstanding partnership between the Jesuits and the crown began to break down during the reign of D. Pedro II and had largely disintegrated by the time the Marquês de Pombal came to power in 1750.

The history of the Jesuit order in Brazil may be divided into three periods. The first, 1549 to 1580, applies to the whole colony (rather than to regions within it) more neatly than the two subsequent stages; it marks the period preceding extensive Portuguese settlement in Brazil. The second period, 1580 to circa 1680, corresponds to the beginning and end of the sugar cycle in Brazil. The 1680s brought a decade-long crisis in the sugar industry that adversely affected the Society. The Society owned sugar mills, as well as slaves who worked in them. This period also saw the weakening of the Jesuits' partnership with the crown and a concomitant reduction of the Society's authority in the Amazon mission system.[4] The third period, circa 1680 to 1758, covers the sustained decline of Jesuit influence, in the cities as well as the

[2] Manuel da Nóbrega, *Cartas do Brasil e mais escritos do P. Manuel da Nóbrega*, ed. Serafim Leite, 34.

[3] Dauril Alden provides a detailed analysis of the attack on the Jesuits throughout the Portuguese Empire in *The Making of an Enterprise*.

[4] See Dauril Alden, "Indian versus Black Slavery in the State of Maranhão During the Seventeenth and Eighteenth Centuries"; and Stuart Schwartz, *Sugar Plantations in the Formation of Brazilian Society: Bahia, 1550–1835*.

missions, culminating in Pombal's expulsion of the Society from Portugal, from Brazil, and from the rest of the empire.

The Founding Generation

The first Jesuits in Brazil arrived in Bahia in March 1549 with Tomé de Sousa, the colony's first governor general. The Superior of this group of six missionaries was Manuel da Nóbrega (1517–1570), an unproven preacher from Coimbra who would become the dominant figure in the early history of the Brazilian church. Among the leaders of the founding generation, only José de Anchieta (1534–1597) would achieve comparable importance. He was a gifted linguist and poet, but he lacked Nóbrega's administrative skills and therefore was not called on to make decisions about the fundamental questions of missionary strategy that shaped the first decade of Jesuit activity in Brazil. Anchieta also lacked Nóbrega's university training. He never completed the standard Jesuit curriculum in philosophy and theology, and was admitted to solemn profession (the profession of the three traditional vows of poverty, chastity, and obedience, as well as a special vow of obedience to the pope) "because of his talent and natural gifts."[5]

Nóbrega came from a family that was closely tied to D. João III (1521–1557), whose treasury paid for Nóbrega's university education.[6] His father, Baltasar da Nóbrega, was a judge, and one of his cousins served as chancellor of the realm. Despite successfully reaching ordination and distinguishing himself in canon law at the universities of Salamanca and Coimbra, Nóbrega was denied a position at the Santa Cruz monastery in Coimbra because of a stutter, which would also plague him later in his pastoral work.[7] Nóbrega's first biographer, António Franco, claims that this experience made Nóbrega resolve to leave university life.

[5] Leite, *HCJB*, 8: 16. No adequate biography of Anchieta has been written. The best-known account of his life is Vasconcelos's hagiographical *Vida do veneravel P. Joseph de Anchieta*.

[6] Nóbrega's life, like Anchieta's, has not yet been the subject of a scholarly study; much basic information (including his birthplace) remains unknown. The best survey is Serafim Leite, *Breve itinerário para uma biografia do P. Manuel da Nóbrega*. See also idem, *Nóbrega e a fundação de São Paulo*, and *HCJB*, 2, and 9: 3–14; and the brief biography in António Franco, *Imagem da virtude no noviciado da Companhia de Jesus*, 2.

[7] See Vasconcelos, *Crônica*, 1: 174–75, 184–85.

This is the means that Divine Providence used to take him from the world and make him one of her great servants. He thought to himself that the world had dealt him a blow when he expected honors from it, and he determined to avenge himself and to scorn it, and to put it under his feet.[8]

Although Franco overstates the importance of Nóbrega's failure at Coimbra, he provides the first view of the strand of anti-intellectualism that would become a central feature of Nóbrega's career. As a result of his decision to leave the academy and devote himself to mission work, Nóbrega joined the Society. From his first writings as a preacher in Portugal and throughout his letters and papers in Brazil, Nóbrega did little to disguise his contempt for religious who remained in universities rather than devoting themselves to pastoral work as he had done. Not until Vieira's *Sermão da sexagésima* would another Portuguese religious criticize his colleagues as Nóbrega did, particularly after he arrived in Brazil. The very language and cadences in which Nóbrega stated his message—attacking those who stayed home rather than venturing forth into the New World, demanding sacrifice from the church hierarchy in Portugal—would reappear in the attacks on the hierarchy that Vieira unleashed more than a century later.

Nóbrega served as administrator and spiritual director at the Jesuits' Coimbra college and as an itinerant preacher throughout northern Portugal.[9] At Coimbra, Rodrigues chose him to lead the first Jesuit mission to Brazil.[10] His appointment came at a time when the Portuguese province of the Society was the only one that had sent missionaries outside Europe.[11]

Nóbrega's career in Brazil consisted of two distinct ten-year periods.[12] The first (1549–1559) established him as the key figure in the development of the Jesuits' missionary strategy. From his base in Bahia, Nóbrega created a mission system that ranged from Pernambuco in the

---

[8] Franco, *Imagem da virtude*, 158.

[9] On the Jesuits' early emphasis on itinerant preaching in Europe, see John W. O'Malley, *The First Jesuits*, 15.

[10] Leite, *Breve itinerário*, 44–47.

[11] Portugal was the most successful of the Society's provinces during the founding decades. No other province would send missionaries overseas until three Spanish Jesuits (including Fr. Pedro Martínez, who would be the first Jesuit killed by Indians in North America) were sent to join the expedition of Pedro Menéndez de Avilés in Florida in 1566. See William V. Bangert, S.J, *A History of the Society of Jesus*, 93.

[12] See Leite, Introduction to Nóbrega, *Cartas*, 15–27.

north to São Vicente in the south. During the second period (1560-1570)—with the exception of the 1567 debate with fellow Jesuit Quirício Caxa which led him to write his last defense of the freedom of the Indians—Nóbrega was occupied primarily with administrative duties in southern Brazil, and few of his letters from this period survive.[13] He died in 1570 at the Jesuit College of Rio de Janeiro.

Nóbrega's early writings concerning his own activities and those of the Jesuits under his authority are among the most important surviving documents related to the introduction of formal Portuguese colonization in Brazil. Despite his avowed preoccupation with the Society's mission to the Portuguese settlers, Nóbrega's efforts during that first decade were directed toward converting the Indians. Although he never explicitly rejected the society of the Portuguese or urged his fellow Jesuits to do so (as Vieira later would), Nóbrega's mission work and writings between 1549 and 1559 suggest that soon after his arrival, he decided that the Jesuits would do best, at least in the short term, to relegate their mission to the Portuguese to secondary importance.

Students of the missionary enterprise in Brazil have generally assumed that the Jesuits were determined from the outset to minister primarily to the Indians. The wide acceptance of this view has helped to obscure the Jesuits' protracted effort to define their ministries. The conflicting impulses Nóbrega expresses in his letters provide ample evidence that as the leader of the early colonial church, Nóbrega did not come easily to his decision to focus the work of the Society on ministry to the Indians.

Like other aspects of the Jesuit enterprise at a time when the Society's pastoral ideals and practices were still being defined, the question of who would make up the flock was open. The answer had more immediate and wider-ranging effects in Brazil than in Europe. In both places, the Jesuit emphasis was meant to be on people (both Christian and non-Christian) outside the reach of traditional ministries.[14] But be-

[13] Leite argues that Indian conversion was "fundamental, but subordinated" to political concerns during this period (ibid., 25). For Caxa's argument and Nóbrega's response, see ibid., 397–429.

[14] This emphasis was most forcefully articulated by Jerónimo Nadal, an intimate of Ignatius who bore much of the responsibility for codifying and implementing Ignatius's ideas. O'Malley notes, "one of the most striking features of the early Jesuits is the wide variety of people to whom they ministered, including many of the poor and outcast. . . . For [Nadal] the Jesuit task par excellence was to search for

yond this basic signpost, individual Jesuits were left to accommodate their own goals and pastoral strategies to the particular conditions of the people whom they served.[15] The first Jesuits in Brazil needed to develop a vocabulary for addressing this new, heterogeneous flock. Conveying the received meanings of ideas and institutions that were central to Jesuit ministry was even more problematic than it had been in Europe.[16] In Brazil, not only the Indians but also the European settlers confounded the Jesuits' expectations. On arrival in Bahia, Nóbrega noted skeptically, "we found some sort of church."[17] He was unable to place the skeletal institution he encountered in a familiar definition of the nature and structure of the church.

In his first letter to Rodrigues, Nóbrega wrote that the Indians "have no knowledge of God, nor have they idols. . . . I have tried to put the prayers and some of the words of Our Lord in their language, but I cannot find an interpreter to do it, for they are so barbarous that they do not even have terms [for religious concepts]."[18] Yet Nóbrega ultimately assigned little importance in the conversion process to language barriers or to doubts about the Indians' spiritual capacity. He determined, as he told Rodrigues, that the Jesuits must apply themselves immediately to learning the Indians' languages, and that he expected help in this task from Diogo Alvares, the most famous of the early settlers of Brazil.[19]

As Vieira would later, however, Nóbrega viewed mastery of Indian languages more as a symbol of the Jesuit vocation than as an end in it-

---

the 'lost sheep'—whether pagan, Muslim, heretic, or Catholic" (O'Malley, *First Jesuits,* 73).

[15] The notion of the first Jesuits "taking shape for ministry" effectively conveys the nature of their task. The phrase serves as the title for O'Malley's chapter about the formative period of Jesuit theory and practice concerning the Society's "customary ministries" (*consueta ministeria*) (ibid., 51–90).

[16] O'Malley's observation that "the vocabulary [the Jesuits] inherited was inadequate for the reality they lived, or at least wanted to live" is thus particularly applicable to Brazil. Ibid., 75.

[17] Nóbrega, *Cartas,* 19.

[18] Ibid., 21.

[19] Alvares, who was known by his Indian name, Caramuru, arrived in Bahia in 1513 and married the daughter of an Indian chief. He and his many children established close ties with Nóbrega and the Jesuits and served as intermediaries between the Portuguese and the Indians. See Francisco Adolfo de Varnhagen, *História geral do Brasil,* 1: 125. For an early account that celebrates the adventures of Alvares and the religious devotion of his wife, see Vasconcelos, *Crônica,* 1: 192.

self. The problems that concerned him most were the conduct of the Portuguese (including the clergy) of Bahia and the strength of his fellow Jesuits' commitment to the missions. In concluding his first letter to Rodrigues, for example, Nóbrega wrote, "I only fear the bad example that our Christianity gives them [the Indians], because there are men who have not confessed in seventeen years, and it seems to me that they find their happiness in having many women. I hear shameful things about the priests."[20] Within two weeks of arriving in Bahia, Nóbrega had begun to question the idea that Christians could serve as examples to Indians. It would take more than four years, however, for him to abandon his efforts to bring together Portuguese and Indians for pastoral purposes.

The Letter to the Settlers of Pernambuco and the *Diálogo sobre a conversão do gentio*

While Nóbrega's views on the Indians developed gradually—and sometimes in contradictory directions—during his first decade in Brazil, his grim initial assessment of the Portuguese settlers and of the non-Jesuit clergy continued to inform his pastoral practices and most of his writings. Nóbrega's theory and practice of mission were shaped, however, by his direct experience. Unlike Vieira, who arrived in Maranhão in 1653 already resolved not even to ask in confession about illegal slaves, Nóbrega decided to use his sacramental office as a way to register opposition to the settlers' treatment of the Indians. He also intended to underscore the differences between the Jesuits and the other clergy in the colony.[21]

Nóbrega's most notable efforts to express these concerns were his 1552 pastoral letter to the settlers of Pernambuco and, four years later, the *Diálogo sobre a conversão do gentio* (*Dialogue on the Conversion of the Gentiles*). The pastoral strategy Nóbrega proposes in the letter to the Pernambucans is at odds with that of most of his other writings, particularly the better-known *Diálogo*. Yet the letter and the *Diálogo* are complementary texts, for nowhere in his writings would he make the

---

[20] Nóbrega, *Cartas*, 24. The last line refers to the handful of non-Jesuit clergy who preceded the missionaries in Pernambuco.

[21] See his letters to Miguel de Torres and Tomé de Sousa in Nóbrega, *Cartas*, 293–360.

link between missionary ideals and practice more apparent. Both texts—the first addressed to a contentious group of settlers, the second to Nóbrega's Jesuit intimates—explore the bonds that are possible between disparate groups of people in a colonial society in which secular and religious authority are tenuous. Both texts express Nóbrega's maximum hopes for the unity of the Brazilian colony. But during the four years between the letter and the *Diálogo*, Nóbrega determined to leave behind the letter's meditations on Portuguese society to concentrate on the Jesuits' faltering ministry to the Indians.

From June 1551 to January 1552 Nóbrega lived among the settlers of Pernambuco, and his work there caused him to reflect on the real and potential conflicts between the Jesuits' work among the Indians and their pastoral obligations toward the Portuguese. The pastoral letter was a Pentecost exhortation preached to the settlers by Fr. António Pires after Nóbrega had returned to Bahia.[22] Nóbrega had criticized the settlers with increasing force during the first two years of his mission; now he wished to revive his original pastoral project in Brazil, in which the Portuguese laity were to be partners with the Jesuits in the missionary enterprise.[23] Indeed, he proposed a pastoral project in which the Jesuits were to be followers, not leaders.

In this respect, the letter marks the beginning of a crucial transition in Nóbrega's missionary strategy. During the period following its composition, 1552 to 1556, Nóbrega grew increasingly frustrated with the Jesuits' pastoral work. Although this frustration applied to the Society's work among all sectors of colonial society, Nóbrega became convinced that the Jesuits could minister more effectively to the Indians than to the Portuguese. By the time he began writing the *Diálogo*, his pastoral work had focused on the Indians, and on the singular role that the Jesuits were to play in the conversion process.

The problems of the Pernambuco mission resembled those elsewhere in Brazil: a corrupt secular clergy, illegal slavery, and concubinage. Nóbrega wrote to Rodrigues in 1551 that the settlers might have killed the Jesuits had it not been for the governor's support. But shortly thereafter, writing to the Jesuits in Coimbra, Nóbrega focused on the

---

[22] For evidence about the date and occasion of the letter, see Leite's bibliographical note in *Cartas*, 104.

[23] Baêta Neves's survey of Jesuit missionary work under Nóbrega emphasizes the "laicization" of catechesis. See *O combate dos soldados de Christo na terra dos papagaios*, 115.

missionaries' successes in preaching to the Indians.[24] In these letters Nóbrega expresses wonder that Indians who had been enslaved by Christians frequently traveled long distances to hear the missionaries preach. He thereby makes a claim about Jesuit ministry (as it was presented to the Indians) that is not found elsewhere in his writings: "We tell them that we have come to this land principally for them and not for the white men."[25] This pastoral strategy provides the point of departure for the critical literature about the Jesuits in Brazil. Yet Nóbrega and his immediate successors rarely identified their flock with anything approaching this kind of explicitness. More typically, their writings underline the conflicting demands of their ministries to the Indians and to the settlers during this first generation.[26] Thus Nóbrega reported that the Jesuits had "many friends" among the settlers in Pernambuco, that at least some of the Portuguese had "reformed," and that the settlers had asked him to stay on.[27]

Nóbrega's continuing preoccupation with his ministry to the Portuguese, his recent experience in Pernambuco, and his respect for the

[24] Nóbrega, *Cartas*, 89.

[25] Ibid., 95.

[26] The assumption that the Jesuits' ministry was not centrally concerned with the Portuguese is shared by writers from Serafim Leite, Gilberto Freyre, and Sérgio Buarque de Holanda to Dauril Alden and David Sweet in more recent studies. The casualness with which Leite posits the central goals of the 1549 mission is particularly striking in his introduction to Nóbrega's letters, where he states, "during the first period, without neglecting the whites, the conversion of the gentiles was [Nóbrega's] immediate goal, the principal object of his worries and efforts" (Introduction to Nóbrega, *Cartas*, 15). This formulation (particularly the incorrect claim that the Jesuits' mission to the Indians did not significantly affect their work among the settlers) ignores Nóbrega's frequently expressed preoccupation with the viability of ministering to both Portuguese and Indians (see Leite, *HCJB*, 2: 3, 141). Writers such as Freyre and Buarque (despite their fundamental differences with Leite about the role of the Jesuits in Brazil) have likewise left unchallenged the basic premise that the Jesuits, leaving Lisbon, were not centrally concerned with establishing ministries among the Portuguese in Brazil (Freyre, *The Masters and the Slaves*; Buarque, *Visão do paraíso*. See also Alden, "Changing Jesuit Perceptions of the Brasis During the Sixteenth Century"; and Sweet, "A Rich Realm of Nature Destroyed: The Middle Amazon Valley, 1640–1750"). Baêta Neves is a rare exception to this tendency to ignore the Society's ministries among the settlers, but he understates the increasing level of conflict between settlers and the Society during the first generation of Jesuit mission work. See especially his analysis of the lay and religious participation in the settlement of Brazil as "two complementary faces of the same act of Creation" (O *combate*, 149).

[27] Nóbrega, *Cartas*, 92; Vasconcelos, *Crônica*, 1: 231.

man who held the donatary captaincy of Pernambuco, Duarte Coelho, were the central factors in his decision to write to the settlers after returning to Bahia in 1552.[28]

The unconventional nature of Nóbrega's exhortation is not evident in the letter's opening passages. Nóbrega enjoins the Portuguese to seek confession and apologizes for sending a set of ecclesiastical laws rather than addressing the settlers in person. This no doubt led the Pernambucans to expect that the letter would contain nothing more than a restatement of past pleas for reform. The letter's opening gloss on Pentecost is framed in similar self-deprecating terms, which may have sounded familiar to Nóbrega's listeners of the year before.

> My dear Brother and Father António Pires will speak to you from closer by, and with more charity, than I do in writing. Listen to him, whom I believe the Lord will give a tongue to tell you what I have to say, for He gave many [tongues] of fire to some poor and ignorant fishermen. He will also give [Pires] courage to weep for your sins, together with his own and mine.[29]

This rendering of Fr. Pires as an instrument of the Holy Spirit notwithstanding, Nóbrega's purpose is to identify the settlers themselves—not the Jesuits—as the successors to the Apostles. To do so, Nóbrega takes an approach to the Pentecost lesson that anticipates Vieira's approach in his famous Pentecost sermon of 1688.[30] Speaking to the novices in the Jesuits' Bahia college, Vieira focused on the tongues of fire as a symbol of the Jesuit enterprise, intending to turn his listeners' attention away from society. But where Vieira makes the hard-won knowledge of indigenous languages part of a missionary strategy that would further separate the Jesuits and the Portuguese, Nóbrega focuses on the fire itself (rather than the tongues) in an effort to bind Jesuits and settlers in a shared mission.

This effort is intelligible only if religious and laity share the assumption that economic and ethical norms in the colony are linked, regardless of whether the settlers actually change their treatment of the Indians.[31] Because the Brazilian colony and the missionary enterprise are

---

[28] Nóbrega had recently praised Duarte Coelho in a letter to D. João III (*Cartas*, 99).

[29] Ibid., 109.

[30] Vieira, *Exhortação primeira em vespora do Espírito Santo* (1688), *Sermões*, 8: 514. See Chap. 6.

[31] Baêta Neves, who is often critical of the missionary enterprise, nonetheless emphasizes this point. "Sixteenth-century Christian ideology does not see the

so new, Nóbrega argues, both the Jesuits and the settlers face choices similar to those the primitive church confronted. Nóbrega places the prehistory of Brazil (the time before the arrival of the Portuguese) in a Christian framework, then discerns the workings of divine providence in the colony during his own time.

> And because only from these lands (so forgotten by Our Lord many thousands of years ago) has such a fire not risen up or even been known, I fervently wish that those to whom Our Lord gives it should take great care that it not be extinguished. . . . I wish that you [settlers] might burn with charity in such a way that even the forests might be aflame [with the Spirit]. . . . You are the new seed that the Lord placed and planted in these lands! Who detains you that you reap no fruit worthy to be presented at the table of the Celestial King? These are the principal riches that you must harvest in Brazil.[32]

At no other point in his writings does Nóbrega issue a comparable appeal to the settlers to be partners in the missionary project. Except for the brief introductory reference to Pires, the letter assigns no special status to the Jesuits in fulfilling the New World's evangelical promise. Nóbrega here advances a vision of colonial society that well exceeds the preoccupation with the contingencies of mission life to which necessity and his own temperament had confined him thus far. A century later, Vieira will have a series of similar confrontations with the Amazon settlers. And in opting to withdraw from colonial society, Vieira will look to Nóbrega and his contemporaries as models. As for Nóbrega, the letter to the Pernambucans suggests that he has carefully elaborated a project of coexistence with the settlers, rooted in the apostolic benefits—for the Indians, and by extension for colonial society as a whole—that such coexistence will bring. His inability to implement this project by navigating successfully between the Portuguese and the Indians (particularly in the matter of Indian slavery) would lead him at the end of the decade to condemn the colony's reception of the missionary church and to escalate his attacks on the settlers.

The letter to the Pernambucans concludes with an ambiguous reference to Paul, in which Nóbrega seems to be arguing for the radical

---

agents of production as social groups in conflict; it sees persons who have relationships. . . . The regulation of socioeconomic relations is thus a regulation of the ethical rather than of the economic order." *O combate*, 133.

[32] Nóbrega, *Cartas*, 110.

separation of Christian mission and economic gain. Nóbrega ends, however, with a conciliatory gesture to the Pernambucans, for he also affirms the human differences in the New World that may be apprehended through the lesson of Paul. Alluding to the "varieties of gifts," Nóbrega writes,

> From that small portion distributed by the Holy Spirit, we pass to another great and perfect gift. [The Spirit,] which "bloweth where it listeth" and gave much to the Apostles, also gives to this land its portion. With [the Spirit] wishing, and with you seeking to hear it, I know that you will make joyful the City of God. . . . Now we wait for a Bishop, and also Fathers from the Society, which will help us all.[33]

The exhortation is the consummate expression of Nóbrega's hopes for colonial society. The role of the Jesuits is inserted obliquely in the last sentence, which narrows the focus from a broad meditation on colonial society to the immediate necessities of the mission. The shift is characteristic of Nóbrega, who was solely responsible for the development and execution of the Jesuits' missionary strategy throughout their first decade in Brazil. With his closing words, Nóbrega presents the Society as a collaborator with the Portuguese rather than an obstacle to the settlers' unimpeded use of Indian labor.

The *Diálogo sobre a conversão do gentio* is generally considered "the first work of literature to have been written as such in Brazil."[34] Written in Bahia in 1556–57 after Nóbrega's return from a three-year mission to São Vicente, it contains a strong affirmation of the Indians' spiritual capacities. Nóbrega asserts that the Indians are easier to convert than the pagans to whom the Apostles were sent, and he is encouraged that many Indians in Brazil have embraced Christianity despite having

---

[33] Ibid., 111–12 (quotation from Jn 3.8). Cf. 1 Cor 12.4–7: "Now there are varieties of gifts, but the same Spirit; and there are varieties of services, but the same Lord; and there are varieties of activities, but it is the same God who activates all of them in everyone. To each is given the manifestation of the Spirit for the common good." Leite writes that the four occurrences of the word *City* in the letter are an "index of a specific culture and spirituality, and their first historic manifestation in Brazil" (Nóbrega, *Cartas*, 112, n. 2).

[34] Serafim Leite, Introduction to Nóbrega, *Diálogo sobre a conversão do gentio*, ed. Leite, 7. The *Diálogo* has received little critical attention. Leite's introduction to the 1954 edition remains the most important discussion. Leite argues that the *Diálogo's* central thesis is the comparative aptitude for conversion to Christianity of the Romans and the Brazilian Indians. See also Fred Gillette Sturm, "'Estes têm alma como nós?' Manuel da Nóbrega's View of the Brazilian Indians."

been mistreated by Europeans. These are the only elements of the text that have been analyzed in any depth in the critical literature. Yet Nóbrega's discussion of the Indians' affinity for Christianity is of secondary importance in the *Diálogo*. The central purpose of the text is to present Nóbrega's arguments concerning the role of the Jesuits in colonial society.

The *Diálogo* is, in effect, a long memorandum to Nóbrega's fellow Jesuits. Without the personal and institutional criticisms that run through it, the *Diálogo* would constitute a comparatively minor contribution to the contemporaneous European debate about the Indians' intellectual and spiritual potential. That debate was pursued more systematically within the Society by José de Acosta and by other Jesuits who succeeded Nóbrega in the New World and shared his preoccupation with developing a vocabulary suited to communicating religious ideas to the Indians.[35] Nóbrega's true interests in writing the *Diálogo* lay elsewhere. The fundamental tensions in the Society and the church that Vieira would later identify are already clearly visible in the *Diálogo*, and these tensions would continue to shape Jesuit thought in Brazil well into the eighteenth century.[36]

The first words of the *Diálogo*, like the first words of Vasconcelos's

[35] José de Acosta's 1577 treatise on mission theory and practice, *De procuranda indorum salute*, systematically develops many of the *Diálogo's* central concerns. Acosta was in Lisbon and Coimbra in 1557–58, and his interest in the Jesuits' missionary experience in the Portuguese Empire (particularly Xavier's experience) dates to this time (see book 4, p. 132, n. 298). In this treatise Acosta also makes several references to Brazil; although he does not cite the *Diálogo*, he may have had access to the text or heard a reading of it at one of the Jesuit colleges.

[36] The most notable of those thinkers in the generation after Vieira were André João Antonil and Jorge Benci. Antonil was the pseudonym of João António Andreoni (1649–1716), author of *Cultura e opulencia do Brasil por suas drogas e minas*, an economic treatise that is one of the most important books about Brazil of the colonial period. Benci (ca. 1650–1708), whose occupation is listed as "moralist" in Leite's brief bio-bibliographical essay, wrote *Economia cristã dos senhores no governo dos escravos*, an inquiry into the theory and practice of slavery in Brazil (Leite, introduction to the 1954 edition. See also *HCJB*, 7: 45, 95). For a defense of Benci's arguments, see Leite's introduction to the 1954 edition of *Economia cristã*. For a comparison of Vieira and Antonil that addresses some of the questions discussed here, see Alfredo Bosi, *Dialética da colonização*. Bosi's argument that a division existed within the social thought of the Society—with Vieira and Antonil representing opposite poles—leaves aside the problems that threatened the Jesuits' various ministries (particularly the backland missions) and informed the views of Vieira and Antonil; but Bosi provides a suggestive analysis of the thought of these two Jesuits in its institutional context.

Crônica, lay the foundations for the author's interpretation of Jesuit ministry. In the only passage not spoken by the dialogue's two inter-locutors, Nóbrega offers a veiled apology to his fellow Jesuits: "Because the times have given me a place in which to rest, I wish to speak with my Brothers about what my spirit feels."[37] This uneasiness stems not from the content of his argument but from the act of writing itself, and in the context of the times, it is well founded. It was characteristic of the first generation of Jesuits to encourage letter writing while assign-ing less importance to other written forms. All writing, in turn, was secondary to speech.[38] In the *Diálogo,* moreover, Nóbrega will take this line of reasoning one step further, posing the argument—a rhetorical argument, to be sure, but one that points to his own sympathies—that physical labor is an even higher calling than preaching.

Nóbrega was wary of how a work such as the *Diálogo* would be re-ceived during the Jesuits' first decade in the New World. His writings during the 1550s had focused on the immediate problems of establish-ing the mission; and the *Diálogo,* despite its speculative elements, does not shift that focus. But in presenting a literary work more ambitious in both theme and structure than his letters, Nóbrega found it necessary to explain the origin of his effort. Going on in this passage to describe how the *Diálogo* was fortuitously written after his return to Bahia from the São Vicente mission, Nóbrega thus does more than adopt a stan-dard literary device; he highlights the differences between the condi-tions of literary production in Brazil and Portugal. Ministry was valued over learning in both colony and metropolis, but writing, in the col-ony—even writing about pastoral issues—removed the writer from the exigencies of mission work. For this reason, departures from the stand-ard epistolary form that would have required little justification in Europe needed to be explained in Brazil.[39]

---

[37] *Diálogo,* 1. Line numbers refer to the text as published in Nóbrega, *Cartas,* 215–50.

[38] "In their pastoral activities . . . the Jesuits preferred the spoken word to the written, direct human contact to a page of print" (O'Malley, *First Jesuits,* 115). Nó-brega did not seek to publish the *Diálogo,* which first appeared in the *Revista do In-stituto Histórico e Geográfico Brazileiro* in 1880.

[39] Thus, in the late sixteenth century, the three Jesuit colleges in Brazil (located in Bahia, Recife, and Rio de Janeiro) continued to emphasize preaching and other pastoral skills, and the course in speculative theology was suspended "due to a lack of students, for at that time many contented themselves with only moral theology

Thus, like Vieira, whose millenarian tract *Esperanças de Portugal* took the form of a private letter begun while he was traveling down the Amazon in a canoe, Nóbrega presented his most profound reflections on Jesuit ministry in the form of an in-house instruction. Also like Vieira, Nóbrega sought to reach well beyond his immediate audience.

After the opening apologia, the dialogue begins. Nóbrega's choice of speakers reinforces the practical focus of the text: they are not priests but laymen of limited learning who live and work with the Jesuits. Gonçalo Alvarez, formerly married to an Indian woman, has been preaching to the Indians of Espírito Santo; Mateus Nogueira is a blacksmith who, "although he does not preach with words, does so with works and with hammer blows." It is the unlettered Nogueira (called "blacksmith of Jesus Christ" in the opening section) who speaks for Nóbrega, as his initials suggest. The two men really existed, however; Jesuit documents place them in Brazil during the 1550s and give their occupations. Alvarez is described only as a "layman in the service of the house," but Nogueira's activities are better known. He participated in fighting against the Indians of Espírito Santo, where he apparently was living when Fr. Leonardo Nunes conducted a mission to the captaincy several months after the Jesuits arrived in Brazil. Nunes admitted Nogueira to the Society, and the tools Nogueira traded to the Indians for food helped sustain the Jesuit houses of São Vicente. At Nóbrega's request, Nogueira was formally named a temporal coadjutor of the Society in 1560, the year before he died.[40]

Although the *Diálogo*'s prose makes little attempt at artfulness, the

---

and some abbreviated studies of dogma" (Leite, *HCJB*, 1: 79). It was this educational orientation that Vieira sought to revive in the 1650s.

[40] See Serafim Leite, *Artes e ofícios dos jesuítas no Brasil*, 221–23, and Introduction to Nóbrega, *Diálogo*, 45–47. António de Aldama notes that "the idea of coadjutors," which was first introduced in the 1550 final text of the Society's founding statement of principles, "was a novel element, peculiar to the Society, with nothing like it in any other religious order" (*The Formula of the Institute: Notes for a Commentary*, 99). For a discussion of the complex issue of grades of membership during the first decades of the Society, see O'Malley, *First Jesuits*, 60–61, 77–80, 345–47. Nóbrega concluded early in his mission that crown subsidies and local alms would not sustain the Jesuits and that members of the Society would have to master trades. His later letters produced a running commentary on his differences with Fr. Luis da Grã about how to support the mission. See Nóbrega, *Cartas*, 354–96; and Vasconcelos, *Crônica*, 1: 211.

text has an aesthetic appeal that derives from its direct language, its effective use of uneducated speakers as vehicles for exploring religious and social issues, and the dramatic tension that develops almost imperceptibly from their conversation.[41] The first exchange suggests that the two men agree in their views of the missionary enterprise. "It is too much to work with these [Indians]," Alvarez begins. Nogueira responds that he, too, doubts the Indians' capacity to understand Christianity.[42] Alvarez laments that preaching to the Indians "is like preaching in the desert to stones," and Nogueira expands on the theme.

> As they do not know what it is to believe or to worship, they cannot understand the preaching of the Gospel, since this is founded in making them believe in and worship one God, and in their serving only this God; and as these gentiles worship nothing, and believe nothing, all that you tell them amounts to nothing.[43]

Nogueira continues to criticize the Indians in language that is similar to that of Alvarez, comparing them to the unworthy animals in the Gospel of Matthew. (Although he does not refer explicitly to the attendant threat to the preacher, the lesson for his Jesuit readers is clear.[44]) Alvarez declares that the only effective teaching instrument available to the Jesuits is corporal punishment, and Nogueira offers no immediate objection. Alvarez consoles Nogueira when he asks,

> Is there then no remedy? Shall we exhaust ourselves in vain? Shall I work at my forge night and day, and will my work among [the Indians] give me nothing to bring before Christ when He comes to judge us, so that I may at least endure some of my sins?[45]

[41] The critical literature on the *Diálogo* does not address Nóbrega's rhetorical strategy, particularly the way he develops the differences between the speakers. Leite, one of the few scholars who have written extensively about the *Diálogo*, focuses on the historical context in which the text was written (Leite, Introduction to Nóbrega, *Diálogo*). Sturm seeks to convey something of the text's dramatic quality but misreads Alvarez's opening words as a personal lament (translated as "I've had it!") rather than as a formulation of the central questions of missionary strategy ("'Estes têm alma como nós?'" 74).

[42] Nóbrega, *Diálogo*, 12.

[43] Ibid., 18.

[44] "Do not give what is holy to dogs; and do not throw your pearls before swine, or they will trample them underfoot and turn and maul you" (Mt 7.6); Nóbrega, *Diálogo*, 33.

[45] Nóbrega, *Diálogo*, 81.

Alvarez assures Nogueira that his labors will not be lost. Alluding to Nogueira's work at his furnace, Alvarez equates Nogueira's body with the burnt offerings of the Israelites and tells Nogueira that his sacrifice will be similarly pleasing to God.[46] This emotionally charged evocation underscores one of the central preoccupations of Nóbrega's career as a Jesuit: the relationship between thought and action and, more specifically, between the work of the theologian and that of the pastor. Nogueira's observation that the Indians "have shown few signs of being able to become Christians" begins an exchange that suggests some of the ongoing tensions of the missionary enterprise.

> Alvarez: Of what use to me, then, is my tongue?
> Nogueira: Ha, ha, ha. . . . Do you know why I laugh? Because you ask me of what use is your tongue, for I ask you: of what use is my forge?
> Alvarez: I have already answered this question for you.
> Nogueira: Take the same answer.
> Alvarez: No, for our offices are different, because mine is to speak, and yours is to make.
> Nogueira: Yet there is no difference in the goal, toward which each one of us must give what he can.
> Alvarez: And what is this goal?
> Nogueira: Charity and love of God and neighbor.
> Alvarez: And you, Brother, are you already a theologian?[47]

In reminding Nogueira of the hierarchy that is maintained even in the self-contained Jesuit world of the colony, Alvarez is doing more than merely mocking his companion. The debate about the relative merits of speaking (*falar*) and making (*fazer*) would continue to shape debates about the Jesuit vocation throughout the colonial period. It is Alvarez, not Nogueira, who introduces the suggestion that the words of the lay preacher might not be equal in the eyes of God to the hammer blows of the blacksmith. In keeping with the *Diálogo*'s constantly shifting dramatic tension, Nogueira now assures Alvarez that they are both working toward the same end.[48]

[46] See Lev 1.3–9.

[47] Nóbrega, *Diálogo*, 146.

[48] Diogo do Couto, one of the most famous students of the Portuguese Jesuits in the sixteenth century, also questioned the connection between learning and wisdom in an exchange that echoed Nóbrega's theme. Couto's soldier advises his interlocutors (one a nobleman, the other a steward),

Through the mouths of humble men God often reveals great secrets that he has

The distinction in the *Diálogo* between speaking and making assumed particular importance in the Brazilian context. Nóbrega's initial
hopes of building a church that would include all members of colonial
society were frustrated, as Vieira's would be a century later, by the settlers' demand for unrestricted access to Indian labor. In the years preceding the arrival of Governor Mem de Sá in 1557, Nóbrega's inability
to limit the illegal slave trade led him to begin to seek the physical
separation of Indians and Portuguese, as well as a reduction of the
Jesuits' reliance on the crown's financial support.[49] The art of speaking,
particularly of speaking Portuguese—to the settlers in Brazil or to his
fellow Jesuits in Coimbra—quickly sank to second place in Nóbrega's
pastoral strategy. The type of speech of greatest value to the missionary enterprise was communication with the Indians by learning their
various languages.[50]

---

hidden from the great and the learned. In this there is no higher philosophy
than the truth. The truth, spoken through the mouth of one so small as myself,
produces the same effects that it would have if it were pronounced by one of
the wise men of the land; and in this matter I rely on nothing more than the
truth, which gives voice to the mute and teaches the ignorant (*O soldado prático*,
ed. M. Rodrigues Lapa, 70).

The soldier's words reflect the Jesuit view that learning is a means, not an end. This
view is outlined in the *Formula* and explored in detail in the *Constitutions*. The *Formula* states that Jesuit colleges "are to be dedicated to labor in God's vineyard and
not to the pursuit of scholastic studies" (*Formula*, 15; cf. Mt 20.1: "For the kingdom
of heaven is like a householder who went out early in the morning to hire laborers
for his vineyard." See also Aldama's commentary, in *Formula*, 84). The *Constitutions*
warn of the rigors of Jesuit education and make clear the order's wariness of
would-be religious who seek a comfortable way of life in the Society; in "The instruction of those who are retained in the Society, in learning and in other means
of helping their fellowmen" (part 4), the text explicitly links study to pastoral work,
beginning with the observation in the preamble,

in comparison with others, those who are both good and learned are few; and
even among these few, most of them already seek rest from their previous labors. As a result, the increase of the Society from such men of letters who are
both good and learned is, we find, something very difficult to achieve. . . .
Therefore . . . our procedure will be to admit young men who because of their
good habits of life and ability give hope that they will become both virtuous and
learned in order to labor in the vineyard of Christ our Lord (Ignatius of Loyola,
The Constitutions of the Society of Jesus, ed. George E. Ganss, 308).

[49] For a survey of this period, see Vitorino Nemesio, *O campo de São Paulo: A
Companhia de Jesus e o plano português do Brasil (1528–1563)*.

[50] Nóbrega thus reserves particularly high praise for the gifted Jesuit linguist

The discussion of speaking and making in the *Diálogo* and the question it provokes about his qualifications as a theologian bring a gently ironic response from Nogueira, who thus far has been deferential to Alvarez. Much of what he knows, Nogueira allows, has come from the learned Jesuits who approach him at his forge. Invoking a second biblical passage, the parable of the Good Samaritan, Nogueira explains that he thinks of the Indians as neighbors. Alvarez then questions Nogueira's use of this term.

> Alvarez: Tell me, Brother Nogueira: these people are neighbors?
> Nogueira: It seems so to me.
> Alvarez: For what reason?
> Nogueira: Because I never find myself without them, with their hatchets and scythes.
> Alvarez: And for this reason you call them neighbors?
> Nogueira: Yes, because "neighbors" means people who have drawn near, and they always draw themselves near to me, that I might do for them what is needed. And I do for them as I do for neighbors, making sure that I follow the precept to love my neighbor as myself. I do for my neighbors what I would wish them to do for me, if I were to suffer a similar hardship.[51]

João de Azpilcueta Navarro, nephew of Martín de Azpilcueta Navarro, Nóbrega's professor in canon law at Salamanca. See Nóbrega, *Cartas*, 21. Leite notes the importance of language study among the Jesuits in Europe and in the New World. He concludes, "language is the apt and accessible instrument for the conquest of souls. This is the reason why the Jesuits in Brazil so urged the study of Tupi, the indigenous language" (*HCJB*, 1: 72; cf. Leite, *Breve itinerário*, 26).

[51] Nóbrega, *Diálogo*, 170. See Lk 10.30–37. In looking to the language of the parable, Nóbrega draws on a central element of Jesuit pastoral practice, also found in Ignatius's prayer, at the end of one of the two surviving letters Nóbrega received from him, "that you [missionaries in Brazil] might always be useful instruments of divine providence in order to help your salvation and the salvation of your neighbors" (Nóbrega, *Cartas*, 509). O'Malley places the help of souls at the heart of the Jesuits' understanding of their work, and his criticism of scholarship on the Jesuits provides an apt characterization of the literature on the Brazilian missions. Of the expressions that the Jesuits used to define themselves, O'Malley writes,

> none occurs more frequently in Jesuit documentation—on practically every page—than 'to help souls'. . . . They helped souls through their ministries. . . . Their ministries and how they went about them were quintessential to the Jesuits' self-definition. . . . What the Jesuits did will tell us what they were. This thesis needs to be stressed because, for the Jesuits as well as for other religious groups and institutions in the sixteenth century, scholars have directed their investigations to other issues—to politics, organization, doctrine and theology, ethics, spiritual teachings, social composition and setting. Important though

This exchange is the turning point in the *Diálogo*. Nogueira proposes that the very proximity of the Indians (*proximos*) at once confirms their humanity and defines the missionary enterprise. Put differently, with this play on words Nóbrega's unlettered blacksmith dispatches a set of theological and juridical questions that occupied Bartolomé de Las Casas and his successors for more than a century after the Europeans' arrival in the New World. Instead of looking to learned investigations of the Indian to address the problems of the missionary enterprise, Nóbrega reaches back to Jesus and the Apostles, and rejoices (like Jesus before telling the parable of the Good Samaritan) "that you have hidden these things from the wise and the intelligent and have revealed them to infants." Nóbrega draws on the same series of verses from Luke in an appeal for more missionaries that focuses throughout on the sacrifices that Jesuit ministry in Brazil requires.[52] All Nóbrega's writings in Brazil may ultimately be understood as an effort to create a missionary church rooted in both the pastoral ideal of the gospel of Luke and the specific "way of proceeding" (*modo de proceder*) of the Society of Jesus.[53]

Pastoral Work, 1557-1559

Nóbrega's decision to focus Jesuit ministry in Brazil on the Indians assumes ever greater importance in the letters he sent to Portugal after writing the *Diálogo*. The letters Nóbrega wrote between 1557 and 1559 may be read as a codicil to the *Diálogo*. In these letters, Nóbrega provides a practical gloss on his criticisms of colonial society to the Provincial in Lisbon and vents his frustration to the former governor of Brazil.

The first of these letters, written from Bahia in August 1557 to Fr. Miguel de Torres, who succeeded Rodrigues as Provincial in Lisbon, appears to address the same themes as the letters from São Vicente written the previous year.[54] But after a routine account of the Jesuits'

---

these issues are, they are not ministry, the activity by which the Jesuits largely define themselves (*First Jesuits*, 18).

[52] See Lk 10.2: "The harvest is plentiful, but the laborers are few; therefore ask the Lord of the harvest to send out laborers into his harvest."

[53] On the Jesuits' "way of proceeding," see O'Malley, *First Jesuits*, 8.

[54] Writing about Torres, who was also confessor to the queen, Leite recapitulates the sixteenth-century missionary ethos in language that recalls Nóbrega's own. Leite refers with contempt to Torres's participation in court life and expresses

ongoing work in Bahia, Nóbrega offers a despairing view of the Society's pastoral work among the Portuguese. In a passage about the settlers of Espírito Santo, the letter makes explicit the missionary strategy that until now has been left unstated as the Jesuits have pursued their work among the Indians: "With the [Portuguese] Christians we do little, for we have closed the doors of confession to most of them, and only by a miracle do we find one who is capable of receiving absolution."[55]

The increasing exclusion of the Portuguese settlers, not only from confession but from Jesuit ministry as a whole, provides the framework for Nóbrega's criticisms of the Indians during the same period. He writes that the Indians are "a kind of people whose condition is more like that of wild beasts than of rational men." He laments the Jesuits' inactivity among the Indians with the same refrain he used in reference to the Portuguese: "With the gentiles we also do little [*se fas pouco*], because most of those [Indians] who were in [the Jesuits'] two parishes have fled."[56] But here, more ominously, it is the "evil proximity of the Christians" that has driven the Indians to flee the villages (*aldeias*) the Jesuits created.

> Thus we have no help from the Christians, but rather many hindrances, both from their words and from the example of their lives, teaching many [Indians] nothing but how to rob and commit adultery and fornicate ... which scandalizes the gentiles. We are weary of hearing the gentiles tell us shameful things about the Christians; and it is certain that [the Indians] shame us and seal our lips. We dare not reprove them for their sins, which are much fewer [than those of the Portuguese].[57]

This attack on the settlers is one of the most powerful statements of its kind in the colonial period. Nóbrega indirectly acknowledges a problem he will analyze more and more explicitly during the last two years of the decade. The Indians cannot be converted unless they are "subjected" to Portuguese rule; but the act of subjection brings them into contact with settlers who seek to remove them from Jesuit control

---

skepticism about his ability to understand the exigencies of the missionary enterprise. Leite's acerbic contrast of court intrigues in Lisbon and mission work in Brazil provides as critical a view of the Jesuit hierarchy as he ventures in any of his writings (Introduction to Nóbrega, *Cartas*, 25).

[55] Nóbrega, *Cartas*, 254.

[56] Ibid., 257.

[57] Ibid., 255.

and who are themselves living outside the church. The question of how to subject the Indians while protecting them from the settlers' abuses sometimes led Nóbrega to adopt contradictory views. These views, however, were rooted in the analysis of the Society's ministry to the Indians that Nóbrega began to refine in the *Diálogo*. They are key concepts for making sense of Jesuit pastoral strategies in Brazil during the first decades of the missionary enterprise.

The letter to Torres allows for the use of force against the Indians and notes that the Jesuits may rightfully serve the crown as agents in the subjection of Indians who refuse "the yoke of reason." Nóbrega cites Spanish Peru as an example of the successful integration of Indians into Christian society.[58] He does more than simply recommend Spanish policies: he urges Torres to help him send Portuguese Jesuits to Paraguay, where Spanish settlers had requested them. (Although such an action would no doubt have met opposition from the Spanish crown, it would have presented no jurisdictional problems for the Society, because Ignatius had named Nóbrega Superior in Brazil and "all further regions" of South America.)[59] Torres, however, responded by forwarding criticisms of the plan from the court in Lisbon. As a result, Nóbrega began to doubt the strength of Torres's support for the missionary enterprise in general and his own activities in particular.

Nóbrega's closing reference to the Paraguayan missions conveys, as forcefully as his direct attacks on the settlers, the extent of his disillusionment with the missionary strategy he had pursued until 1557, when he completed the *Diálogo*. The São Vicente mission is failing, he

[58] He also cites the Carijós, with whom the Jesuits had had contact in southern Brazil, as having been successfully "subjected by the Castilians" in the region bordering on Spanish territory. Nóbrega's vague impressions of the church in Peru were formed before the arrival of Viceroy Toledo and the campaigns of extirpation of the second phase of missionary activity. For a periodization of Andean church history that emphasizes the Spaniards' shifting missionary strategies during the early colonial period, see MacCormack, *Religion in the Andes*. Nóbrega is impressed mainly by the Spaniards' success in imposing order. The foundations of this order—the incorporation into colonial society of key elements of the preconquest Inca hierarchy, the civil war that was fought among the Spaniards, and the increasingly violent repression of Inca religion—raise questions about the particular issues Nóbrega addresses in his letters and the larger differences between the missionary strategies available to the church in Brazil and in Spanish America. The level of subjection to which Nóbrega refers in the case of Peru was not achieved in many areas of Brazil until the late colonial period.

[59] Nóbrega, *Cartas*, 257–58, 505; cf. Leite, Introduction, ibid., 25.

writes, because of lack of support from the king or from Martim Afonso de Sousa, who held the donatary captaincy there.[60] Instead of trying to rescue the doomed enterprise, however, Nóbrega proposes to establish new missions in Paraguay.[61] Foremost among the attractions of the Paraguayan missions is the possibility of severing most of the Jesuits' ties to the Portuguese settlers in the south, the region in which Nóbrega had invested his highest hopes for the success of the missions after leaving Bahia with Mem de Sá.[62]

Nóbrega's subsequent letters to Torres contain the same harsh assessments of Indian culture but do not ultimately compromise the view of Jesuit ministry among the Indians that Nóbrega has been developing over the course of the decade. In May 1558, the opening salutation of Nóbrega's report to Torres is the most forceful—and abrupt—in his letters: "First, the gentiles must be subjected and made to live like creatures who are rational."[63] Amid his familiar litany of Indian

[60] Martim Afonso de Sousa has since come to be seen as one of only two successful *donatários*, or lord proprietors, among the original twelve who received land grants from D. João III in 1534. (The other successful *donatário* was Duarte Coelho Pereira of Pernambuco.) The land grants were made "to encourage permanent settlement and better defense from pirates. The lord proprietors who received these grants were required to defend and settle the land at their own expense, to found and charter townships, administer justice, collect tithes, and license sugar mills." Patricia Mulvey, "Donatários," in *Scribner's Encyclopedia*, ed. Tenenbaum, 2: 401.

[61] At the same time, he notes that he lacks the manpower to make even a preliminary investigation of the possibility of removing Jesuits from São Vicente to Paraguay, and that in any case he has delayed action in anticipation of possible opposition from the Portuguese crown. Nóbrega's position was further complicated because Cardinal Henrique had assumed the regency for D. Sebastião on the death in 1557 of the Jesuits' patron, D. João III.

[62] For an account of the Jesuits' continuing battle with the settlers of the south during the late sixteenth and seventeenth centuries, see Boxer, *Salvador de Sá and the Struggle for Brazil and Angola, 1602–1686*. Among the Jesuits' principal supporters during this period were Salvador de Sá; his father, Martim de Sá; and his grandfather, Salvador de Sá (nephew of Nóbrega's ally Mem de Sá, who arrived in Brazil in January 1558). Boxer states,

> It is evident from the complaints of the Jesuits and from the reports of seventeenth-century colonial officials in Brazil and Paraguay, that nearly every able-bodied male settler in the captaincy of São Vicente was liable to be a slave-raider some part of the time, and a reasonably peaceful citizen the rest. All the municipal officials of São Paulo, and even many of the clergy (the Jesuits alone and always excepted), often went on the raids; and the judges who were supposed to stop them were often their chief promoters (p. 18).

[63] Nóbrega, *Cartas*, 270. The letter is dated May 8, 1558, from Bahia. Torres may

sins he emphasizes the continuing practice of cannibalism. While Nóbrega criticizes cannibalism and other Indian practices in his other writings, generally in measured and somewhat formulaic terms compared with his attacks on the settlers and even on his fellow Jesuits, the present letter is an exception. The opening section distinctly shifts his narrative voice. He describes the Indians as the common enemy of the settlers and the Jesuits; as "bestial" and "bloodthirsty." In a striking departure from previous writings, he argues that with the arrival of the colonial administration in 1549, the abuse of the Indians ended, and that it is now the innocent settlers who live in fear. The letter sets forth an uncompromising argument for political subjection and religious coercion.

> These gentiles are of such a quality that they do not surrender willingly, but rather through fear and subjection, as experience has shown. And for this reason if His Majesty wishes to see them all converted he should order that they be subjected and should send Christians throughout the interior and give them the service of Indians who will help them to conquer and rule, as has been done in other parts of the new lands. I do not know how it is permitted that the Portuguese nation, which among all nations is the most feared and obeyed, should suffer along all this coastline, virtually subjecting itself to the most wretched and sad gentiles in the world.[64]

From these general assertions, Nóbrega turns to a specific grievance: the death in June 1556 of Brazil's first bishop, D. Pedro Fernandes Sardinha, who was killed and eaten by cannibals (along with as many as one hundred shipmates) after being shipwrecked between Bahia and Recife en route to Lisbon.[65] Nóbrega calls for the speedy punishment of those responsible for the attack. The apparent impunity with which the bishop and his companions were killed and the implications for the nascent colonial church provide the most convincing explanation for Nóbrega's uncharacteristic harshness toward the Indians in this letter.

Heretofore, Nóbrega has generally treated cannibalism as a cultural rather than a religious problem, repeatedly referring to the need to

---

have been impatient with lapses in correspondence. In the opening passages of the August 1557 letter, Nóbrega states that the personnel changes in Lisbon—not his own failure to report—have caused any breaks in communication. Ibid., 251.

[64] Ibid., 280–81.

[65] See John Hemming, *Red Gold: The Conquest of the Brazilian Indians, 1500–1760* (Cambridge: Harvard University Press, 1978), 82; and Alden, "Changing Jesuit Perceptions," 214. The new bishop would not arrive until December 1557.

transform the Indians' "evil customs." The bishop's death, however, causes Nóbrega to ponder whether the missionary enterprise can move forward in a society in which new converts continue to tolerate cannibalism (particularly when the Jesuits were unable to impose effective punishment). Focusing on the murder of innocent Portuguese (including priests and others, "of such appearance that brute animals would delight in them and would not harm them"), Nóbrega warns that the Jesuits' teachings may finally be ignored even by those Indians among whom the missionaries have had their greatest successes.

> They kill and eat everyone without exception, and no kindness sways them or causes them to abstain from their evil customs. Rather it seems—and experience has shown—that they grow more proud and evil with caresses and good treatment. And the proof of this is that these [Indians] of Bahia, who are well treated and instructed in church doctrine, have grown worse, seeing that those who are evil and guilty of past deaths have not been punished and made humble and subjected with severe treatment.[66]

Nóbrega also refers uncritically here to "legitimate slaves, taken in just war," although he contests the legitimacy of slavery and the conditions for the conduct of war throughout his writings.[67] His comments on the Indians, however, do not finally support the argument of Gilberto Freyre and other writers that contempt for the Indians was characteristic of the Jesuit missionary enterprise.[68] Instead, Nóbrega provides a new gloss on two central themes: the conflict between the settlers and the Jesuits, and the missionary strategies and ultimate goals of the Society in Brazil.

In contrast to his next surviving letter to Torres, which is dated July 5, 1559, and addressed to Torres and the entire Jesuit community in Portugal, the May 1558 letter is for Torres alone. In it Nóbrega experiments with ideas that will appear in the later one, as well as in a companion letter (also dated July 5) to Tomé de Sousa, the former governor

[66] Nóbrega, *Cartas*, 279.

[67] Ibid., 281.

[68] Freyre's attack on the paternalism and "religious imperialism" of the Jesuits is the best-known discussion of this issue. He concludes that the Jesuits were complicit in the "racial and cultural degradation of the aborigines in Brazil" and that the Indians would have fared better had the Franciscans controlled the Brazilian missions (*Masters and the Slaves*, 108–9, 161). Buarque provides a more subtle criticism of Jesuit perceptions of the Indians and the effect of those perceptions on missionary strategies (*Visão do paraíso*, 301–3).

general, who had returned to Lisbon. The 1558 letter is an attempt to gain a kind of balance. Nóbrega does not propose a policy of unrestrained coercion, but he acknowledges more explicitly than ever before the missionaries' dependence on the crown and tries, as Vieira would in the 1650s, to turn this dependence into a virtue. He looks for examples of successful collaborations between the missionary church and the crown; finds them in Paraguay and Peru; and concludes that if he cannot establish this kind of partnership in Brazil, he would prefer to move with his fellow Jesuits to Spanish America or even to India. Nóbrega's attack on the Indians thus occurs in the context of his effort to map out for the Lisbon hierarchy a new pastoral strategy.

Among the innovations he advances is the creation in the colonial administration of a new post, Protector of the Indians, to be held by someone "chosen by the Jesuits and approved by the Governor." In keeping with his preoccupation with Indian attacks on the Portuguese and particularly on the clergy, he states that this official should be charged with the punishment as well as the protection of the Indians. Nóbrega provides a succinct overview of how the colonial administration should proceed in matters concerning the Indians.

> The law which must be given to them is meant to prohibit them from eating human flesh and from making war without the approval of the Governor; to make them have only one wife; to make them dress (for they have much cotton, at least since the arrival of the Christians); to take away their *feiticeiros* [shamans]; to maintain justice among Indians and between Indians and Christians; and to make them live quietly and not move around, unless it is to live among Christians who have lands to support them and Fathers from the Society to instruct them.[69]

Noting that Mem de Sá has done much to impose order among the Indians, Nóbrega asks the crown to reward the governor by strengthening his authority over Indian communities.[70] Under the Mem de Sá regime, Indians were required to live among Christians whenever possible. The principal purposes of this requirement were to make peace among Indian groups that had traditionally been enemies by bringing them together in a single aldeia, and to assist the Society's attempt to

[69] Nóbrega, *Cartas*, 282.

[70] Mem de Sá apparently arrived in Brazil with legislation from D. João III containing the central elements of Nóbrega's program, but this document has not been found (ibid., 283, n. 1). For an excellent discussion of Mem de Sá's Indian policies, see Hemming, *Red Gold*, 139–61.

integrate the Indians from the interior into European society. The Portuguese settlers opposed this effort because they feared that in the absence of traditional rivalries, the Indians would make more powerful enemies.

Nóbrega's decision to lead the effort to integrate Indians and Europeans—an effort that he will soon oppose—underscores the ongoing transformation of his pastoral strategy. The Jesuits' alliances with the Indians have been unstable, and the missionary enterprise has encountered opposition, not only from the settlers but also from among the secular clergy. Nóbrega therefore has come to view Mem de Sá's campaign to force the Indians into aldeias as the only means to incorporate them into the church. Instead of arguing (as he did in the early years) that the best strategy for converting the Indians was to protect them from the settlers, Nóbrega now proposes forcing the Indians to live in close proximity to the Portuguese, albeit under controlled conditions, including a legally mandated role for the Jesuits in the colonial administration. And with few exceptions, Nóbrega's initial vision of a mixed society—in which aldeias would be established near Portuguese communities and the Jesuits would control the distribution of Indian labor—was implemented by the crown throughout Brazil long after Nóbrega had abandoned hope that the settlers could help the missionary enterprise.

If Torres wondered whether Nóbrega's proposals reflected a more hopeful assessment of the relationship between the Jesuits, the crown, and the settlers, his questions were answered when Nóbrega addressed the practical obstacles ahead. Discussing the details of Jesuit administration, particularly the establishment of the aldeias, Nóbrega summarizes the tensions in colonial society.

> I say again that the hatred that the people of this land feel for the Indians is so great that in all things these people consider the Indians to be the enemy of all good, and to be responsible, moreover, for obstructing their own conversion. For I am unable to express to you how the settlers fought Mem de Sá in every way when he tried to bring four aldeias together in one place and several others in another place. In this case it seems to me that what Mem de Sá is doing (and what I and D. Duarte advised) is correct, because otherwise [that is, without consolidating the aldeias] it would not be possible to teach our religion to the Indians or to subject them and put them in order. The Indians are placing themselves under the [Portuguese] yoke with good will, "But this crowd, which does not know the law" or possess mercy or piety, considers that these [Indians] have no souls. They do not

venture what [these souls] have cost, and have no feeling except for what serves their own gain.[71]

Nóbrega sought additional crown legislation to protect the Indians and to codify the Jesuits' role in the colonial administration. By the end of the century, most of Nóbrega's demands had indeed become law in Brazil. The Jesuits' complex relationship with the crown during the early colonial period supports Charles Boxer's conclusion that although "the crown was not absolutely consistent" in upholding its own laws in favor of the Indians, "on the whole . . . it supported the Jesuits in their efforts to protect the natives, and by 1600 it had given the effective control of its aldeias to the Company [sic] which, in turn, contracted with the colonists for the labour of their mission Indians, under certain safeguards."[72] The aldeia system, with all its inherent conflicts between Jesuits and settlers, was still the organizing principle of colonial society when Vieira arrived in Maranhão.

Nóbrega's May 1558 letter to Torres shows that even at the end of his term as Superior, he sought to emphasize the common concerns of settlers and Jesuits. He states that he shared the settlers' fear of increased unity among the Indians until he learned of the successful colonization of Paraguay, where a small number of Spaniards established settlements containing previously warring Indian groups (including the Carijó, who had been fighting the Portuguese in the south).[73] Once again, Nóbrega provides a new gloss on a familiar subject: the quality of the settlers being sent to Brazil. The settlers "want the land ruled and subjected, and they want the service of the Indians, but they want all this to happen without their planting a single mandioca root." The crown therefore either must send a different kind of

---

[71] Nóbrega, *Cartas*, 284–85. D. Duarte da Costa was the second governor of Brazil (1553–57). Hemming expresses admiration for the first Jesuits and for Mem de Sá despite arguing that the former "became obsessed with their personal soul-count" (to the detriment of Indian survival) and that the latter was responsible for a series of bloody military campaigns against the Indians. Emphasizing the collaboration between Mem de Sá and the Society during the governor's "outstanding fifteen-year administration," Hemming concludes, "Although [Mem de Sá] conquered the Bahia Tupinambá, he also tried to stop the indiscriminate slave-raiding that had provoked so many Indian wars" (Hemming, *Red Gold*, 145, 147). The moral in Nóbrega's letter paraphrases the gospel of John: "But this crowd, which does not know the law—they are accursed" (Jn 7.49).

[72] Boxer, *Salvador de Sá*, 125; cf. Leite, *HCJB*, 6: 225–43.

[73] Nóbrega, *Cartas*, 285.

settler—one who is willing to work the land—or provide more material support to Mem de Sá, "who appears in this matter to be illuminated by Our Lord."[74] In addition, Nóbrega asks that the king write to the town council of Bahia prohibiting the settlers from interfering with the Jesuits' work, and states that if this support is not forthcoming, he wants to abandon Brazil and move with his fellow Jesuits to a more viable mission field.

> For if this [mission] continues the way it has until now, I am of the opinion that the Society's college will be dispensable and that we should be given permission to go to Peru or to Paraguay; or if some ship from India should come to this harbor (as has happened every year for the last twelve years) we might go there, for here we will do no good either among the Christians or among the gentiles.[75]

Nóbrega's next letter to Torres demonstrates that he did not continue to pursue the possibility of abandoning the Brazilian missions. This letter, dated July 5, 1559, focuses on certain hopeful signs in the development of the Jesuit aldeias and the immediate prospects for the missionary church. Addressed both to Torres and to the entire Jesuit community of Portugal, the letter is a prototype of the "edifying letters" that Ignatius himself had requested. (Ignatius's 1553 letter to Nóbrega distinguished between *letras de edificación* and private communications.)[76] The edifying letters were generally read aloud in Jesuit refectories at mealtimes, along with passages from the church fathers and other writers.[77] But Nóbrega's public letter also serves as a kind of counterweight to its companion piece, the letter to Tomé de Sousa of the same date. The letter to Sousa is written in an intimate, almost con-

[74] Ibid., 286. The unintended results of some of these efforts would later become clear. As Hemming notes, "Mem de Sá's very successes as governor undermined his protection of the Indians. The colony prospered. With the Governor's crushing victories the colonists lost some of their fear of the Indians" (Hemming, *Red Gold*, 147). This set the stage for more illegal expeditions against the Indians and for the rapid expansion of sugar cultivation in the Recôncavo district of Bahia.

[75] Nóbrega, *Cartas*, 286.

[76] Ibid., 510.

[77] "At the beginning of both [dinner and supper] a chapter was read in the vernacular from a book of the New Testament. At dinner this was followed by a reading from a book chosen by the superior. . . . Edifying letters from 'the Indies' were read when they arrived. Instead of reading, Xavier occasionally had Jesuits from Goa tell each other the stories of their lives and vocations." O'Malley, *First Jesuits*, 358.

fessional style. In contrast, the letter to the Jesuits is a public exhortation that makes reference to the Jesuits' struggle with the settlers only in the course of surveying specific pastoral strategies.

In addressing his fellow Jesuits, Nóbrega credits Mem de Sá for strengthening the missions: "After the arrival of Mem de Sá, the Governor, three churches were built in three Indian villages, and there will be many more if there are Fathers and Brothers to live in them."[78] Yet Nóbrega does not reproach the Coimbra Jesuits for not sending more volunteers; instead, he provides a point-by-point survey of the state of the Brazil mission, aimed at inspiring his listeners to join him in the New World by recounting Jesuit successes there.

The collaboration between Nóbrega and Mem de Sá extended to the governor's campaigns against the Indians of the interior. Nóbrega's account here of the Indians' bloody defeat at Paraguaçu provides one of the few instances in his letters in which the interests of the Jesuits, the crown, and the settlers appear to converge in a military context. The outcome in Paraguaçu, he writes,

> is such a great thing that the Christians of this land never could have wished for or desired so much, for they considered it to be impossible to subject [the Indians]. Nor could they make war in the Indians' Aldeas, because the paths to reach them were full of brush and water and steep hills. . . . Our catechumens from the three villages [created during the Mem de Sá administration] have helped very much. They serve in these wars with great loyalty and diligence, and at their own cost. They already fight in a manner that is different [from that of other Indians], for they go armed with the name of Jesus, and when they leave they commend themselves to God and ask that we pray to God for them. And Our Lord listens to them and to us, for until now He has always given them great victories.[79]

Still, the sense of solidarity that emerges from this account is short-lived. In the letter's opening passages, Nóbrega has stated that the only Indians who continue to pose a problem for the Jesuits are the slaves of the Portuguese, and he has attributed the Indians' opposition to "the neglect of their masters."[80] Now he brings the letter to a sober conclu-

---

[78] Nóbrega, *Cartas*, 295. Within five years of Mem de Sá's arrival in Bahia, approximately 30,000 Indians had come to live in 11 newly established Jesuit aldeias. See Alden, "Changing Jesuit Perceptions," 216.

[79] Nóbrega, *Cartas*, 302.

[80] Ibid., 297.

sion (in the idiom of his previous affirmation of the Jesuits' separation from the Portuguese) by explaining the pastoral consequences of the dispute over Indian enslavement.

> With the Christians of that land we do little, for we have closed the door of confession because of the slaves they hold illegally, and because almost all of them (married and unmarried alike) live in concubinage in their homes with their Indian women. Their slaves, too, live in concubinage. In neither case have any doubts of conscience been shown, and they find Fathers there who are more liberal [than the Jesuits] in granting absolution and who live in the same manner. Even so, I did not fail to preach and to remind them of the law of God last Advent and at Easter and holidays and most Sundays. Only women and poor people who are unable to have slaves are confessed by us.[81]

With this admission, Nóbrega reaffirms the pastoral strategy that he developed during the first years of the mission. "We are waiting," he concludes, "for the bishop to put everything in order."[82] These words contain an element of sarcasm, particularly given Nóbrega's contentious relationship with the first bishop, D. Pedro Fernandes Sardinha. Nóbrega argues in the letter to Tomé de Sousa, moreover, that the future of colonial society will be determined by whether the colonial administration—working not only with the Jesuits but also with the secular clergy—succeeds in its effort to establish order among the Portuguese.

Nóbrega's letter to Tomé de Sousa (one of the last of his surviving letters, and the only one to Sousa) offers a retrospective survey of the church's development in Bahia—the most detailed and intimate survey of his missionary career. It begins on a plaintive note:

> Since I have been in this land, two desires have tormented me always: one, to see that the Christians of these parts be reformed and adopt good customs, and that good seeds that might provide a good example be transplanted to these parts; the other, to see a disposition among the gentiles that will enable us to preach to them the word of God and make them capable of grace and of entering the Church of God, for Christ our Lord also suffered for them. For this reason I was sent to this land with my Brothers, and this was the intention of our most Christian King who sent us. And be-

[81] Ibid., 312. For Nóbrega's first statement of this view, see his 1550 letter from Porto Seguro (ibid., 80).
[82] Ibid., 313.

cause I have seen how both these desires are so little capable of being fulfilled on these shores, Oh how many chalices of bitterness and anguish my
soul has drunk![83]

The two central elements of the Jesuit enterprise in Brazil—ministry to
the Portuguese and ministry to the Indians—receive equal weight
here. It is the Jesuits' failure in the former project that accounts for the
differences between the two letters written on the same day. In his
public appeal to his fellow priests, Nóbrega emphasizes the pastoral
successes among the Indians in an effort to instruct his listeners and
draw them to the mission field. Confiding in Tomé de Sousa, by contrast, Nóbrega is more somber. The failed promise of the 1552 letter to
the Pernambucans—not the difficulties of the mission to the Indians—
informs this letter and accounts for its particular cadences, which recall
those of a classical lamentation.[84]

In recounting to Sousa the history of the colonial church, Nóbrega for
the first time depicts the ministry to the settlers as a project he has ceded
to the bishop and the secular clergy. On arriving in Bahia, he decided on
two strategies: "One was to seek a bishop of the kind you and I hoped for
to reform the Christians. The other was to see the gentiles subjected and
placed under a yoke of obedience to the Christians."[85] Nóbrega has never
before explicitly accepted this division of labor. This letter thereby
shows that Nóbrega and the Jesuits serving under him still wish to be
part of the church's ministry to the Portuguese. Nóbrega insists, however, that the Society set the terms of this engagement.

In the context of the debate over Indian slavery, Nóbrega's quarrel
with the church hierarchy intersects his quarrel with the settlers. Re-
viewing the history of the mission under governors Sousa, Duarte, and
the present regime of Mem de Sá, Nóbrega argues that Sardinha and
the other non-Jesuit clergy in Brazil never accepted their pastoral responsibilities to the Indians.

> With regard to the gentiles and their salvation [Sardinha] took little trouble,
> for he did not consider himself to be their Bishop, and they seemed to him
> incapable of understanding church doctrine because of their brutishness

[83] Ibid., 318.
[84] "I wish to lament [*fazer pranto*] this land," Nóbrega writes in his salutation
(ibid., 317).
[85] Ibid., 318.

and bestiality. He did not consider them to be sheep in his flock, nor did he think that Christ would have considered them as such.[86]

The responsibility for ministry to the Indians thus fell exclusively to the Jesuits, and Nóbrega speculates that D. Pedro's death may have been a divine punishment for his rejection of that task.[87] Nóbrega reserves his harshest criticism, however, for the clergy who own slaves, father children with Indian mistresses, and routinely grant absolution to the settlers for these practices. Recalling words spoken by Tomé de Sousa himself, Nóbrega concludes, "it would have been better for us if [the other priests] had never come here."[88]

With respect to the Portuguese, the central theme of Nóbrega's history is that the settlers encouraged cannibalism and intertribal warfare for the purpose of obtaining slaves. Nóbrega refines his previous criticisms of these practices, arguing that the Portuguese are responsible for the survival of cannibalism, and even that the settlers have engaged in cannibalism themselves to set an example to the Indians. The Indians "are now subjected and fearful and disposed to receive the Gospel," but the settlers are worried by Mem de Sá's success in gathering the Indians into aldeias, "saying that they should be allowed to eat [each other], for in this [practice] lay the security of the land."[89] Nóbrega asserts, moreover, that the Portuguese have introduced an evil—the sale of captives—previously unknown among the Indians.

Those of Porto Seguro and Ilhéus never sold themselves, but the Christians taught them to attack and sell those from the interior (*sertão*) who come to gather salt. It is now customary that those from the coast sell as many of those from the interior as they can, for it seems good to them, this plunder that the Christians have taught them. And because this is the conduct of all [the settlers] I decided to stop hearing their confessions, because no one

[86] Ibid.
[87] Ibid., 319–20. Although Nóbrega had frequently criticized D. Pedro in his letters, this interpretation of his death is offered here for the first time.
[88] Ibid., 321. Nóbrega's survey reveals that his opposition to D. Pedro's pastoral practices and to the corruption of the clergy, not his disinclination to minister to the Portuguese, was what led him to leave the city for São Vicente with Sousa in 1549. "You will well remember that . . . despairing of being able to do anything in this land with the Christians or to reap fruit among the gentiles, I went down the coast with you to São Vicente, letting everything go from my hands and commending Bahia and its Prelate to God" (ibid., 322).
[89] Ibid., 331, 337.

wishes to do what is required in this matter, and they have the other clergy who absolve them and approve of what they do.[90]

Nóbrega observes that even the Portuguese in whom he had placed the greatest trust have been corrupted by colonial society.[91] And yet, in keeping with his longtime pastoral concerns and his present meditative tone, he closes by reflecting on the Jesuit project and his own missionary vocation as a way to make sense of the history of the colonial church.

Two elliptical passages—inserted like parenthetical asides in his larger narrative about slave labor—convey the view of Jesuit ministry that emerges in Nóbrega's later writings. The first passage concerns a dispute with the Bahian administrator and landowner Garcia de Avila. Nóbrega had helped Garcia de Avila to acquire several slaves, on condition that he continue to allow them to receive religious instruction. When this condition was not met, Nóbrega asked that the slaves be removed from Garcia de Avila's plantation. The colonial administration did not comply with this request, but Nóbrega writes that Garcia de Avila "was very offended at me anyway, so that I no longer have him or any other [friend among the settlers], nor do I seek more than the Lord, and reason, and justice (if I might have it)."[92]

By underscoring the contingent nature not only of his relations with the Portuguese but also of the law itself in colonial society, Nóbrega distances himself from the Portuguese without abandoning his ministry among them. His words recall his first surviving letter from Coimbra.[93] Like Vieira, who urged the Jesuits into the backlands and postponed his hopes for the conversion of the settlers to an indefinite point in the future, Nóbrega views the missionary enterprise as something best pursued by religious working in relative isolation, even as the Society continues to rely on its partnership with the Portuguese crown.

The second passage that expresses Nóbrega's changing view of his ministry is a panegyric about the new governor, Mem de Sá. As his history of the mission reaches the present day, Nóbrega's criticisms of the Portuguese grow more pointed. Accompanying these criticisms, however, are Nóbrega's briefly stated hopes for the mission.

[90] Ibid., 327.
[91] Ibid., 342–43.
[92] Ibid., 343.
[93] "I wish not to know what I love, but in all cases only to love Jesus Crucified" (ibid., 2).

Since I have seen this [progress] in the land [under Mem de Sá], I have begun to come back to life. I no longer want to be preoccupied with ethics, or to die; rather I want to give thanks to Our Lord and to praise his mercies and to be happy not about one sinner who repents, but about many who from paganism convert to Christ.[94]

Thus, as he does throughout his writings, Nóbrega moves in this letter from a broad meditation about law and society in Brazil to an intimate expression of the rewards of ministry to the Indians. He renounces both the burden of judgment that has been placed upon him as the founder of the missionary church and the desire for martyrdom that he lamented had eluded him when he told of Sardinha's death. This renunciation is somewhat disingenuous in a letter laced with uncompromising attacks on his fellow Portuguese; but the disingenuousness must be weighed against Nóbrega's effort both to do battle with the Portuguese and to implement the Jesuit commitment "to help souls." Nóbrega focuses here on his own vocation, leaving talk of justice to his interlocutors in Portugal, and assumes in his own right the voice of Mateus Nogueira as imagined in the *Diálogo*. Now Nóbrega seeks to act rather than to speak.

The letter to Tomé de Sousa occupies a place in Nóbrega's correspondence similar to that of the 1694 circular letter to the Conde de Castanheira in Vieira's letters.[95] Nóbrega would send few letters to Portugal during the next ten years, and the letter to Sousa remains the consummate expression of his understanding of Jesuit ministry and of the church in Brazil. Scholars have not yet adequately analyzed Nóbrega's pastoral thought, but Sérgio Buarque de Holanda's treatment of the Jesuits in the context of early colonial perceptions of the Indians offers a fundamental insight: the Jesuits' evaluation of Indian society was not the determining factor in the development of their pastoral strategy in Brazil.[96] In focusing on Nóbrega's criticisms of the Indians, how-

---

[94] Ibid., 335–36. The scriptural allusion is to the parable of the lost sheep (Lk 15.3–7).

[95] See Chapter 6; Vieira, *Cartas*, 3: 661–62.

[96] It is emblematic of the Jesuits' centrality to Buarque's comparative themes that *Visão do paraíso* concludes with a discussion of Nóbrega and the first generation of Brazilian missionaries. Buarque here states a simple truth that received scant attention from previous writers: the Portuguese contributed virtually nothing to the European "idealization of the American Indian," which had gathered full force by the time Nóbrega accompanied Tomé de Sousa to Bahia. Emphasizing the differing views of the Indians advanced by Bartolomé de Las Casas and the Jesuits in Brazil,

ever, Buarque misrepresents him, and ignores the criticism of the Jesuits themselves that is at the heart of the *Diálogo* and the letters.

Unlike the Jesuits in Spanish America, who did not even establish their missions in Mexico until 1572 (6 years after the death of Las Casas and 50 years after the arrival of the Franciscans), the Jesuits in Brazil were the first missionaries in the colony. Despite their conflicts with settlers and the crown, their preeminent role (particularly in the backland missions) was not seriously threatened until late in the seventeenth century. Nóbrega, however, received little material support from the crown during the early years of the mission, and the Jesuits suffered from a chronic lack of personnel. D. João was preoccupied with pursuing the riches of empire in the East, and after his death the nation's future lay in the hands of the unstable D. Sebastião, for whom Cardinal D. Henrique served as regent. Although the appointment of Mem de Sá as governor of Brazil provided the Society with vital political support, the economic and physical obstacles to the Jesuits' ministry were such that the Jesuits remained in precarious circumstances throughout Nóbrega's 21 years in the colony. Had the missionaries in Brazil encountered Indian civilizations like those the Spaniards found in Mesoamerica and the Andes, their missionary strategy and the writings it inspired would have been different. But they did not; and what is striking is not the contempt and frustration that surface with increas-

---

Buarque observes that the persistence of cannibalism and other vices caused the Jesuits to abandon theoretical treatises defending the Indians in favor of the practical demands of mission work.

> That practical activity—the catechization and defense of the Indians—was pursued by the Portuguese Jesuits independent of any good or bad conception that these gentiles might merit from them serves clearly to separate the position of the Jesuits [from that of Las Casas]. The fact that the work of Nóbrega and his auxiliaries on behalf of our Indians proceeded independent of (and despite) the opinions the Jesuits were able to form about them does not discredit—much to the contrary—their efforts (*Visão do paraíso*, 302).

This statement aptly characterizes the first Jesuits' course of action in Brazil, but it ignores the main factors that explain why the Jesuits did not produce more texts defending the Indians. Buarque integrates his interpretation of Jesuit history into his larger argument about the practical bent of the Portuguese who were part of the imperial enterprise: early in the colonization process, the Jesuits adopted an attitude of "disenchanted obstinacy" in their negative portrayal of the Indians. The Jesuits, Buarque concludes, thought like Las Casas but acted like Sepúlveda; and in advocating religious coercion, "it is to be believed that in the gentiles [they] saw much more the 'dirty dog' than the 'good savage'" (ibid., 303).

ing frequency in Nóbrega's work but the conspicuous absence, from the beginning, of the questions that occupied Las Casas.

Nóbrega's most enduring concern emerged in the opening lines of the *Diálogo*, where he chose a blacksmith to speak for him. Mateus Nogueira was an ideal articulation of Nóbrega's vision of colonial society because Nóbrega provided a simple response to the central question facing the first Jesuits in Brazil: "Who is my neighbor?"[97] The *Diálogo*'s instruction about the Indians as neighbors (and the letters that followed) acknowledged the difficulty of reconciling ministry to the Indians with ministry to the settlers. In urging the Society to concentrate on the Indians, Nóbrega laid the foundations for the debate about ministry that was still shaping Jesuit pastoral thought throughout the Luso-Brazilian world when Vieira began his work.

[97] See Lk 10.29.

CHAPTER TWO

A Society of Apostles

T HE PERIOD between the death of Manuel da Nóbrega in 1570 and the arrival of António Vieira at the court of D. João IV in 1641 was notable for an absence of Jesuit missionary theorizing to accompany the Society's rapid growth in Portugal and Brazil. Indeed, it was Vieira himself who, at the age of sixteen, penned the most notable text produced by a Brazilian Jesuit during this period: the famous annual letter from Brazil, in which he wrote not about the missionary church but about the Dutch invasion of Bahia in 1624 and the expulsion of the attackers the following year.[1]

These events, along with the Dutch occupation of Pernambuco from 1630 to 1654, played an important role in mobilizing resistance to the rule of the Spanish Habsburgs in Portugal and the empire. Other contributing factors included the lower classes' longstanding antipathy to the Spanish; the provincialization of the Portuguese nobility; the strength of the Sebastianist movement; shipping losses to the English, Dutch, and French; and Portuguese political aspirations that focused on the Bragança house in general and the duke D. João (the future D. João IV) in particular.[2]

---

[1] Vieira, *Cartas do Padre António Vieira*, 1: 3–74.

[2] Stuart Schwartz has noted that the period of Habsburg rule in the Portuguese Empire has been little studied. The so-called Voyage of the Vassals that led to the recapture of Bahia by the Spanish and Portuguese nobility "was the last great enterprise in the Iberian world in which the traditional feudal obligations and military values of the nobility were effectively mobilized by the crown. . . . The expedition marked a break in the transition of the seventeenth century, a historical moment in the transformation of European society and political organization." See Schwartz, "Luso-Spanish Relations in Habsburg Brazil, 1580–1640," 33, and "The Voyage of the Vassals: Royal Power, Noble Obligations, and Merchant Capital Be-

The growth in size and influence of the Society in Brazil under the Habsburgs was concentrated—like the growth of the colony as a whole—in the sugar-producing regions of the northeast.[3] The exploration and settlement of the peripheral captaincies in the north and south languished far behind that of the plantation zones. By about 1610, European settlers in Rio de Janeiro, under the leadership of the Correia de Sá family, had created a settlement that was safe from Indian attacks; but the region was poor and slow to develop, particularly compared to the prosperous captaincies of Bahia and Pernambuco.[4] São Vicente during this period remained a frontier society dominated by bandeirantes (backwoodsmen who prospected for gold and raided Indian communities for slaves). Decades of Jesuit efforts to enforce crown legislation restricting the enslavement of Indians led in 1640 to the expulsion of the Society from São Paulo and Santos by militant settlers. Settlers in Rio de Janeiro also threatened to drive out the Jesuits.[5]

The Amazon was the fifth great mission field the Jesuits entered in Brazil. Drawing on the lessons of Bahia, Pernambuco, Rio de Janeiro, and São Vicente, the Society sought to institutionalize its partnership with the crown more firmly than before. The missionary enterprise in Maranhão and Pará was, in turn, more carefully regulated by Portuguese administrators than it was elsewhere in Brazil (including other

fore the Portuguese Restoration of Independence, 1624–1640," 748. The subject of Habsburg rule has been inadequately investigated, in relation not only to the Portuguese Empire but also to the metropolis. Despite recent studies by Hespanha, Oliveira, Reis Torgal, and others, important aspects of the period, including messianic and millenarian literature and the roles of the Jesuits and New Christians in the opposition to Habsburg rule, require further research. See António Manuel Hespanha, *As vésperas do Leviathan*; António de Oliveira, *Poder e oposição política em Portugal no período filipino (1580–1640)*; and Luis Reis Torgal, *Ideología política e teoria do estado na Restauração*. Eduardo d'Oliveira França's *Portugal na época da Restauração* remains indispensable, especially for the religious, cultural, and social background of the Restoration.

[3] By the 1620s, Brazil had approximately 50,000 European settlers and 200 sugar mills. Boxer writes that the colony in 1612 "can fairly be described as prosperous," with striking regional variations (*Salvador de Sá*, 17–18). The sugar industry in Bahia and Pernambuco grew rapidly under Habsburg rule and remained generally strong until the 1680s. See Schwartz, *Sugar Plantations and the Formation of Brazilian Society*, 160–64.

[4] Boxer, *Salvador de Sá*, 19–21.

[5] Only the intervention of Salvador Correia de Sá, the Society's perennial patron in the southern captaincies, prevented the Jesuits' expulsion from Rio de Janeiro (ibid., 121–37).

peripheral regions) because its success here was directly linked to the establishment of the colonial administration in the region. One result of this partnership with the crown was that despite the strains that developed between the missionaries and the settlers, the Jesuit aldeias in the north did not experience the persistent attacks that those in the south suffered at the hands of the bandeirantes.

The history of the Jesuits in the Amazon in the seventeenth and eighteenth centuries may be divided into three periods. The period from 1607 to 1638 may be called the prehistory of the Society in the Amazon. The period 1638 to 1686 was the era of Jesuit dominance, ending with the publication by D. Pedro II of the *Regimento das missões*, which broke the Jesuit monopoly in the Amazon missions. The third period lasted from 1686 until the expulsion of the Society in 1759 by the Marquês de Pombal, whose brother-in-law, Francisco Xavier de Mendonça Furtado, had battled the Jesuits as governor of Maranhão.

The Jesuit missions of the Amazon were plagued by conflict from the time the first two missionaries, Padre Francisco Pinto and Padre Luiz Figueira, arrived in Maranhão in 1607. Pinto died in 1609 in an Indian ambush instigated by the French, who sought to increase hostilities between the Portuguese and the Indians.[6] Figueira, however, returned thirteen years later, and became one of the legendary figures of the Brazilian missions.

In the years following Pinto's death, the exploration and defense of the Amazon was conducted by lay captains with little participation by religious. In 1614 Jerónimo de Albuquerque and Diogo de Campos Moreno defeated the French near Ceará and negotiated an uneasy, one-year truce. At the end of that time, the Portuguese induced the French to surrender without a fight, thus bringing to an end French ambitions in the Amazon. In 1617 the Franciscans sent four missionaries to work in Pará, where the crown had placed the order in charge of the missions.[7] In 1621 the State of Maranhão was created as an administrative entity separate from the State of Brazil.[8] The Franciscans faced many of the same problems the Jesuits in the Amazon would confront during the latter half of the century: lack of manpower and money, and opposition from the slave trader turned captain major Bento Ma-

---

[6] Leite, *HCJB*, 3: 9; Mathias Kiemen, *The Indian Policy of Portugal in the Amazon Region, 1614–1693*, 9–10.

[7] Kiemen, *Indian Policy*, 19–20.

[8] Leite, *HCJB*, 3: 104.

ciel Parente and other settlers over the distribution of Indian slaves. The missionaries' clashes with the settlers culminated in the murder of a Franciscan during a settlers' riot in São Luiz in 1637. This event marked the effective suspension of Franciscan mission work in the Portuguese Amazon.[9]

The Franciscans in the Amazon also clashed with the Jesuits throughout the 1620s and 1630s. The most important Franciscan missionary of the period, Fr. Cristovão de Lisboa, accused Luiz Figueira of meddling in the Franciscans' administration of the missions and of treating their Portuguese opponents with excessive leniency.[10] Figueira traveled to Lisbon in 1637 to persuade crown officials to place Indian administration in the Jesuits' hands. His petition was granted, but objections to Jesuit control and the return of the controversial Amazon expedition of Pedro Teixeira delayed his departure for Maranhão until after the 1640 Restoration. D. João IV granted sweeping powers to the Jesuits in the administration of the aldeias, as well as salaries for missionaries and other concessions. Figueira finally set sail in April 1643, but died with twelve of his fifteen Jesuit companions in a shipwreck off the island of Marajó, before reaching Maranhão.[11]

The physical dangers of the environment and the continuing interreligious rivalries kept the Jesuits inactive in the Amazon for the next decade. The Society inevitably became embroiled in national rivalries in the region; at various times their Portuguese enemies accused the Jesuits of being agents of the French, the Dutch, or the Spanish. The potentially disruptive effects of these rivalries were demonstrated by the Jesuit Samuel Fritz, whose travels into disputed areas of the Amazon led to his being detained by the Portuguese on suspicion of spying.[12] The years between Figueira's voyage to Lisbon in 1637 and Vieira's arrival in 1653 thus constituted an "interim period," during which the colonial and ecclesiastical administrations in the Amazon were virtually powerless. For practical purposes, the Portuguese settlers in the state of Maranhão lived in a stateless society.[13] This was the

[9] Kiemen, *Indian Policy*, 44.

[10] Ibid., 36–37.

[11] Ibid., 55.

[12] See Leite, *HCJB*, 3: 7, 345–47; idem, *Luiz Figueira: a sua vida heróica e a sua obra literária*, 60; Kiemen, *Indian Policy*, 9, 55; Samuel Fritz, *Journal of the Travels and Labours of Father Samuel Fritz in the River of the Amazons between 1686 and 1723*, ed. George Edmundson; and Sweet, "A Rich Realm," chap. 7.

[13] Kiemen, *Indian Policy*, 66. As late as the 1660s, the entire state of Maranhão

society that António Vieira confronted when he arrived in Maranhão in 1653 with a set of privileges similar to the ones that D. João IV had granted to Luiz Figueira ten years before.

The Reestablishment of the Jesuit Missions 1653-1655

Until recently, the dominant theme in historiography of the Amazon was the perceived heroic element in the Portuguese project of creating a broad-based society in the region. The Amazon colony was to be, at least in theory, a creation not of the Jesuits alone but of the Portuguese community as a whole. In his introduction to a volume of key documents in Amazon history, Artur César Ferreira Reis observes,

> The incorporation of Maranhão and Amazonia was not a surprise that was brought about, *grosso modo*, by the religious orders. These were official enterprises that included the participation alongside the religious (and with magnificent results) of *sertanistas* [backlanders], settlers, soldiers, and governors, who all showed themselves to be capable of the task that had been entrusted to them.[14]

Ferreira Reis's triumphal paean to the Portuguese empire builders should not obscure his accurate characterization of the social nature of the colonization. He leaves out, however, the preponderant Indian influence on the European settlers.[15] Miscegenation and the settlers' lack

---

contained perhaps seven hundred Europeans (Azevedo, *Os jesuitas no Grão Pará*, 159–60). For a breakdown of this figure in the captaincies of Maranhão and Grão Pará, see Sweet, "A Rich Realm," 90–93. Alden estimates a European population of eight hundred in 1682 ("Indian versus Black Slavery," 73).

[14] Artur César Ferreira Reis, ed., *Livro grosso do Maranhão*, 10.

[15] Stuart Schwartz emphasizes this Indian influence (and the sense of independence that accompanied it) in contrasting São Paulo and the Amazon with the more densely settled regions of Brazil.

> In both São Paulo and the state of Maranhão e Pará, the levels of miscegenation and of Indian cultural impact on the colony were greater than in the plantation zones. With a small European population and constant contact with the Indians, mamelucos in the first generations held a somewhat different position in these peripheral regions. Often they were accepted as Portuguese and, in truth, there was little to distinguish them from the colonists. ... The truculent independence of both São Paulo and the state of Maranhão caused both to be called the 'La Rochelles' of Brazil in the 1660s, and more than one governor accused

of ties to the Lisbon market made for considerable autonomy in the Amazon. Over the course of the colonial period, the settlers proved increasingly ready to do battle with the crown administrators and their Jesuit partners in their efforts to regulate the Portuguese-Indian relationship.

Ferreira Reis, João Lucio de Azevedo, and David Sweet have made important contributions to Brazilian historiography by reconstructing the Amazon's political and economic development during the seventeenth century.[16] Each of these writers has made extensive use of Jesuit sources, especially letters and travel narratives. This study, by contrast, analyzes the issues at stake as the Jesuits returned to the Amazon by focusing on Vieira's sermons. The sermons show more clearly than Vieira's state papers or even his letters that he arrived in the Amazon at a crucial juncture in his own life and the life of the colony.

Pulpit oratory was an important forum for political and religious discussion throughout Europe during the sixteenth and seventeenth centuries.[17] The Portuguese critic Sampaio Bruno has observed that "to be a preacher was the old way of being a journalist, just as to be a journalist is the modern way of being a preacher."[18] Most sermons in sev-

---

them of obeying no law, justice, or holy commandment ("Formation of a Colonial Identity," 30–31).

It was Vieira who compared São Paulo and Maranhão to La Rochelle, a Huguenot stronghold during the religious wars in France. See his April 1654 letter to D. João IV, in *Cartas*, 1: 422.

[16] Azevedo, *Os jesuitas*; Artur César Ferreira Reis, *História do Amazonas*; Sweet, "A Rich Realm." Azevedo also devotes much of the first volume of his biography of Vieira to a discussion of the Amazon missions. See *HAV*, 1: 195–366.

[17] G. Lanson aptly defines preaching as "the living source of public speech" (*Histoire illustré de la littérature française*, 1: 422, quoted in Hilary Dansey Smith, *Preaching in the Spanish Golden Age*, vii). Preaching has only recently begun to receive the scholarly attention it deserves. While the critical literature on English preaching is extensive, the literature on France and Spain is limited and the literature on Portugal even more so. Smith's book, which focuses on ten preachers, is the best study on preaching in the Iberian world. Peter Bayley's *French Pulpit Oratory, 1598–1650* includes a brief but valuable survey of various methodologies for studying sermons. On Portuguese preaching, see Maria de Lourdes Belchior Pontes, *Fr. António das Chagas: um homem e um estilo do séc. XVII*; and the comprehensive studies by João Francisco Marques: *A parenética portuguesa e a dominação filipina* and *A parenética portuguesa e a Restauração, 1640–1688*.

[18] Sampaio Bruno, *Portuenses ilustres*, 2: 333, quoted in Marques, *A parenética portuguesa e a dominação filipina*, 9.

enteenth-century Portugal were intended to reach a wide audience.[19] The baroque period, however, also witnessed a long-running debate in the Iberian world and beyond about the appropriate use of the *concepto predicable* (preaching conceit). Many preachers tried to bring to their sermons the linguistic complexity and wit that characterized the secular literature of the day, such as the reconciliation of apparent opposites. For practitioners of *conceptismo*, entertaining the audience was as important as traditional instruction. Opposing this emphasis on artfulness were those who favored plain speaking and moral edification without *delectatio*. They favored an emphasis on the preacher's natural gifts.[20] An exemplary life—not only erudition—was required for the effective instruction of the flock.

> The infused qualities are the necessary ones, especially all the virtues: much and continuous prayer; the great and living spirit of our Lord; a burning desire to win souls; a supernatural gift for moving, as it is written of Christ our Lord: "mighty in deed and word."[21]

The proponents of plain speaking discouraged preachers from engaging in theology—in the pulpit or elsewhere—because most religious were not adequately trained for theological speculation. Such speculation, moreover, did not advance the pastoral purpose of the ministry of the word, which the Council of Trent defined simply as the teaching of "all that is necessary for salvation . . . leaving aside any useless disquisitions."[22]

Preaching was central to the self-definition of the Society of Jesus. It was the first ministry that the Society's founding documents (the 1539 and 1550 versions of the *Formula*) charged all Jesuits to perform.[23]

---

[19] "If the sermon is to be seen as a banquet of the Word of God," Smith notes, "it ought to be a banquet to which all are admitted (*para todos*—a popular catch-phrase of the secular literature of the age) and from which all receive sustenance fitting to their needs" (*Preaching in the Spanish Golden Age*, 12).

[20] Ibid., 91–93.

[21] Lk 24.19; Francisco Terrones del Caño, *Instrucción de predicadores* (Madrid, 1617), 19, quoted in Smith, *Preaching in the Spanish Golden Age*, 93.

[22] Sess. 5, Cap. 2 (17 June 1546), in Juan Tejada y Ramiro, *Colección de canones de la iglesia española, publicada en latín*, 5 vols. (Madrid, 1849–55), 4: 47–49, quoted in Smith, *Preaching in the Spanish Golden Age*, 138.

[23] Aldama, *Formula*, 3. John W. O'Malley states, "Almost all the other ministries that follow in both [the 1539 and 1550 versions] relate to this one. The subsequent history of the order testifies to the earnestness with which this commitment was

Members of the Society made notable contributions to both sides of the debate over preaching styles. The Spanish Jesuit Baltasar Gracián wrote the seminal text of the *conceptista* school, while Vieira and a number of lesser-known preachers argued for a more direct style.[24] The Jesuit General Mutio Vitelleschi, sympathetic to complaints he received about young Jesuits who adopted *conceptista* mannerisms, recommended that "our preachers preach with more spirit" rather than "with ostentatious display of their language and wit."[25]

Ironically, Vitelleschi's immediate predecessor, Claudio Aquaviva (1581–1618), was one of the few seventeenth-century religious to voice objections to the publication of sermons in the vernacular.[26] Aquaviva was a nonetheless strong proponent of preaching. In the *Ratio Studiorum* (1599), he helped reinforce the importance of preaching in Jesuit education. That year and again in 1613, he also issued instructions on the training of Jesuit preachers.[27] His successor, Gian Paolo Oliva, served as *praedicator apostolicus* at the papal court and was an important exponent of the formal exhortations that had been pioneered by Jerónimo Nadal.[28] Oliva was also a patron of Vieira, and he proposed that Vieira succeed him at the papal court. After leaving Rome and returning to Brazil, Vieira preached the only two exhortations that he ever published.

---

taken and to the attempts to employ both new and traditional ways of fulfilling it" ("Preaching," in *Encyclopedia of Jesuit History*, forthcoming).

[24] See Baltasar Gracián, *Agudeza y arte de ingenio*. O'Malley writes, "the three men most responsible for a simplification or change in style were three men generally considered the greatest preachers the order has produced—Paolo Segneri in Italy, Louis Bourdaloue in France, and António Vieira in Portugal and Brazil" ("Preaching").

[25] Miguel Batllori and Ceferino Peralta, "Baltasar Gracián en su vida y en sus obras," in Gracián, *Obras completas*, ed. Batllori and Peralta (Madrid: Ediciones Atlas, 1969), 1: 157–58, quoted in Smith, *Preaching in the Spanish Golden Age*, 91; see also O'Malley, "Preaching."

[26] In 1604 Aquaviva wrote to the Provincial of Castile, "I have already written to you that it serves no purpose for our men to publish sermons in the vernacular. Now I add that they should not review their sermons until after they have translated them into Latin" (A. Astraín, *Historia de la Compañia de Jesus en la asistencia de España*, 7 vols., Madrid, 1902–25, 4: 15, n. 1, quoted in Smith, *Preaching in the Spanish Golden Age*, 38).

[27] O'Malley, "Preaching."

[28] Ibid. Nadal's exhortations were a central feature of his inspections of Jesuit communities throughout Europe during the early years of the Society. See O'Malley, *First Jesuits*, 64.

Vieira's letters refer several times to Oliva, and though Vieira does not cite Oliva's *Sermoni domestici* or any discussions he may have had with Oliva in Rome concerning preaching styles, Oliva was arguably the decisive influence on the form of these "in-house" sermons.[29]

In Portugal, the death of D. Sebastião in 1578 and the 60 years of Habsburg rule that followed the brief reign of his successor, Cardinal Henrique, created a climate in which preaching on topical subjects found a ready audience. Between 1580 and 1640, a large body of sermons advanced the Bragança claim against Spain. An even larger corpus defended the new dynasty during the Restoration war (1640–1668). Preaching in Portugal served both as an "instrument for the expression of certain collective anxieties" and a means of shaping public opinion.[30] Although the size of the audience is generally difficult to determine, it is clear that sermons were widely diffused in seventeenth-century Portugal, and they played a key role in mobilizing support for independence.[31]

In the New World, preaching became a particularly important means of communication. In isolated settlements such as São Luiz do Maranhão, where the number of literate settlers was small, preaching was the best vehicle available for Vieira to express his differences with the Portuguese. As will be seen, however, it was central to his work in Europe as well. During a 60-year preaching career, Vieira addressed from the pulpit virtually every issue of contemporary concern, from the Dutch invasion of Brazil and the Restoration war to the corruption of church and state in Portugal. The breadth of his subject matter and the ease and immediacy with which he communicated with a large public show that preaching was the foundation of Vieira's work as missionary, pastor, theologian, and politician.

With Vieira's appointment as Superior in Maranhão, the Society began a sustained effort to establish itself in the far north and northwest of Brazil. In leading this effort, Vieira pursued a missionary strategy that sought to convert not only the Indians but also the Portuguese of the backlands (*sertão*). Like Nóbrega, who ministered to the settlers of Pernambuco and appealed to them to lead the Jesuits in the conversion of the Indians, Vieira looked to the creation of a society of apostles.[32]

---

[29] The exhortations were preached to the novices at the Jesuit college in Bahia. See Chap. 6.

[30] Marques, *A parenética portuguesa e a dominação filipina*, x.

[31] Ibid., 5–7.

[32] Vieira's project also resembled in many respects the pastoral project of the

The *Sermão das tentações*

Vieira arrived in Maranhão just before the publication of a royal decree that freed all Indian slaves in the colony. The settlers in the capital city of São Luiz therefore assumed that Vieira was responsible for the legislation. As Mathias Kiemen has observed, "both in Maranhão and Pará . . . it was to be an axiom that whoever controlled the Indians became the target of much opposition."[33] This opposition was never more potent than during Vieira's tenure in the Amazon, nor did it ever fix on a more combative target. Yet Vieira had already decided that during his first two years in Maranhão he would not exercise the full range of powers D. João IV had granted him. In particular, he was willing, in the interest of social peace, to compromise the Jesuit monopoly on the distribution of Indian labor in the colony. During the 1650s, Vieira was at the height of his powers as a preacher. Between the *Sermão das tentações* (*Sermon of the Temptations*) of 1653, preached in São Luiz, and the Lenten sermons of 1655, preached in Lisbon, Vieira began to develop the central elements of his pastoral theory and practice. Taken as a group, his sermons demonstrate that Vieira's pastoral thought changed continuously in the course of his nine years in the Amazon.

Early in his stay in Maranhão, Vieira revealed the conciliatory strategy he had adopted in planning the new missions. He would preach on this strategy in the *Sermão das tentações*. In a letter to the Jesuit Provincial for Brazil, Vieira noted that he had renounced the responsibility for distributing Indian labor "to avoid conflicts in this matter with the Portuguese, whose souls, before those of the Indians, we have come to Maranhão to seek."[34] This is a vitally important statement of Vieira's initial missionary purpose. Vieira restated this argument in his famous 1662 defense of his actions in Maranhão (written immediately after the expulsion from the Amazon), in which he noted that throughout his initial conversations with D. João he had specifically asked that the Jesuits be exempted from any temporal jurisdiction over the Brazilian Indians, so as to avoid the inevitable conflicts with the settlers.

In the year . . . 1649, Father António Vieira tried to restore the Maranhão

---

Andean missionary church. See MacCormack, *Religion in the Andes*, and "The Heart Has Its Reasons."

[33] Kiemen, *Indian Policy*, 35.
[34] Vieira, *Cartas*, 1: 334.

mission. His Majesty ordered that [Vieira] be granted the same provisions that Father Luíz Figueira had been granted, including the administration and instruction of all the Indians. The aforementioned Father [Vieira], however, accepted only the provisions that touched on the instruction of the Indians. He renounced the administration of the Indians, just as he renounced the title of Father of the Christians [*Pai dos Christãos*] ... and the reason the aforementioned Father gave for not accepting this administration was that he wished totally to avoid conflicts with the Portuguese, having been informed how poorly their interests could accommodate justice and freedom for the Indians.[35]

In other words, Vieira wished to assume his post as Jesuit Superior unburdened by the powers that previously had caused tensions in the colony.

In a controversial incident that shows a similar independence from European assumptions about the colonial economy, Vieira took the side of the Brazilian Jesuits in a dispute with their colleagues in Lisbon over the disposition of the estate of Governor Mem de Sá. Vieira's position in this dispute (which dated to 1618, or five years before Vieira entered the college in Bahia whose position he now supported) is an important example of his long-term advocacy of the economic rights of both settlers and religious in Brazil.[36] His frequent attacks on the Portuguese in his sermons and state papers of the 1650s notwithstanding, it was not until the following decade that Vieira began to shift decisively away from ministry to both Europeans and Indians and toward an exclusive preoccupation with the protection of the new converts.

The first action Vieira took in 1653 to ensure the peaceful coexistence of the Jesuits and the Portuguese was to request the suspension of the crown decree freeing the Indians. This request (like Vieira's discussion of the early plans to reestablish the Maranhão mission) was to

[35] Vieira, *Resposta aos capítulos que deu contra os religiosos da Companhia, em 1662, o procurador do Maranhão Jorge de Sampaio,* in *Obras escolhidas,* 5: 240. Sampaio's charges included an account of the Jesuits' public humiliation of two settlers who falsely accused Vieira of raping an Indian woman. For the text of the charges, see "Representação de Jorge de Sampayo e Carvalho contra os padres da Companhia de Jesus, expondo os motivos que teve o povo para os expulsar do Maranhão," in *Documentos para a história do Brasil e especialmente a do Ceará,* ed. Barão de Studart, 4: doc. 267.

[36] Azevedo, *HAV,* 1: 198. For an account of the estate's complex history and the legal battle among the Jesuits (which produced a unique body of documentation on the workings of the plantation economy), see Schwartz, *Sugar Plantations,* Appendix A, "The Problem of Engenho Sergipe do Conde," 488–97.

figure in his response to the settlers, who contended that Vieira had schemed before arriving in Brazil to deprive them of their labor supply. Vieira's claim that he was ignorant of the legislation cannot be taken at face value, but it is clear that he did not intend to enforce the new law on his arrival in São Luiz.[37] Nevertheless, when the legislation was published, the settlers took to the streets and threatened to seize the Jesuit college. It was in response to this near-riot that Vieira preached the *Sermão das tentações*, his first sermon in the Amazon. The sermon was preached on the first Sunday of Lent. Vieira took as his text the devil's words to Jesus in the desert: "All these I will give you, if you will fall down and worship me."[38]

Vieira begins the sermon by situating himself squarely in the colonial milieu while reminding his listeners of the court circles from which he has recently come. He tells the settlers that he takes no satisfaction in coming to the pulpit "to bring displeasure ... to people for whom I wish only pleasures, and all good things." But he wants the settlers to know that while he has no reason to believe that the Portuguese community will not welcome the Jesuits back to the Amazon, he will have recourse to powerful friends in Lisbon if the need arises.

In the sermon's opening passages, Vieira stresses that the settlers themselves had asked him to preach about slavery. He acceded to the request, he says, despite his initial resolve to proceed directly to the aldeias.

> To rise to the pulpit and not speak the truth is to go against duty, against obligation, and against conscience, particularly for me, [I] who have spoken so many truths, and to such great ears. For this reason I resolved to exchange one service to God [his mission to the Portuguese in both Lisbon and São Luiz] for another, and to set out to teach the Indians in those Aldeias.[39]

[37] Azevedo dismisses Vieira's avowal of ignorance (*HAV*, 1: 216). It should be noted that Vieira in his response was as methodical in pointing out his enemies' logical inconsistencies as in reconstructing his own missionary strategy. Even if he had wished to insist that Captain Major Baltasar de Sousa publish the regimento in Maranhão, he points out, someone else would have had to persuade Captain Major Inácio do Rego to publish the same law in Pará. Vieira's rhetorical purpose throughout his *Resposta* is to make Sampaio appear a buffoon as well as a criminal. He sums up his argument by stating, "neither in Portugal, nor at sea, nor in Maranhão did the aforementioned Father [Vieira] have any knowledge of this *regimento* until after it was published in Portugal" (*Resposta*, 194).

[38] Mt 4.9.

[39] Vieira, *Sermão das tentações*, in *Sermões*, 12: 325.

Vieira's abandonment of this resolve was an early example of his wish to minister to the Portuguese and of his willingness to address his accusers' grievances directly instead of seeking to enforce the *regimento* that threatened to increase unrest in the colony. At the outset of his Amazon mission he placed his pastoral responsibilities to the Portuguese before his right to resort to the authority with which the king had invested the Jesuits and him.

As he will do in all his sermons in the Amazon, Vieira assumes the role of the lonely prophet, telling his listeners that divine providence has led him to draw not only on the text from Matthew but also on God's command to Isaiah—"Cry aloud, spare not, lift up your voice like a trumpet; declare to my people their transgression, to the house of Jacob their sins"—to preach on the sins of colonial society.[40] Vieira never abandons his fellow feeling for the *povo* (poor settlers) of Maranhão, in part because he separates their actions from their intentions as he is unable or unwilling to do with the clergy and the rest of the colonial elite. The crown administrators occupy a shifting middle ground in this schema of intention and blame. Vieira creates a seamless connection between Israel and Maranhão, loosely translating God's instruction to Isaiah to warn the Portuguese settlers about the dangers around them.

> There are some men, God says, who seek me every day, and who do many things in my service, and though their sins of injustice are most grave, they live without fear, as if they were in my grace: "As if they were a nation that did righteousness." Do you know, Christians—Do you know, nobility and *povo* of Maranhão—what fast God desires from you this Lent? That you loose the bonds of injustice, and that you let those whom you hold captive and oppressed go free. These are the sins of Maranhão. These are the sins that God sends me to announce to you: "declare to my people their transgression." Christians, God sends me to undeceive you, and I undeceive you on the part of God. You are all in a state of mortal sin. You all live and die in a state of damnation and go directly to hell. Already many [settlers] are there, and you too will soon be with them unless you change your lives.[41]

Vieira takes a fundamentally practical approach to the Lenten lesson. He follows his claim to divine inspiration by setting forth the cen-

---

[40] Is 58.1.

[41] Vieira, *Sermões*, 12: 327; cf. Is 58.2: "Yet they seek me daily, and delight to know my ways, as if they were a nation that did righteousness and did not forsake the ordinance of their God."

tral idea around which the sermon is constructed: Christian conduct need not conflict with economic gain. He argues that Christian apostleship and the accumulation of wealth must be complementary enterprises in Brazil, and that the sins of the Portuguese threaten not only the settlers' individual salvation but also the economic well-being of colonial society as a whole.

In advancing this argument, Vieira shifts stances between the uncritical accomplice and the distanced observer. He identifies himself with the economic interests of his audience to show these Portuguese traders that if they are going to bargain with the devil, they must be sure that their bargain makes good business sense. Instead of presenting himself as the tiresome moralist, he insists that if the settlers are going to sell their souls they should sell them for their full value. The question for both preacher and settlers then becomes, "On what scales shall a soul be weighed?" Vieira's answer provides the key to the sermon, as well as to the mystery of Jesus' temptation in the desert. The soul must be weighed on the scales of the devil himself. The devil offered Jesus the whole world in exchange for his soul. An individual soul, then, is worth more than the world.

In these passages and throughout his first two years in the Amazon, Vieira's pastoral purpose was to make the value of the soul as real to his listeners as the money and land for which they were struggling. Perhaps this is why his sermons of this period are full of question marks. Vieira seems to be giving his listeners every opportunity to explain their sins to him. Having identified himself with his audience so as to help them confront the temptation offered by the devil, Vieira now identifies Jesus with his audience in an effort to make the lesson even more vivid.

> Let us suppose . . . that Christ were not God but a mere man, and so weak that he could and would have fallen into temptation. I ask: If this man had received all the world and become the master of it, and had delivered his soul to the devil, would he have been a good trader [*ficaria bom mercador*]? Would he have made a good deal? Christ himself answered us on another occasion: "For what will it profit a man, if he gains the whole world and forfeits his life?" What does it profit a man to be lord of all the world, if his soul is captive to the devil? Oh what a divine matter to consider![42]

Between 1653 and 1655, Vieira continued to signal his intention to

[42] Vieira, *Sermões*, 12: 321; Mt 16.26.

minister to the Portuguese, even while acknowledging the unprece-dented dilemmas slavery created for the missionaries. Perhaps the most dramatic example of this pastoral strategy was his resolve not to ask about the settlers' ownership of slaves, not even in the confes-sional. Vieira realized, probably before arriving in Maranhão, that just as the legality of slavery in colonial society could not be resolved by standard legislation from Lisbon, the pastoral problems that the insti-tution created in the New World could not be resolved by traditional religious acts, such as the sacrament of penance. Far from a temporary concession designed to ensure the Jesuits' survival in the colony, this policy was a characteristic feature of Vieira's ministry during these years. For Vieira, the New World called for new pastoral ideals and practices.

The process of creating those ideals and practices had been inter-rupted several times since the first Jesuit missionaries arrived in Ma-ranhão in 1607. In reestablishing the Jesuit mission almost 50 years later, Vieira was creating, out of necessity, a set of religious and social guidelines for living alongside the Portuguese settlers of the north. His concession about penance was of a piece with the compromises Nóbrega had made in the south and other Jesuits had made in China at the beginning of the seventeenth century. At no other time in his ca-reer did Vieira attend with such painstaking care to the sacramental is-sues raised by the need to reconcile Christian faith with colonial sur-vival. Thus the Jesuits, he wrote in the *Sermão das tentações,*

> did not have an obligation to ask those who did not confess the sin of slav-ery to talk about it, because we are unable to determine for certain whether a particular penitent is in a state of bad conscience, and because we assume that to try to rouse in the penitent a bad conscience would be of no benefit; and we held that these are the cases in which the church authorities not only excuse the confessors, but actually oblige them not to ask.[43]

Vieira's determination not to ask the settlers about their ownership of slaves represented an abdication of one of the principal elements of Jesuit ministry as it had developed in Europe: the resolution of "cases of conscience." He was willing to make such a concession and to explain it directly to his Provincial because, during his first years in Maranhão, he assigned as much or greater importance to his min-

[43] *Sermões,* ibid., 328.

istry among the Portuguese as he did to his mission to the Indians.

The critical literature on the Jesuits has provided an accurate picture of the order's systematic attempt to accommodate the settlers' economic interests, particularly just after the missionaries returned to the Amazon. Although the Jesuits frequently argued before crown administrators (and the court in Lisbon) on behalf of Indians who had been unjustly enslaved, the Society resolved to avoid sustained confrontations with the settlers in the Amazon because this would prevent the attainment of "greater goods."[44] This position became increasingly untenable, however, with the legal ransoming by the Portuguese of *índios de corda* (Indians captured and held hostage by their enemies). This practice promoted intertribal warfare and prevented the missionaries from gaining the Indians' trust (*índios de corda* were the only captives the Portuguese could legally enslave). Nóbrega had argued in the 1550s that the legal status of these Indians was questionable, because Portuguese slavery laws effectively encouraged Indians to take captives for ransom. Much of the modern debate about the Jesuits and slavery in colonial Brazil hinges on whether the writer views distinctions such as these as useful tools for analyzing colonial politics, or simply as props the Jesuits used to defend the colonial order in general and the institution of slavery in particular.[45]

During the first year of the Amazon mission, Vieira saw that the Portuguese *entradas* (official expeditions) into the backlands in search of slaves could not be effectively placed under Jesuit supervision, as the law required. In a famous letter, Vieira informed the king of the continuous Portuguese abuses and the Jesuits' inability to exercise their legal mandate.[46] Vieira recognized, however, that his protests were futile. By the time the king could respond with new legislation, for example, a new spate of problems would arise.

In an excellent analysis of the development of Portuguese Indian policy during the first three years of the Maranhão mission, Serafim Leite writes that the law moved from "total liberty" (the first 1653 law) to "disguised slavery" (following the settlers' rejection of the *regimento*

[44] Leite, *HCJB*, 4: 122. Kiemen has similarly observed, "Vieira and the Jesuits gave the benefit of the doubt in Indian matters to the colonists wherever they could" (*Indian Policy*, 101).

[45] For the latter view, see Freyre, *Masters and the Slaves*; and José Honorio Rodrigues, "António Vieira, doutrinador do imperialismo português."

[46] Vieira, *Cartas*, 1: 306–15; cf. Azevedo, *HAV*, 1: 219.

and the crown's formal withdrawal of the law). Vieira advocated a third course of action, which Leite calls "impeded slavery," whereby a fragile equilibrium might be established. But the initial failure of this endeavor prompted Vieira to decide, late in 1654, to return to Portugal to persuade D. João IV and his court to provide him with legislation designed to withstand the settlers' opposition.[47] Equally important, Vieira hoped to bring back to Maranhão a governor who would enforce such legislation.

The *Sermão da sexagésima* and the Lenten Sermons

Vieira produced a torrent of sermons following his return to Lisbon in 1655. As soon as he arrived, he went to the royal chapel to preach the *Sermão da sexagésima* (Sermon for Sexagesima Sunday), the title paragraph of which reads, "This sermon was preached by the Author in the year 1655 when he came from the Maranhão Mission, where he found the difficulties that are recounted in it. When these difficulties had been overcome he returned immediately to the same Mission."[48] He selected it as the first text to appear in his collected sermons, and it is the sermon for which he is best known today.[49] In addition, Vieira preached a series of seven Lenten sermons in 1655 that have received comparatively little attention.[50] These sermons express even more accurately the complexity of Vieira's pastoral concerns as they developed during his sojourn in Lisbon.

Vieira chose the occasion of his return to court to launch an unsparing attack on his fellow religious in both Brazil and Portugal. The *Sermão da sexagésima* provides the clearest statement in the sermons of

[47] Leite, *HCJB*, 4: 54.

[48] Vieira, *Sermão da sexagésima*, in *Sermões*, 1: 1.

[49] The sermon has been analyzed in detail in the critical literature. See especially António José Saraiva, *O discurso engenhoso*, chap. 4; Azevedo, *HAV*, 1: 262–65; Buarque, *Visão do paraíso*, 226–27; Cidade, *Padre António Vieira*, 1: 92 and 3: 447–48; and Baêta Neves Flores, "Palavra, mito e história no *Sermão dos sermões* do Padre António Vieira."

[50] The sermons are the *Sermão da primeira dominga da quaresma*, in *Sermões*, 2: 53–85; *Sermão da terceyra dominga da quaresma*, 1: 449–558; *Sermão da quarta dominga da quaresma*, 3: 179–215; *Sermão da quinta dominga da quaresma*, 11: 432–69; *Sermão do bom ladrão*, 3: 317–54; *Sermão do mandato*, 4: 318–56; and *Sermão segundo do mandato*, 4: 357–95.

Vieira's belief that words are meaningless unless they lead to actions.[51] It is both a systematic attack on the homiletic conventions of his time and a brief on behalf of the Brazilian Jesuits whom he has come to Lisbon to represent. This latter project has been largely overlooked in the critical literature on the sermon.[52]

[51] Saraiva begins his fine essay on the *Sermão da sexagésima* by observing that for Vieira, "the word was an instrument of action. Although historians of Portuguese and Brazilian literature consider him a typical example of the 'baroque,' Vieira was able to be clear and convincing. Using the same words and the same type of structure, he made himself understood both by men of the court and by illiterate settlers in the Brazilian aldeias. In spite of being 'baroque,' nothing was more foreign to him than the idea of 'art for art's sake'" (*O discurso engenhoso*, 113).

[52] Merquior's brief discussion of the *Sermão da sexagésima* succinctly conveys the extent to which this sermon was informed by Vieira's work as a missionary in Brazil (*De Anchieta a Euclides*). In the most striking tribute to Vieira's preaching to appear in recent years, Merquior suggests that the sermons,

> which are always nourished by themes that have a direct connection to Brazilian reality (the expulsion of the Dutch, the abuses of the settlers, the customs of the captaincies), irrevocably linked to Brazil one of the most perfect and complex constructions of baroque prose. . . . Vieira's sermons, which are full of verbal games and inventive expressions of ideas, converted [traditional] meditation on the atemporal meaning of the Christian message into a critical consideration of historical circumstances (18–19).

Buarque writes that much of the power of the sermons derives from their intimate connection with the Brazilian landscape, which provided Vieira with the "authentic images" that all preachers must appropriate in order to instruct their flocks.

> These images, which are created by God himself, may have more power than those created by the art and wit of men as witnesses to the sacred mysteries, such that the shape and similarity of things that are perceptible come to provide a foretaste of those that are spiritual and eternal. Should the means of powerfully moving the piety of the faithful be added to the miracle of the holy image, this power would of course be even greater (*Visão do paraíso*, 227).

Cidade notes the Brazilian aspect of the *Sermão da sexagésima* but emphasizes the metropolitan rivalries that Vieira engaged rather than the sermon's importance in the larger body of Vieira's preaching during his return to Lisbon. Cidade repeats the standard view that the sermon was a polemic against the Dominicans in general and against Vieira's rival Fr. Domingos de S. Thomás in particular. Looking ahead to Vieira's imprisonment by the Inquisition, which was controlled by the Dominicans, Cidade concludes,

> If the Sermon did not fail to yield fruit in Court in the form of legislative measures designed to remove the obstacles to evangelization, in the city, among rival orators and particularly among the Dominicans who were singled out for attack, the reverberations were powerful and long-lived (*Padre António Vieira*, 1: 92).

Azevedo suggests that the rivalry with the Dominicans was more important to the

As he often does in his more combative sermons, here Vieira takes his text from Luke: "The seed is the word of God."[53] He immediately links the sermon's message to the gospel, and he insists that all good preachers should do the same. The sermon begins in midsentence, as it were.

> And may God grant that this large and most illustrious audience leave today as undeceived by preaching as it is [now] deceived by the preacher [tão desenganado da pregação, como vem enganado com o Prégador]! Let us listen to the gospel, and let us listen to it all. For in the gospel is the entire affair that brought me from so far away.[54]

Vieira spars with his audience even as he flatters it. The incantatory quality of his instruction to listen to the words of the gospel (it will also be a key rhetorical feature of the upcoming Lenten sermons) is woven into the very substance here. Vieira argues that what the congregation hears will have no impact unless the preacher exemplifies the connection between words and actions.

> The definition of the preacher is his life and example. This is why Christ in the Gospel did not compare the preacher to the sower, but rather to the one who sows. . . . The sower, the preacher are mere names; but the one who sows, the one who preaches, this one acts. And it is actions that give the preacher his being. To have the name of preacher, or to be a preacher by name, means nothing. Actions, way of life, example, and works are what convert the world. . . . In ancient times the world converted. Why does no one convert today? Because today words and thoughts are preached; in ancient times words and actions were preached. . . . Do you know, Father Preachers, why our sermons cause so little excitement? Because we do not preach to the eyes, we preach only to the ears.[55]

Lisbon public than to Vieira himself. He rightly minimizes the importance of S. Thomás's attacks on Vieira and emphasizes the Lenten sermons' significance beyond the interreligious rivalry, particularly with regard to Vieira's Amazon mission.

> The sermons of this religious [S. Thomás] more than justify the criticisms of his Jesuit rival. There followed other orators from the [Dominican] Order, and throughout Lent the churches of Lisbon resounded with bitter gibes and thinly veiled allusions to the aggressor. The whole city was amused, and each Sunday it awaited a response from Vieira. This response, however, never came (HAV, 1: 266).

[53] "Semen est verbum Dei" (Lk 8.11).

[54] Vieira, Sermões, 1: 1.

[55] Ibid., 27–29, 33. The Revised Standard Version and the King James Version translate qui seminat as sower, and thus do not suggest the distinction between the

In the parable of the one who sows—*qui seminat*—Vieira finds a natural vehicle with which to express his scorn for the pretensions of his listeners. Vieira requires them not only to pay attention to the entire gospel—"Let us listen to it all (*Ouçamolo todo*)"—but also to listen in a way that will move them to imitate the action of the one who sows. Vieira returns throughout the sermon to the theme of the apostle's departure from the comforts of the world to sow his seed: *Exiit qui seminat, seminare semen suum*. The parable expresses the fundamental choices Christianity presents to the believer.

Having prompted his audience in Lisbon to consider its response to the parable, Vieira moves seamlessly from the one who goes out and sows to the missionaries whom he has temporarily left behind. Not even the sower suffered as the Jesuits have suffered, for the missionaries in the Amazon are both the sowers and the seed.

> The misfortune of the sower of our Gospel is not the greatest one. The greatest misfortune is the one that has been suffered in the field where I was, and to which I am going. All that the seed has suffered here, the sowers have suffered there. If you note well, you will see that here was seed that was withered, seed that was choked, seed that was devoured, and seed that was trodden upon. . . . All this the Evangelical sowers of the Mission of Maranhão have suffered in the last twelve years.[56]

Vieira here provides the only specific discussion of the sufferings of the Jesuits of the Amazon to be found in the Lisbon sermons of 1655. Its inclusion is in keeping with the combative tone of the rest of this

---

sower and the one who sows on which part of Vieira's interpretation turns. Betendorf's reference to the sermon as the *Sermão do semeador* likewise ignores this distinction. The Revised Standard Version reads, "And when a great crowd came together and people from town after town came to him, he said in a parable: 'A sower went out to sow his seed; and as he sowed, some fell along the path, and was trodden under foot, and the birds of the air devoured it. And some fell on the rock; and as it grew up, it withered away, because it had no moisture. And some fell among thorns; and the thorns grew with it and choked it. And some fell into good soil and grew, and yielded a hundredfold.' As he said this, he called out, 'He who has ears to hear, let him hear'" (Lk 8.4–8; cf. Mt 13.1–23; Mk 4.1–20); and Betendorf, *Chronica*, 85).

[56] Vieira, *Sermões*, 1: 8. Vieira takes as his time frame the twelve years since the death of Luiz Figueira in 1643. This passage constitutes one of Vieira's more sustained early arguments for the singular place of the Jesuits in the history of the postprimitive church. He will develop these arguments (albeit never systematically) in the *História do futuro*, in the Inquisition defense, and in the later letters.

sermon.[57] Vieira compares the Jesuits to the seed that was trodden underfoot. In addition to suffering the misfortunes inflicted by nature, the Jesuits have been trodden upon by men. This last injustice, inflicted by the Portuguese settlers and their sponsors at court, has brought Vieira to Lisbon; yet he states that his concern is with the soil rather than with those who walk on it, and still less with those who sow. In his anger on behalf of the Jesuits, Vieira turns away from his listeners in the royal chapel and, for a brief moment, descends from the pulpit to conduct a private colloquy with the God for whom the missionaries suffer.

> I do not complain for the sowers, nor do I speak for them. Only for the field do I speak, only for the field do I have feeling. For the sowers, these are glories. Withered, yes, but withered for love of you; choked, yes, but choked for love of you; devoured, yes, but devoured for love of you; trodden upon and persecuted, yes, but trodden upon and persecuted for love of you.[58]

To which field is Vieira referring? This question pinpoints the anomalous character of the *Sermão da sexagésima* both among Vieira's sermons of 1655 and in the larger body of his writings on the Amazon. Vieira repeats, with increasing anger, the two words of the parable—*conculatum est*—that forced him to return to Lisbon. Because the seed was trodden underfoot by men, Vieira appears ready to turn his concern away from those men and to devote himself entirely to the field—that is, to the Indians whom the Jesuits served as sowers and seed.[59] Absent from this passage is the pastoral engagement with the Portuguese that will suffuse even the most combative passages of the upcoming Lenten sermons.[60] In these sermons, Vieira's harsh words will be spoken with an unequivocal concern for his listeners in the royal chapel, as well as for the Jesuits—and Indians—whom he has left in the field and whose history is contained in the parable.

[57] Baêta Neves has noted that the *Sermão da sexagésima* figures in Vieira's attempt to challenge the Lusocentrism of his Portuguese audience and to identify the New World as the "privileged locus of religious and personal development"; but Baêta Neves's suggestion that the text treats the Jesuits' specific problems in Maranhão "in hidden form" is more applicable to the Lenten sermons of 1655 than to the *Sermão da sexagésima* ("Palavra, mito e história," 174–79).

[58] Vieira, *Sermões*, 1: 9–10.

[59] Vieira emphasizes the traditional interpretation that the deed was done by men (*ab hominibus*). Ibid., 7.

[60] Vieira's address to Lisbon in the *Sermão da quinta dominga da quaresma* is among the most striking examples of this kind of tempered anger. See *Sermões*, 11: 462.

In the uncompromising rhetoric of the *Sermão da sexagésima* it is possible to discern the beginnings of the transformation of Vieira's theory and methodology of conversion. This transformation would not be complete until the writings of Vieira's last years in Bahia. His early setbacks in the Amazon missions had forced Vieira to ask for the first time: Whom am I seeking to convert? Before assuming his post as Superior, he had had a clear sense of the difficulties he and the Jesuits were likely to encounter in their mission to the Indians. The Society's bloody history among those Indians demonstrated the difficulties of creating a viable network of missions in a region that was only nominally under European control. Vieira, however, had not anticipated with comparable accuracy the obstacles to conversion that would be posed by the Portuguese themselves. Thus one of the central goals of the *Sermão da sexagésima* is Vieira's attempt to salvage a pastoral agenda from the defeats of his first two years in the Amazon. To this end he employs the language of the battle-weary apostle.[61]

The anger that suffuses the *Sermão da sexagésima* plays a particular rhetorical role in the opening passages. Vieira creates in these passages a physical distance between himself and his audience corresponding to the pastoral distance created with his reference to the mission field of the New World. He preaches that his return to Lisbon is as illusory as a flash of lightning. Once he secures the instruments of evangelization he seeks, he will disappear from Lisbon without a trace, "because one who goes out and comes back like a flash of lightning does not turn back. To go and to come back as a flash is not to return, it is to go forward."[62]

The Jesuits in Brazil will be rewarded more than the preachers who remain in Portugal (more, even, than the one who sows in the parable), Vieira continues, because they have gone out to the New World, and their journey did not end there. Since they left behind the ships of Europe, the Jesuits have continued their travels on foot, so as to reach all the non-Christians of Africa, Asia, and America. The discussion here

---

[61] Particularly striking in this regard is his allusion to the limited spiritual capacities of the Brazilian Indians in the context of Jesus' instruction, "Go into all the world and preach the gospel to the whole creation" (Mk 16.15). The language with which Vieira depicts the difficulties of preaching to the Indians recalls the pastoral thought of Nóbrega (as do the detailed analyses of missionary strategy he produced in the 1670s and 1680s).

[62] Vieira, *Sermões*, 1: 11. He refers in this context to Ez 1.14: "And the living creatures darted to and fro, like a flash of lightning."

of God's payment to those who go out to sow juxtaposes the mobile Jesuits and the sedentary court.

> Among the sowers of the Gospel there are some who go out to sow and others who sow without going out. Those who go out to sow are those who go to preach in India, in China, in Japan. Those who sow without going out are those who content themselves with preaching in the *Patria*. All have their reasons, but everything has its reward. Those who seek their field at home shall be paid for the sowing; but for those who go out and seek their field far away, their sowing shall be considered, and their footsteps shall be counted [*hãolhes de medir a semeadura, e hãolhes de contar os passos*]. Ah, Day of Judgment! Ah, preachers! Those of you from here will find yourselves with more Court [*com mais Paço*]; those of you from there, with more footsteps [*com mais passos*]: *Exiit seminare.*[63]

Vieira takes evident pleasure in deploying traditional homiletic word-play for an apostolic purpose. His detailed treatment of those who stay and those who go out serves as a prelude to his larger argument that he himself went out and never really returned. Vieira wants to deprive the skeptics in his audience of the chance to speculate about the reasons he abandoned *passos* for *paço*.

Vieira's assessment of the fitful progress of the missionary church identifies even the gains he hopes to achieve during his Lisbon sojourn as contingent goods, to be lost many times before they are finally secured.

> The sower is a great example to me; because after losing the first, the second, and the third part of the seed, he drew on the fourth and last part, and gathered much fruit from it. . . . The year has a season for flowers and a season for fruits. Why should not life, too, have its autumn? Some flowers fall, others dry up, others wither, others are taken by the wind. The few that attach themselves to the trunk and become converted into fruit, only these are the fortunate ones, only these are the wise ones, only these are the lasting ones, only these are the ones that flourish, only these are the ones that nourish the world. Can it be that the world may die of hunger? Can it be that the last days may be those of the flowers? It cannot be, nor does God wish it to be, nor shall it be.[64]

Vieira's emphasis on the indeterminacy of the missionary enterprise offers his listeners a kind of respite in the sermon. It is a much-needed

[63] Vieira, *Sermões*, 1: 4.
[64] Ibid., 12–13.

respite, for it follows his condemnation of those who impede the work of the sowers and precedes his criticism of preachers and preaching in Portugal. In a remark intended both for the audience in the royal chapel and readers of the published sermons, Vieira states that his argument should serve as a "prologue" to the sermons of other preachers, as well as to his own Lenten sermons. He hopes to leave his audience "disenchanted with the Sermon"; that is, with the homiletic genre as it is presently constituted.[65] But the content of this sermon is not of a piece with that of the sermons that follow. Vieira's effort in the *Sermão da sexagésima* to distance himself from his audience stands in marked contrast to the rhetorical strategy of the Lenten sermons, in which he treats his audience as interlocutors rather than as ignorant dupes, at best, or villains, at worst. Although a number of stock characters (most notably that of the corrupt cleric) will figure in the Lenten sermons, in no instance will they appear as one-dimensional as the complacent preachers of the *Sermão da sexagésima*.

After delivering the sermon and making use of the debate it ignited to speak with the king and his ministers, Vieira largely abandoned his insistence on the illusoriness of his presence in Lisbon. By the time he preached the *Sermão da primeira dominga da quaresma* (Sermon for the First Sunday of Lent), three weeks later, he was pursuing a pastoral agenda that attended to the metropolis as much as it attended to the New World.

Perhaps because Vieira had spent the better part of his anger in the *Sermão da sexagésima*, or because he thought this kind of anger did not suit the Lenten season, the tone of the seven Lenten sermons is conciliatory. In these sermons, Vieira provides a highly self-conscious analysis of the elements of a just colonial order. He wants the society he describes to be believable to his listeners, so he concentrates on the particular problems of Brazilian society and avoids what might be taken as attacks on his audience.

In the *Sermão da primeira dominga*, Vieira repeats the questions about the value of a soul that he posed to the settlers of Maranhão in the 1653 *Sermão das tentações*.[66] But the *Sermão da primeira dominga* shows even

[65] Ibid., 13.
[66] Vieira adds verse 8 to the reading from Matthew: "The devil took him to a very high mountain, and showed him all the kingdoms of the world and the glory of them; and he said to him, 'All these I will give you, if you will fall down and worship me'" (Mt 4.8–9).

more clearly how fully Vieira identified himself with his Brazilian adversaries. If he sought legal remedies, he also sought to coax forth from a shared spiritual tradition the impetus for action that alone would permit any legislation to be effective.

Following the same rhetorical strategy as the *Sermão das tentações*, the first sentence of the *Sermão da primeira dominga* is a question.

> If the devil is so clever that he makes temptations even of our strengths, why shall we not be so prudent as to make strengths of his temptations? This is the conclusion that I draw today from the whole Gospel story.[67]

The juxtaposition in this passage of temptations and remedies suggests the central project of both this sermon and those of the following weeks. On the first Sunday in Lent two years earlier, in Maranhão, Vieira invoked the voice of God in an effort to caution the Portuguese about their sins. Now, in Lisbon, Vieira uses the same occasion to offer a direct challenge to the devil. He searches self-consciously with his listeners for a means of appropriating the devil's temptations as a defense against temptation itself. Vieira arrived in Maranhão as a messenger; he has returned to Lisbon as a seeker who identifies himself with his audience. The combative rhetoric of the *Sermão da sexagésima* gives way to an invitation to action in which Vieira himself is a participant. Vieira's message is that unschooled laypeople are just as prepared to act on the lessons of Scripture as the most learned theologians.[68] For Vieira, acting on faith is a collective as well as an individual enterprise.

> The Divine Scriptures are most powerful arms and most effective defenses against the temptations of the Devil. But as I preach for all people, and not all people can wield these arms or make use of these defenses, my purpose today is to give you other, more available arms, and other easier defenses, with which each of you may resist all temptations.[69]

Vieira seeks to show his listeners—"misguided Esaus"—the differ-

---

[67] Vieira, *Sermões*, 2: 53.

[68] William Sloane Coffin addressed this theme in an Epiphany sermon, preaching, "faith must be lived before it can be understood" (*Sermons from Riverside*). The responsibility to "reconcile our faith with our lives" is the stated theme of the *Sermão da quinta dominga da quaresma*, which Vieira preached one month later. See *Sermões*, 11: 434.

[69] Vieira, *Sermões*, 2: 56.

ence in weight between their own souls and the goods of this world.[70] The ignorance of the Portuguese that he lamented in the *Sermão das tentações* becomes in the *Sermão da primeira dominga* a sign of God's infinite grace. The Portuguese are a pious people who commit impious acts for which there is still time to repent.

In these passages Vieira states more powerfully than anywhere else in his writings the depth of his identification with the laity. The vision of community he presents here, however, carries a prescriptive burden. If we ask the right questions, Vieira preaches, God will lead us to the right answers. As in the *Sermão das tentações*, the central question in the *Sermão da primeira dominga* is the weight of an individual soul, and Vieira again emphasizes that to sell one's soul in exchange for even the whole world is a bad bargain. The difference between the two sermons lies in the latter's inclusive rhetoric. We would not accept such a bargain—"At least, I would not"—if the price were damnation. And yet the Portuguese sell their souls for much less.

> Ah, idolators of the World! who so many times give your souls and bend your knees to the Devil, not for the whole World but only for such small parts of it that they cannot even be called crumbs of the World! . . . Is there any small piece of the World that has not taken many souls to hell? . . . If the whole World does not weigh a soul, how is it that these small pieces of the World weigh so much? In the end [the world] is as clay. Throw a whole clay pot into the sea, and it is as nothing on top of the water; break the same pot, and put it in pieces, and each piece (even the smallest) sinks to the bottom. If the whole World weighs so little, how is it that these small pieces of the World weigh so much that they all sink to the bottom, and take our souls with them?[71]

[70] Ibid., 60–61.
[71] Ibid., 75. Saraiva's analysis of the image of the broken pot incisively conveys Vieira's emphasis in all the 1655 Lenten sermons on familiar physical objects, which made vivid to his listeners the transience of the human body and all other temporal goods. The power of the image, Saraiva writes, derives

> from the fact that the pieces of the broken pot are of clay; that is, of earth, the same substance as the small parcels of land [*alqueires*] for which men are damned. Into the two parts of the text (the one that shows men devouring each other for a piece of land and the one that presents to us the image [of the pot]) is woven an expression that applies equally to the first and to the second and that underlines this identity: "all turn to dust again" [Ec 3.20]. . . . The referents of the image and of the concept are the same, the pieces of the pot and those of the earth are a single reality (*O discurso engenhoso*, 44).

As powerful as is Vieira's preoccupation with the responsibility of each Portuguese for his own soul, it is not the rhetorical center of the sermon. Vieira now turns to the shared responsibility of all Portuguese for the souls of non-Christians; in the sermon's concluding passages, he draws tight the link between salvation and empire that will inform his entire body of prophetic writings. The fundamental Jesuit vocation to help souls informs these passages: for Vieira, it is still possible—in a way it would not be twenty years later—to define Jesuit ministry in terms of the pastoral obligations of the Portuguese nation to new converts in all parts of the empire. Thus, throughout the Lenten sermons, Vieira draws on the vocabulary of Ignatius, Nóbrega, and Acosta to express the specifically Brazilian elements of the Portuguese imperial project.

In the *Sermão das tentações*, Vieira assuaged the fears of his audience by emphasizing that his proposals for colonial reform were intended to promote the economic progress of the Amazon rather than to impede it. He advances a similar argument in the *Sermão da primeira dominga*; but here his purposes are much broader. Vieira focuses on the humanity of Jesus in his depiction of the worth of an individual soul.[72] In the manner of a prudent Jesuit spiritual director who adjusts the rigors of the *Spiritual Exercises* to the capabilities of the exercitant, Vieira calls not for suffering but for heightened awareness. Just as he recognized in São Luiz that forcing settlers to speak of slavery in confession "would be of no benefit," Vieira recognizes in Lisbon that presenting evidence of the settlers' abuses will not cause the government ministers to share his preoccupation with the fate of the Indians. He therefore offers the ministers a practical plan for achieving the Lenten renewal he describes. He proposes this plan in the complicitous tone he has employed throughout the sermon. We should, he preaches, take 30 minutes a day during Lent to "close up within ourselves." And what should we think about during those 30 minutes? Here Vieira makes the crucial transition between the souls in the audience and the souls in Maranhão. Lent has no meaning apart from the action it inspires.

> Now, faithful Christians, let us all observe this [period of prayer and reflection] during Lent, so that Lent, too, might be Christian. Let us consider that our soul is one; that this soul is immortal, and eternal; that the union of this

---

[72] Vieira's emphasis on the humanity of Jesus also informs the two Maundy Thursday sermons he preached five weeks later. See *Sermões*, 4: 318–56, 357–95.

soul with the body (which we call life) can be severed today; that all the things of this present World shall remain, and only our soul shall go with us; that one of two eternities awaits this soul: if we are good, an eternity of glory; if we are wicked, an eternity of punishment. Is this the truth or a lie? Do we believe that we have a soul, or do we not believe it? Are these souls our own, or are they the souls of others? What, then, shall we do?[73]

The penultimate question carries the weight of two years of struggle in the Amazon. Even if the Portuguese continue to scorn their own salvation, they cannot escape their responsibility for the souls of the Indians. Vieira here puts forward with a pastoral intent the interpretation of the Fifth Empire that he will develop in the *História do futuro* and the Inquisition defense. The Portuguese are the temporal vicars of Christ, but it is the human Jesus in the desert whose example is all-important in the present circumstances. The outward forms of Portuguese piety, from the present Lenten observance in the royal chapel to the pious brotherhoods that proliferate throughout the empire, mock the temptations that Jesus overcame: "Truly there is no kingdom more pious than Portugal; but I do not know how to understand our piety, nor our faith, nor our devotion."[74]

Vieira reserves for the peroration the sermon's only extended reference to the New World. He laments that the souls of the Portuguese in purgatory have countless guardians, even as the Indians of Brazil are condemned to hell. The final passage of the sermon reads effectively as antiphonal verses addressed alternately to Christ and to D. João IV.

At this very instant, an infinity of souls is being lost in Africa, an infinity of souls in Asia, and an infinity of souls in America (whose help I come to seek), all due to our fault and negligence. Lord [Christ], have all these souls not been redeemed with your Blood? Lord [D. João IV], have all these souls not been redeemed with the Blood of Christ? Lord, did you not entrust the conversion of these souls to the Kings, and to the Kingdom of Portugal? Lord, are these souls not entrusted by God to you with the Kingdom? Lord, shall those souls be lost and go to Hell because of our negligence?[75]

This mode of dual address brings Vieira to the final step in his metaphorical endeavor to enlist the devil's own weapons in the battle against temptation. The sermon's rhetorical emphasis on the salvation

---

[73] Ibid., 2: 83.

[74] Ibid.

[75] Ibid., 84. A rare editor's note in the margin of the first edition reads, "He speaks alternately with God and the King."

of the Portuguese has given way to a larger argument about the meaning of the empire. Vieira demands nothing less than a Lenten conversion, in which the Portuguese recognize that it is not the non-Christians who must serve them but they who must serve the non-Christians. The enrichment of the metropolis—the heart of the imperial enterprise—is seen here as a precarious good; it will be lost if the Portuguese fail to advance the missionary church. Christ entrusted the empire to the Portuguese to save the souls of non-Christians. The attainment of the temporal and spiritual goods they seek will require the Portuguese not only to profess but also to act (through the legislation and other measures that Vieira has proposed) to uphold the inseparable link between the missionary enterprise and the imperial one.

The rhetorical conceit with which Vieira concludes the sermon reiterates this strategic inversion of the Portuguese view of non-Christians. Once again, Vieira's inclusive language demonstrates that he means to join D. João's government ministers in seizing the devil's weapons.

> Allow me to sanctify the words of the Devil and put them in the mouth of Christ: he "showed him all the kingdoms of the world." God is showing us all the Kingdoms of that New World. . . . And, pointing toward Africa, toward Asia, and toward America, He is telling us: "All these I will give you, if you will fall down and worship [adoraveris] me." Kingdom of Portugal, I promise you the restitution of all the Kingdoms that paid you tribute and the conquest of many other opulent Kingdoms of that New World, if you (for I have chosen you for this task) will make it believe in me and worship me: If it will fall down and worship me [si cadens adoraverit me].[76]

Having put the words of the devil into the mouth of Christ, Vieira now modifies those words to express the temptation of the Portuguese, who have been chosen as Christ's successors. Vieira's substitution of *adoraverit* for *adoraveris* completes the shift in focus from the souls of the Portuguese to the souls of the non-Christians of America, Africa, and Asia.

Vieira's preoccupation with *almas alheas* (the souls of others) provided a characteristically Ignatian foundation for that shift. Throughout the six Lenten sermons that followed the *Sermão da primeira dominga*, Vieira developed his ideas about the humanity of Jesus and the responsibility of the king and his ministers to non-Christian peoples throughout the empire. Those sermons place the defining ministry of

---

[76] Ibid. , 84–85; Mt 4.8–9.

the first Jesuits—the care of souls—in the context of a universal missionary project that the Society cannot complete alone.

In the *Sermão da terceira dominga da quaresma* (Sermon for the Third Sunday in Lent), Vieira took as his text Luke's account of the people's response to Jesus' ministry: "When the demon had gone out, the dumb man spoke, and the people marveled."[77] Vieira repeats the expression of wonder throughout the sermon as he tries to express his understanding of the moral dilemmas facing the king and the royal government.

Vieira begins the sermon by advising his audience of the limits of his own understanding: "The Sermon will not be wonderful but it will be wondering: 'and the people wondered.'" He continues to profess his lack of understanding by ending each successive section of the text with a variation on the stock phrase, "I do not praise, nor do I condemn: I wonder with the People."[78]

The seventh of the sermon's ten sections closes by contrasting the pastoral purposes of preaching and confession. Vieira thereby shows how much his view of penance has changed since the letter from Maranhão two years earlier in which he argued for a flexible practice of that sacrament in the colony. "If I were in the confessional," Vieira now tells his Lisbon audience, "I promise you that I would not absolve but rather would condemn them; as I am in the pulpit, however, I neither absolve, nor do I condemn. I wonder with the People."[79]

As the *Sermão da sexagésima* demonstrated, Vieira knew well how to speak in tones of moral superiority. His purpose in the Lenten sermons is different, though the difference is sometimes obscured by his sharp criticism of the privileged audience to which he is preaching. With three words—*admiratae sunt turbae*—Vieira professes his own failure to understand not the miracles of Jesus but the folly of Jesus' ministers, particularly his ministers in the church. For Vieira, turning characteristically to Luke in preaching on the workings of faith, the gospel lesson is the efficacy of the confession derived from the purity of the mute man's faith. In an indictment that recalls the *Sermão da sexagésima*, Vieira preaches that his listeners' willingness to dissimulate in confes-

---

[77] "Cum eiecisset Daemonium, locutus est mutus: et admiratae sunt turbae" (Lk 11.14). Vieira apparently did not preach on the second Sunday of Lent during his stay in Lisbon.

[78] Vieira, *Sermões*, 1: 485; cf. 474–75, 494, 505, 520, 539, 551.

[79] Ibid., 528.

sion is a graver sin than the sins they confess. Yet he understands the reasons for their omissions.

> Never have there been so many Confessions as today; yet we see little evidence of Grace. What might the reason for this be? . . . The only possible reason is that there are Confessions in which the Mute ones speak but the Devils do not depart. . . . If each day we see you [religious] more entered into and penetrated by the Devil, what do you expect us to gain in your Confessions? Now I shall speak today of Confession, as I promised. But in order that the remedy might be applied according to the wound, I shall preach not of the Confession of sins, but of the Confession of Confessions.[80]

The remedy Vieira prescribes expresses the transformation of his pastoral theory and practice since his 1653 resolution not to emphasize the sacrament of confession in the colonial context. Now he not only argues for the importance of individual confession but calls for a reexamination of the sacrament itself. In keeping with the pastoral purposes of these Lenten sermons, Vieira preaches that he is more concerned with confession than with sin. In Maranhão the reverse was true. What accounts for this change? Vieira's goals are still the same; but he has recognized that he must change his pastoral strategy in Lisbon if he is to influence an audience that professes itself to be the most pious in Portugal. The *Sermão da terceira dominga* is the most abstract of the 1655 Lenten sermons, but Vieira's message to the ministers of the court is clear. He turns the court's outward piety into a source of sin, and shows that the small deceptions its ministers practice in the confessional threaten not only their own salvation but the survival of the empire itself.[81] Throughout the sermon, he emphasizes the pastoral

---

[80] Ibid., 460–61.

[81] In a further gloss on the idea that it is more important to analyze the sacrament than the sin, Vieira declares that he is concerned not so much with money as with the smaller and therefore less detectable forms of corruption among the ministers.

> I do not deny money its powers, nor do I wish to deprive it of its scruples. But my own scruple is neither so common nor so coarse a one as money. I fear not so much what is stolen as what is not stolen. There are many ministers in the world, and in Portugal more than many, who in no way may be bribed with money. But these same ministers allow themselves to be bribed with friendship; they allow themselves to be bribed with recommendations; they allow themselves to be bribed with dependency; they allow themselves to be bribed with respect. And though none of these things are either gold or silver, they are the reasons for all the world's injustice" (ibid., 512).

care all Christians need. It is this willingness to engage his audience, as someone who not only administers the sacraments but also receives them, that separates the *Sermão da terceira dominga* from the *Sermão da sexagésima*.

If Vieira came back to Lisbon as a flash of lightning in the *Sermão da sexagésima*, he may have felt more earthbound as his stay in Lisbon drew to a close. Although the *Sermão da quarta dominga da quaresma* is not the last of the Lenten series, it is the only one in which the title paragraph notes that the preacher is planning his return to the Amazon.[82] This is no innocuous insertion: Vieira is groping for a way to reconcile the demands of public life with the periodic need for withdrawal.

The *Sermão da quarta dominga* is the quietest sermon of the series. It is weighted from the outset with a sense of the inherent sinfulness of human society. The day's reading from Scripture informs Vieira's effort to link Luke, the engaged apostle and doctor; John, the mystic; and a meditation on the consequences of sin. He preaches that the text, "Jesus withdrew again to the mountain by himself," teaches "the lesson not of words but of works."[83] Flight from society is not a sign of weakness but a necessary part of the renewal of every missionary, beginning with Jesus himself.

The *Sermão da quarta dominga* is also a darker sermon than the others; darker even than the *Sermão da sexagésima*. Vieira preaches that society defeats and finally dehumanizes even the best individuals, leaving them no choice but to retreat.[84] Although the retreat is not permanent, it colors the nature of the individual's relationship with the world. This is true above all for the individual whose public life takes him to palaces, churches, and universities, for all these places are peopled with "thinking beasts." Rome, the holiest place in the world, is also a place of corruption.[85]

Such a society offers more limited choices, even to its most privileged members, than the society that figures in Vieira's other sermons

---

[82] Indeed, it was the only one of the series published with a descriptive title paragraph of any kind. The title reads: "Sermon for the Fourth Sunday of Lent, Preached in Lisbon in the Royal Chapel, year 1655. On the occasion when the Author, having made his first departure from the Court for Maranhão, prepared his second one, which he also undertook" (*Sermões*, 3: 179).

[83] Jn 6.15.

[84] Vieira, *Sermões*, 3: 185.

[85] Ibid., 193; cf. Vieira, *Cartas*, 2: 512–17.

of the 1650s. But its restrictions on human action heighten rather than diminish the importance of individual choice. In contemplating the meaning of Jesus' flight into the desert, Vieira offers a stark picture of the multiplicity of human wills and the inability of those who understand the world best to gain a controlling hand in politics. Then, in his peroration, he looks for a way to live in such a world. He reaches for a pastoral application of the day's lesson, albeit more tentatively than is his custom; and he finds it in the injunction to withdraw. Each minister must set aside a few days each year during which he takes the time to retreat and reflect. Whether it is found in the desert or in a place closer to home, solitude is a living companion because it is suffused with God's presence. The punishment for Adam's sin was the loss of human solitude. One of the most urgent tasks for human beings (particularly those entrusted with the affairs of church and state) is to attempt to regain that solitude, even if only fleetingly.[86]

Anticipating those who would suggest that this pastoral ethos would more fittingly be advanced in Bussaco (the king's hunting retreat) than in the royal chapel, Vieira addresses the ministers directly as powerful ones (*poderosos*) who should abandon the hunt and the other traditional diversions of the Portuguese nobility to fulfill the mission that Christ placed on the shoulders of D. Afonso Henriques.

> The work (called recreation) that it takes to catch and wound a Javalí, and to bear it away in triumph once it has been killed, would be better spent in pursuing other beasts that may be brought back from the hunt with as much life as they had when they were led to it.[87]

With this peroration, Vieira recaptures the pastoral energy of the weeks just passed. The responsibilites of empire require the nobility to adopt a new code of leisure: their new quarry is the souls of the Indians of the New World. In this way, Vieira enlists the traditional values of the metropolitan church and the royal court in the service of the missionary enterprise.

Vieira sustains this exhortatory tone the following week in his last Sunday sermon of Lent. Though the *Sermão da quinta dominga da quaresma* is also tinged with a certain sadness, it is characterized above all by an intimate style that is unusual even considering the complicitous tone of the first two Lenten sermons. Vieira reaffirms his identifi-

---

[86] Vieira, *Sermões*, 3: 207–10.
[87] Ibid., 214.

cation with his audience, thereby providing the point of departure for a renewed attack on the outward piety of the Portuguese. The intrigues of his fellow religious, he asserts, show that their lives and their faith are at odds. The Portuguese churches are the most beautiful in the world, but the clergy and their flock "undo" this beauty. Only our actions determine whether our faith is living or dead. Vieira mitigates these high-handed indictments, however, by parenthetical reversions to the conciliatory style of the preceding Lenten sermons.

> Do you wish me, my Lisbon, to tell you without flattery a very sincere truth, and to reveal to you a deception in which your piety finds much glory? This Faith of yours that is so generous, so rich, so beautifully ornamented, and so fragrant, is not a Faith that lives. What is it, then? It is a dead Faith, but one that smells sweet.[88]

It is fitting that Vieira addresses not the individual listeners here but his beloved Lisbon, for the sermon's message is that human understanding means nothing if it does not lead to action.

The argument of the *Sermão da quinta dominga* anticipates Vieira's argument linking faith and action in the 1662 *Sermão da Epiphania* and his interpretation of faith in the postprimitive church in the prophetic writings and later sermons. Taking up a new image, he preaches that in the pillar of fire that appeared to the Israelites in the desert lies the truth that their Portuguese successors must recognize. As throughout the Lenten sermons, Vieira's rhetorical questions have the effect of an incantation; here, they attain maximum force. Vieira wonders what would have happened had the Israelites not pitched their tents when the pillar of fire came to rest and had they not followed the pillar when it moved on. He wonders, too, about the historic choices the Portuguese now face, for "everything in that time [of exodus] was a figure of what was to come in ours."[89] For Vieira, the enactment of this truth will consist in nothing less than the Portuguese exodus into the empire that he demanded explicitly in the *Sermão da sexagésima*. Those who fail to follow the pillar of fire will be condemned.

---

[88] The informal, second-person address with which Vieira personifies the audience in his birthplace suggests the intimate and mournful character of this passage in the Portuguese: "Queres que te diga, Lisboa minha, sem lisonja, huma verdade muito sincera, e que te descubra hum engano, de que a tua piedade muito se gloria? Esta tua Fè tão liberal, tam rica, tam enfeitada, e tam cheirosa, não he Fè viva: pois que he? He Fè morta, mas embalsamada." *Sermões*, 11: 462.

[89] Ibid., 463; cf. 1 Cor 10.11.

For these are the ones who do not accompany their faith with good works; and worse are those who contradict their faith with evil works. Instead of their faith taking them to the Promised Land and to Heaven, with this very faith they will find themselves in hell. Inasmuch as they deny their Faith only with works and not with words, their guilt will not be enough for the Holy Inquisition of the earth to condemn them and send them to burn in the Ribeira [site of the autos da fé]. But it will be not only enough, but certain and without fail, that by the sentence of the supreme Tribunal of Divine Justice they will go to burn eternally in the fire of hell.[90]

With these words Vieira underscores the social nature of salvation for the Portuguese as well as his pastoral commitment to the care of individual Portuguese souls. The commitment is especially striking here because it will appear only sporadically in the later sermons. In the *Sermão da quinta dominga*, Vieira argues that although the Juramento d'Ourique placed an irrevocable blessing on the Portuguese as a nation, the salvation of each individual remains in doubt.[91] Once again, Vieira demands a conversion, with an immediacy matched only by the private sermons he will preach 30 years later to the Jesuits of Bahia.[92] Up to this point, Vieira has been vague about the ecclesiastical institutions he is criticizing. Now, echoing the *Sermão da sexagésima*, he points to the damnation of the Portuguese (particularly those who mouth pieties from the pulpit). The notion of accompanying the faith and reaching the promised land may be taken as both a literal and a figurative reference not only to an otherworldly paradise but also to the New World—a necessary stopping place for all Portuguese (even those who are unable to join directly in the imperial and missionary enterprises) who would follow in the footsteps of the Israelites.

[90] *Sermões*, 11: 464.

[91] At Ourique in 1140, according to legend, Christ appeared to D. Afonso Henriques and promised to establish an everlasting empire in the sixteenth generation of D. Afonso's descendants. Vieira refers frequently to the Juramento in the thanksgiving sermon and in the *Discurso apologético*. For a discussion of previous interpreters, see Cintra, "Sobre a formação e evolução da lenda de Ourique."

[92] Not until the *Discurso apologético* of 1688 will he return to the theme of Portuguese mission and individual salvation in a comparably detailed discussion; and although in the later sermon he will emphasize the reckoning that is to come, his larger focus will be on prophecy as much as on repentance (*Sermões*, 13: 139–276, especially 268–76).

The Maundy Thursday Sermons

No liturgy better expresses Vieira's ideal of apostolic service—for ministers of both the church and the crown—than does the liturgy for Maundy Thursday. It is therefore fitting that Vieira chose to preach two sermons in Lisbon at the Maundy Thursday masses for 1655, in which the liturgy includes the *pedilavium*, the ritual washing of the disciples' feet.[93]

Maundy Thursday falls just after the celebration of the Incarnation, a sequence that particularly suits Vieira's pastoral purposes in the present circumstances. In the first sermon, he takes as his text John's account of the Last Supper: "When Jesus knew that his hour had come to depart out of this world to the Father, having loved his own who were in the world, he loved them to the end."[94] In telling this story, John serves not as a mere historian but "as the Confidant of the soul and love of Christ."[95] Throughout the two sermons, Vieira refers to the *pedilavium* as a sacrament. The Incarnation bound Jesus to a time and place in history, while the washing of the feet at the Last Supper was an act that would be shared forever among all humanity.

> In the Incarnation Emmanuel and God were with us in only one land; in the Sacrament, in every land. In the Incarnation they were only for a few; in the Sacrament, for all. In the Incarnation they were only for those who were present; in the Sacrament for those who were present, and for those who were to come. In the Incarnation they were with us for a brief and limited time; in the Sacrament, without a limit of time, and as long as the world lasts and there are men: "to the close of the age."[96]

[93] *Sermão do mandato*, in *Sermões*, 4: 318–56; *Sermão segundo do mandato*, ibid., 357–95. The first sermon was preached in the morning in the Misericordia, the second sermon in the afternoon in the royal chapel. The only sermon besides the first Maundy Thursday sermon that Vieira preached outside the royal chapel during his journey to Lisbon was the *Sermão do bom ladrão*, also preached in the Misericordia.

[94] Jn 13.1. To facilitate his comparison of the washing of the feet and the Incarnation, Vieira in the first sermon provides a slight gloss on John's text by substituting a passage from verse 3 ("knowing . . . that he had come from God and was going to God") for the first part of verse 1, retaining in both versions the phrase that begins "having loved" (*cum dilexisset*).

[95] Vieira, *Sermões*, 4: 372. The phrase is from the second sermon. Vieira speaks of John in the first sermon as "the one who composed the panegyric of the love of Christ" (ibid., 321).

[96] Ibid., 348; cf. Mt 28.20.

Although in the first Maundy Thursday sermon Vieira makes no direct reference to the New World, the pastoral purpose of the text is unmistakable. His pace is more deliberate and his language more recondite than in the previous Lenten sermons, but once again it affirms the humanity of Jesus. The Incarnation, Vieira argues, was no more than the first example of Jesus' love for men. The most perfect example of this love—the one that would prepare the Apostles for the work of conversion that lay ahead—was the washing of their feet.

> For God to become incarnate was to make himself a man; for him to wash the feet of man was to make himself a servant. For him to become flesh was to clothe himself with our humanity; for him to make himself a servant of men was to shed his own Divinity. . . . For being at once God and man, he made himself a servant, and in making himself a servant he unmade and extinguished himself [fazendo se servo, se desfez, e aniquilou a sy mesmo]. . . . Nature made all men equal; it is fortune that has made the great ones as well as the most humble ones [baixissimos] who are their servants. And in this lies the perfection of the love of Christ today [Maundy Thursday] over that of the day (and the work) of the Incarnation. When he made himself a man he took the conditions of nature; when he made himself a servant and washed the feet of men he took the rudest part of fortune. The former was to make himself, the latter to unmake himself: "[Jesus] emptied himself, taking the form of a servant."[97]

With this interpretation of the *pedilavium*, Vieira returns to the central themes of the first of his published Maundy Thursday sermons, preached in 1650 in the royal chapel.[98] This sermon was the most notable among the Maundy Thursday sermons that, 40 years later, inspired the Mexican poet Sor Juana Inés de la Cruz to write her famous *Carta atenagórica*.[99] The 1650 sermon illuminates the theological thinking that informs the two Maundy Thursday sermons of 1655; the *Carta*, in turn, is important for understanding those sermons and Vieira's preaching career as a whole, because it affords a revealing glimpse of the reception of Vieira's sermons by his contemporaries. Both works, in

[97] *Sermões*, 4: 328–30; cf. Phil 2.7.

[98] Vieira, *Sermões*, 9: 333.

[99] Sor Juana Inés de la Cruz, *Carta atenagórica*. The critical literature on Sor Juana (1647–1695) is extensive and has grown significantly during the last decade. The most important recent study is Octavio Paz's *Sor Juana Inés de la Cruz o las trampas de la fe*, especially 511–33, in which the *Carta atenagórica* is analyzed in detail; see also Robert Ricard, "António Vieira et Sor Juana Inés de la Cruz."

addition, provide a glimpse of the contemporary religious and political milieu.

Two unauthorized volumes of Vieira's sermons appeared in Madrid in 1675 and 1678, before the first volume of the Portuguese edition was published in 1679.[100] The Spanish volumes were dedicated by the publisher to Francisco de Aguiar y Seijas, a well-known patron of the Jesuits in Mexico, who at the time was bishop of Michoacán and was competing with the bishop of Puebla, Manuel Fernández de Santa Cruz, to become archbishop of Mexico. The *Carta atenagórica* was a byproduct of this struggle. The unknown patron of high rank to whom it is addressed was Fernández de Santa Cruz, who wrote the pseudonymous letter that serves as its prologue. The *Carta atenagórica* is a detailed critique of Vieira's 1650 *Sermão do mandato*. By writing about Vieira (who was never made aware of the letter), Sor Juana indirectly was attacking Aguiar y Seijas and his Jesuit friends.[101] Sor Juana, however, was not merely an instrument of Fernández de Santa Cruz. She had her own reasons for attacking Aguiar y Seijas, a well-known misogynist.[102] Sor Juana apologizes that the criticisms of Vieira were penned by a woman ("a sex that is so discredited in the field of letters"), but concludes that she, a "poor woman," is God's chosen instrument for punishing Vieira—and Aguiar y Seijas—for their pride.[103]

Although the *Carta atenagórica* disputes Vieira's 1650 sermon, it begins by praising Vieira.[104] Sor Juana explains that she is writing for three reasons: she feels "no less a 'daughter' of [Vieira's] holy order" than Vieira is a son of the Society; she admires Vieira "so much that I always say that if God were to allow me to choose my talents, I would choose no other than [Vieira's] genius"; and she feels an "occult sym-

---

[100] Pirated translations of Vieira's sermons circulated for decades, particularly in Spain and Spanish America. Vieira stated in the prologue to the first Portuguese volume that he had decided to publish the sermons to fight the circulation of those translations, which were riddled with errors. Still, he was gratified by the interest the sermons provoked and by the honor he received in 1683 from the Real y Pontifícia Universidad de México. In his letters, he lamented that although he was the only Portuguese thus honored in Mexico, he had been burned in effigy by a crowd in Lisbon.

[101] Paz, *Sor Juana*, 525–26.

[102] Ibid., 530.

[103] Sor Juana, *Carta atenagórica*, 434–35.

[104] The letter, Paz writes, reveals "another unsuspected facet of her genius: Sor Juana is a real intellectual pugilist" (*Sor Juana*, 512).

pathy" for the Portuguese nation.[105] Nowhere in the letter do the political and ecclesiastical rivalries come near the surface; moreover, Sor
Juana was ignorant of the sermon's political and religious context—un-
avoidably so, given her lack of access to reliable information about the
Luso-Brazilian world.

That context, however, is as important for understanding Vieira's sermon as it is for understanding Sor Juana's criticisms. After diplomatic
service during the previous decade, Vieira in 1650 was court preacher
to D. João. He steeped himself in the intrigues of court life. Like Sor
Juana, Vieira made no direct references to the religious and political debates that simmered beneath his words. In Vieira's case, the omission
reflects his sermon's fundamental difference from Sor Juana's *Carta*:
the *Sermão do mandato* was not intended to discredit specific members of
the church hierarchy. Instead, the sermon—one of only two from 1650
that Vieira published (the other was an Advent sermon)—exemplifies
the meditation on ministry and the demands of apostleship that dis-
tinguishes Vieira's preaching throughout the decade. In Sor Juana's letter, "theology was the mask of politics."[106] In Vieira's sermon, theology
is not a mask but rather a constituent element of Vieira's pastoral project. Were it not for the *Carta*, which has made the 1650 *Sermão do mandato* one of Vieira's most widely read texts, the sermon would be read
today mainly as a preliminary treatment of the ideas about the *pedilavium* that Vieira would refine in his 1655 Maundy Thursday sermons.

Like the 1655 sermons, the 1650 Maundy Thursday sermon hinges
on Vieira's interpretation of the greatest example of Christ's love for
humanity.[107] In 1650, however, Vieira argues that the greatest example
of this love was not the washing of all the Apostles' feet (as Chrysostom argued, and as Vieira himself would argue in 1655) but the specific
act of washing the feet of Judas. This argument is what provokes Sor
Juana's objections. Vieira's interpretation of the *pedilavium* in the 1650
sermon focuses on Jesus' humanity. Sor Juana's *Carta*, in contrast, focuses on Jesus' divinity. The difference is crucial, because it explains
the pastoral purposes of the sermon that the *Carta* ignores.

---

[105] *Carta atenagórica*, 412–13. "Very occult, in effect," Paz remarks (*Sor Juana*, 513).
Sor Juana's writings make no other reference to this sympathy for Portugal.

[106] Paz, *Sor Juana*, 533.

[107] The text for the sermons is Jn 13.14: "You also ought to wash one another's
feet."

The perfection of the love [of Christ] shows itself in making equal in favors those who are unequal in deserts: not in making deserving men out of undeserving ones, but in treating them as if they were deserving. Love must have some traces of injustice to be perfect.[108]

Following this additional gloss on his interpretation of the *pedilavium*, Vieira takes up the theme to which he will return in the 1655 sermons: Jesus became a servant of humanity. Vieira argues that the highest love is unrequited love, and that the requiting of Christ's love takes away from the perfection of that love. Christ requires not that we requite his love but that we love each other.

Sor Juana does not know of the pastoral project in which the argument is rooted; she treats Vieira's sermon as so much idle theological speculation. She sets out to prove "that Christ wants us to requite his love, and that this is the perfection" of Christ's love. She cites the binding of Isaac and Christ's command to put love of God before love of family to show that "God is very jealous concerning the primacy of his love."[109] For Vieira, the perfection of Christ's love consists in asking that human beings love each other rather than requite his love. Vieira is almost right, Sor Juana states, but

seeing that Christ was disinterested, [Vieira] persuaded himself that He did not want his love to be requited. The author made no distinction between the requiting [*correspondencia*] of love and the utility of that requiting. And it is the latter that Christ renounced, not the requiting itself.[110]

For Vieira, however, God's love is always turned outward. The lesson of the *pedilavium* is that all human beings must be apostles and serve each other as Christ served even his enemies.

I tell you that the perfection of the love of Christ today was in his wishing that the love with which he loved us should become an obligation for us to love each other: "You also ought to wash one another's feet." . . . Let us open our eyes and see the difference between this love and all the other love that has been given and seen in the world. Man's love says: "I have loved you? Then love me." Christ's love says: "I have loved you? Then love yourselves."[111]

[108] Vieira, *Sermões*, 9: 357.
[109] Sor Juana, *Carta atenagórica*, 424, 427.
[110] Ibid., 430.
[111] Vieira, *Sermões*, 9: 365–66.

Vieira fully develops this argument in the 1655 Maundy Thursday sermons. There, the washing of the feet becomes a key symbol of the pastoral project Vieira has brought to Lisbon. In pursuing the legislative reforms he seeks for Maranhão, Vieira narrows the focus of the 1655 sermon to appeal to his listeners—many of whom had also been present in the royal chapel five years earlier—on behalf of the Indians. He argues that Jesus "unmade" himself to serve humanity; the ministers of church and state must also unmake themselves to serve their flocks. Vieira notes that the question of how to interpret God's love in the postprimitive church remains a problem for each succeeding generation. Only the love of Jesus for men is boundless, Vieira preaches, and even this love had to be sacrificed to convert the world.

Vieira argues that God did not dare test Jesus' love for the Father against his love for men; instead God relied on the knowledge that Jesus would obey him. Jesus obeyed because he knew that the work of conversion was to be carried forward with the infusion of the gifts of the spirit that would come only after the resurrection. But Jesus' saving mission, as Vieira also warned in the *Sermão da quinta dominga da quaresma* four days earlier, is something that can never be taken for granted. The washing of the feet represented the additional act of humility that would complete the work of the postprimitive church. It was the act that Vieira, in the culminating Lenten sermons, was demanding from every Portuguese—whether missionary, Amazon settler, crown official, or Inquisitor.

> Because when the time comes for the love of our divine lover to make itself known, as it does today [Maundy Thursday] ... [that love] does not content itself with one crown alone, nor with one victory alone: it crowns itself in order to crown itself again, and it vanquishes in order to vanquish again. This is the unimagined work that takes it at this time not to the same but to another still greater theater. This morning it went forth to win the battle; now it goes forth to claim the victory.[112]

Vieira again anticipates the objections of some of his learned listeners by challenging them (as he would later challenge the Inquisitors) to interpret the signs that were before them. He had already affronted his enemies in the colony in the 1654 *Sermão das verdades* (*Sermon of Truths*). The text for that sermon was Jesus' words to the Jews: "If I said, I do

---

[112] Vieira, *Sermões*, 4: 358

not know him, I should be a liar like you." The sermon explicitly compared his relationship to the settlers and that of Jesus to the Jews.[113] A year later, having returned to Lisbon to establish with crown decrees what his preaching had so far been unable to accomplish, Vieira affronted his more select audiences in the Misericordia and the royal chapel.

The Maundy Thursday sermons show how intimately theology and the contingencies of everyday life were bound up for Vieira, even in his most abstract texts. These sermons prefigured his relationship to the Inquisitors by focusing on a Jesus who was honored by being scorned and who called on men to be converted by recognizing the signs of God's love in the world around them. Vieira preached that these signs would finally be recognized by the Portuguese (and by the rest of the world through the Portuguese). After an intervening decade of defeats in Maranhão and in Lisbon, the Christology of the Maundy Thursday sermons would receive full expression in Vieira's reaffirmation of the apostolic destiny of the Portuguese nation in his Inquisition defense and in the *História do futuro*.

Vieira's last Lenten sermon of 1655 was preached on Good Friday. He chose to preach the traditional *Sermão do bom ladrão* (Sermon of the Good Thief) not in the royal chapel but in the Misericordia.[114] Perhaps, as João Lúcio de Azevedo has suggested, he thought his material was too explosive for the king's sanctuary.[115] Vieira's reluctance to preach in

---

[113] Jn 8.55; *Sermão da quinta dominga da quaresma (Sermão das verdades)*, in *Sermões*, 4: 292–93. Vieira was at once defiant and conciliatory. Truth and lies, he preached, can never stand together. He warned the settlers that their lies were like those of the Pharisees, "because [the Pharisees] did not believe the truth ... because they impugned the truth ... because they affirmed lies ... I too [like Jesus] must speak to you hurtfully. ... And yet, though truths cause hatred, I hope that you will not be angry with me, for I must affront all in order to make each one free" (ibid.). Cf. Vieira, *Representação primeira*, in *Defesa perante o tribunal do santo ofício*, ed. Cidade, 1: 95. There, Vieira cites Luke's account of the reception of Paul in Rome: "And some were convinced by what he said, and others disbelieved" (Acts 28.24). The difference in tone between the Maundy Thursday sermons and the *First Representation* shows in Vieira's warning in the latter text to those who can read but do not understand. The *First Representation* suggests that it may be more difficult to convert the Inquisitors than the settlers.

[114] Vieira, *Sermam do bom ladrão*, in *Sermões*, 3: 317–54.

[115] Azevedo writes that in this sermon Vieira "was at his most audacious, and seemed to exceed himself in the vehemence of his attack. Perhaps recognizing the

the royal chapel, however, was rooted less in practical considerations than in the larger pastoral lessons of the *Sermão da sexagésima* and the six previous Lenten sermons. Vieira takes as his example Jonah, who preached "not in the court, but in the streets of Nineveh." Having taken his message beyond the palace on Maundy Thursday for the first time during Lent, Vieira once again chose the Misericordia to preach the Good Friday lesson—that just as kings may bring thieves to heaven, thieves may bring kings to hell.[116]

Because of the difference in scale between a den of thieves and a kingdom, Vieira begins, people condemn in the first what they praise in the second: "To steal little is a crime, to steal much is greatness."[117] Kings are damned not by their own actions, however, but by the actions of those to whom they delegate responsibility. The *Sermão do bom ladrão* is a lesson about the punishment that awaits D. João IV should he fail to punish the corrupt ministers who surround him, particularly the ones entrusted with the affairs of the empire. Positing an imaginary D. Fulano (Lord Whoever), Vieira asks, If this lord steals in Lisbon, what will he do in Goa? For those who might respond that the crimes of the nobility should be handled differently from those of the common people, he has a ready answer: "Oh how Hell is full of those who, using these and other interpretations to praise the great ones, do not think to condemn them!"[118]

By Good Friday, Vieira had already secured from the king the legislative initiatives he was seeking. In the *Sermão do bom ladrão* he aims to remind D. João once again of the reasons for his return to Lisbon and to strengthen the king's resolve in the face of the attacks on Vieira and the Jesuits that will gain force after his departure.

In the Lenten sermons that followed the *Sermão da sexagésima*, Vieira had adopted a pastoral strategy in which the combative rhetoric of that first sermon was attenuated or absent. In the Good Friday sermon,

---

sermon's excesses, he did not wish to preach it in the Royal Chapel; he took himself to a place where his liberties would be viewed less harshly" (*HAV*, 1: 270).

[116] "Kings cannot go to Heaven without taking thieves with them; nor can thieves go to Hell without taking Kings with them. This is what I shall preach" (Vieira, *Sermões*, 3: 319).

[117] Ibid., 326. This statement anticipates the nineteenth-century Brazilian adage, "Furta pouco é ladrão, furta muito é barão" (He who steals a little is a thief; he who steals much is a baron).

[118] Ibid., 341.

however, he abandoned his moderate approach. As he prepared to return to Maranhão he preached a sermon that was consistent with the *Sermão da sexagésima* and with his adversarial discourse of the 1680s, rather than with the discourse of the first two years of his Amazon mission. The transformation of Vieira's pastoral thought had begun.

CHAPTER THREE

The Lessons of Epiphany

VIEIRA'S JOURNEY to Lisbon advanced the cause of the Brazilian Jesuits in two significant ways. First, it led to the publication, in April 1655, of a new law protecting the Indians. Second, it led to the appointment of André Vidal de Negreiros as governor of Maranhão. Vidal proved to be a tough-minded administrator who successfully enforced the new legislation and brought the activities of the Portuguese settlers under the control of the crown and its Jesuit partners. But Vidal spent only two years in the Amazon. After he departed, the settlers would increasingly defy the Jesuits and finally, three years later, would expel them from the Amazon. The confrontations that led to the expulsion and the impact of that event on Vieira's missionary strategy would receive their fullest expression in Vieira's 1662 *Sermão da Epiphania* (Epiphany Sermon).

The 1655 law represented a sweeping effort by D. João IV to reinforce the Jesuits' authority in the Amazon and to install a set of clear guidelines for the procurement and use of Indian labor.[1] The enslavement of Indians was to be permitted only under four sets of circumstances: when the crown ordered the enslavement; when the Indians had prevented the preaching of Christianity (though even when this occurred, the law prohibited forced conversion); when the Indians were captives of other tribes and at risk of being ritually eaten; and when the Indians were captured by the Portuguese in a just war.

Vieira left Lisbon on the sixteenth of April, exactly one week after the new legislation was published. Publication had provoked a con-

---

[1] The text of the law is in Reis, *Livro grosso do Maranhão*, 25–28.

certed attempt by the settlers' agents in Lisbon to prevent enforcement. In response, Vieira wrote two state papers aimed at persuading D. João IV not to modify the provisions of the new law.[2] Nevertheless, in the Amazon itself the Jesuits and the settlers were able to forge an "uneasy truce" that lasted until 1660. During this period, the Jesuits established 54 missions in which 200,000 Indians came to live.[3]

The Jesuits owed their success in both enforcing the crown legislation and establishing the new missions largely to Vidal's support. Born in Brazil and a hero in Portugal's recent war against the Dutch, Vidal became one of the most effective administrators of the colonial period.[4] Enforcement of the 1655 laws, however, did not resolve Vieira's dispute with the settlers over Indian labor, nor did it provide answers to the pastoral questions concerning his ministry to the Portuguese that continued to preoccupy him. Despite the indications to the contrary in the *Sermão do bom ladrão*, Vieira continued to pursue a conciliatory strategy in his dealings with the settlers following his return to Maranhão. He had won an important legislative victory in Lisbon, but in São Luiz he was determined to realize his potential gains as a collaborator with the settlers rather than as an adversary.[5]

[2] The settlers' response to Vieira's first paper led to the second paper, which reiterated his original argument. See *Obras escolhidas*, 5: 1–27; Azevedo, *HAV*, 1: 277; Kiemen, *Indian Policy*, 98–103.

[3] Alden, "Indian versus Black Slavery," 76.

[4] Kiemen argues that because of Vidal, "the law and the *regimento* [governing Indian slavery] were immediately put into practice. The choice of governors had been a wise one. ... The presence and prestige and determination of [Vidal de] Negreiros were sufficient to ensure the carrying out of the royal will in both Maranhão and Pará" (*Indian Policy*, 100–101). Azevedo is similarly admiring, describing Vidal as "not only a valiant soldier but also a noble character" (*Os jesuítas*, 275).

[5] Azevedo, summing up the situation on Vieira's return to Maranhão, argues that although Vieira sought "absolute and unconditional freedom" for the Indians, he recognized the need to attend

to the necessities of the colony, which for lack of active laborers could not prosper; and to the inveterate habits of the population, which in its indolence had enslaved itself to the forced labor of the indigenous people. So it was that Vieira accepted the evils that he could not avert; he looked to time, hoping that as it passed he would be able to direct the spirits of the Portuguese toward the solution that his own instincts favored (*Os jesuítas*, 276).

From Conciliation to Expulsion, 1655-1661

Nowhere was Vieira's continued interest in conciliation more evident than in the *Sermão da primeira oitava de Pascoa* (Sermon for the First Monday of Easter), preached in Belém in 1656.[6] In 1654 the settlers had launched (with Vieira's assent) what came to be known as the *Jornada de Ouro* (Gold Expedition), hoping to discover riches in the Amazon backlands. The expedition returned in 1656 after eighteen months of fruitless exploration. João de Souto Maior, the Jesuit Vieira had assigned to accompany the expedition, died before the battered group reached Belém. Vieira preached the *Sermão da primeira oitava de Pascoa* to commemorate the return. It is striking that while the sermon addresses the hardships of life in the colony, it provides a foretaste of the rhetorical style and even the scriptural passages that would figure in Vieira's Inquisition trial and later sermons.

Vieira's text for the sermon is the exchange between Jesus and the Apostles on the road to Emmaus.[7] The sermon provides a meditation on the Easter lesson of hope and doubt that keeps the settlers' present troubles constantly in view. Vieira preaches that the very indeterminacy of human life is one of God's greatest blessings. Vieira seeks not only to console the settlers but also to reassure them: they are better off without riches that would benefit only the colonial elite and its patrons in Portugal. The *povo*—the poor settlers with whose lot he explicitly associates himself throughout the sermon—were unwittingly preparing to impoverish themselves further, Vieira declares, by seeking to bring money and its attendant evils into a colony that had never known them.[8]

Vieira goes on to emphasize that the greatest hardships of mining are imposed on the Indians who are forced to work for the Portuguese. At no point, however, does he high-handedly condemn the sins of the settlers. Instead, he advances a means of reform designed to be attainable within the constraints of colonial society. He continues to envision

[6] Vieira, *Sermão da primeira oitava de Pascoa*, *Sermões*, 4: 396–433.

[7] "'What is this conversation which you are holding with each other as you walk?' And they stood still, looking sad ... 'we had hoped that he was the one to redeem Israel.'" (Lk 24.17, 21). Cf. *Representação segunda*, in *Defesa*, 2: Exame 17, 334; and Chap. 4.

[8] Vieira, *Sermões*, 4: 417. For an account of the development of a money economy in the Amazon, see Sweet, "A Rich Realm," 65–70.

a society of apostles, and he asks only that the contribution of each European to that society be commensurate with his position in the community.

> We must all wish that these Souls be saved, and for each of them we must offer our sacrifices and prayers to God. But since each one of us cannot work toward the salvation of all, at least let us not fail those neglected Souls to which (because they are closest to us) we most owe our charity. Above all, let each one care with true Christian zeal for the instruction and salvation of at least those Souls that he has in his own home, and especially for his own Soul (which many forget). Let us finally understand (and let us not deceive ourselves) that these alone are the true treasures and that there are no others, though our blindness might give them this name.[9]

The *Sermão da primeira oitava da Pascoa* would be Vieira's last major statement about colonial society while in the Amazon.

As the truce between the Jesuits and the settlers stretched thin, the missionaries looked increasingly to André Vidal de Negreiros to uphold their authority. Vidal had succeeded where every administrator before him had failed: he regulated the Portuguese slaving expeditions into the backlands and punished settlers who impeded the Jesuits' work.[10] Meanwhile, Vieira's stock in Lisbon had actually risen after the death of D. João IV because of his influence over the king's pious widow, D. Luísa de Gusmão. Even Vieira and Vidal together, however, could not meet the settlers' mounting demands for Indian labor.[11] The settlers eventually resolved to wait for the end of Vidal's term as governor to take the Indian labor problem into their own hands.

Vidal left Maranhão in 1657. By the time D. Pedro de Melo arrived to replace him in 1658, the fate of the Jesuits in the Amazon was effectively sealed. Even though the Society continued to control the balance

[9] Vieira, *Sermões*, 4: 432.

[10] An especially striking example was Vidal's swift punishment of the settlers who expelled two Jesuits from Gurupá. The guilty parties were sent to Lisbon to answer for their crimes against the Indians. "In this way Vieira, who finally had at his side an energetic government, maintained the respect of the settlers and was able to nourish hopes of a more wide-ranging freedom that would be won in the future" (Azevedo, *Os jesuítas*, 81).

[11] Assessing Vidal's tenure in Maranhão and the battles that followed his departure, Azevedo writes, "during the year and a half that he was there he had done what was possible to enforce the laws and to better the sad lot of the Indians; but the facts demonstrated the fruitlessness of his efforts" (ibid., 86).

of power in the colony from a legislative point of view, and even with the publication in 1658 of a *provisão* affirming the measures decreed in the law of April 1655, the settlers were willing to risk punishment in Lisbon to rid themselves of the Jesuits.[12]

The settlers seem to have recognized before Vieira did that D. Pedro de Melo was a duplicitous administrator whose character flaws could be turned to their advantage. The new governor at first played the role of a staunch ally for the Jesuits. Vieira, indeed, was so confident of the status quo in 1659 that he undertook his longest and most successful journey into the backlands, the mission to the Nheengaiba Indians, who had killed Father Francisco Pinto in 1609 and had remained implacable enemies of the Jesuits ever since.[13] The fundamental reason for Vieira's confidence in D. Pedro was that, like Vidal, the new governor refused to allow the settlers a free hand in the backlands.[14] This refusal, however, led to a revolt in São Luiz in July 1661, during which the Jesuits were imprisoned in their college. The settlers demanded an end to all Jesuit temporal jurisdiction in the colony.[15]

At the time of the revolt, Vieira was on his way by boat from Belém to São Luiz. He failed to negotiate with the settlers, who had already decided for expulsion. When he reached São Luiz, he was refused permission to land and placed in custody on a small boat in the harbor.[16] He remained there for several days, during which time he saw a more seaworthy vessel depart for Lisbon with his less dangerous Jesuit colleagues aboard. Vieira realized that the settlers were intent on sending their agent, Jorge de Sampaio, to present their case at court before their most important prisoner (whose influence with D. Luísa was well known) could arrive.[17]

After seeing Sampaio's ship depart, Vieira (writing from what he called his "Setubal sardine boat") addressed a letter to the town council of São Luiz in which he accused the leading settlers of trying to kill

---

[12] For the text of the new *provisão*, see Reis, *Livro grosso do Maranhão*, 29.

[13] Vieira claimed that he converted one hundred thousand Indians during this expedition. For an account of the journey, see "Relação da missão da Serra de Ibiapaba," in *Obras escolhidas*, 5: 72–134.

[14] B. Pereira de Berredo, *Annaes históricos do Estado do Maranhão*, 2: 144. For the basic documents concerning the conflict between the Jesuits and the settlers during the period preceding the expulsion, see ibid., 106–45.

[15] Azevedo, *Os jesuítas*, 97–100; Kiemen, *Indian Policy*, 115–16.

[16] Azevedo, *HAV*, 1: 343–47; Berredo, *Annaes históricos*, 2: 151.

[17] Vieira, *Obras escolhidas*, 5: 169; Azevedo, *HAV*, 1: 350.

him. (He also commented acidly that Sampaio's ship had room for 50 passengers, including 9 gypsies, but no room for António Vieira, preacher to the king.) By the time he reached Lisbon, he had developed the somewhat equivocal response to the expulsion that he put forward in two key documents of 1662. Vieira was enraged with the settlers and determined to justify his conduct before D. Luísa in the *Resposta aos capítulos*. At the same time, he advocated pardoning the guilty settlers and addressed, in the *Sermão da Epiphania*, the central pastoral concerns of the Amazon mission as a whole.

The *Sermão da Epiphania*

The *Sermão da Epiphania* (1662) is the most important sermon on Brazilian society that Vieira ever preached. It was the first sermon he preached after his forced return from Maranhão, and his anger over the expulsion animates the text from the beginning. The sermon ranges so widely that it resists the kind of summarizing to which texts such as the Lenten sermons lend themselves. Its eight subsections are more rigorously organized than most of Vieira's sermons, but they also contain several digressions and contradictions, as befits a text encompassing the most important themes of a missionary career that already spanned four decades. Vieira's arguments had both a long-term and an immediate purpose: he wanted to leave an indictment of the settlers for posterity and to inspire the queen to a new resolve to reinstate the Jesuits and revive the Amazon missionary enterprise. The strength of the sermon lies in Vieira's success at creating and sustaining a tension between his anger toward the settlers and his continued determination to enlist all Portuguese society in the Jesuit project.

The first edition of Vieira's *Sermões* generally provides only minimal information about the time and place in which a given sermon was preached. Many sermons remain undated, despite historians' efforts to place them through internal clues and references in Vieira's letters. The *Sermão da Epiphania*, however, presents no such problems. The reader is informed in the title note that the sermon was preached to D. Luísa and D. Afonso VI before the young king had assumed the responsibilities of the throne (*na menoridade d'ElRey*). After stating the sermon's occasion—Vieira's return from the Maranhão missions—the note provides an unusual indication of the animus with which the sermon itself will be suffused. It states that Vieira and his Jesuit companions were expelled "by the fury of the *Povo* for having prohibited unjust enslavement and for having defended the freedom of the Indians who were in their charge."[18] That the sermon's introduction asserts the irony of the Society's confrontation with the Portuguese indicates the importance Vieira attached to the arguments he would pursue in the main text. No other sermon by Vieira carries such a charged title paragraph.

The exordium is equally emotional. It begins with a warning to the audience that the preacher today will be silent.

> So that Portugal in our time might hear a Gospel preacher, today the Gospel will be the preacher. This is the novelty that I bring from the New World. The customary style has been that the preacher should explain the Gospel: today the Gospel shall be the explanation of the Preacher. It is not I who shall comment on the Text, but the Text that shall comment on me. I will not say a word that is not the Gospel's own, because there is not a clause in it that is not mine. I will echo its voices, and it will shout out my silences. May it please God that men on earth might listen to them, that they might not come to be heard in Heaven.[19]

This passage presents in a few words the tension between anger and conciliation that runs throughout the sermon. What exactly is the novelty the preacher brings from the New World? On one level, Vieira presents himself as a passive carrier of a new form of expression, one that grants direct access to the meaning of Scripture. On a deeper level, he works to incorporate the violence he has suffered into his discourse to the queen. He has been subjected to treatment that he claims has silenced him, but he finds in Scripture a way to instruct the Portuguese with his silence. The Brazilian settlers, moreover, have rendered meaningless, for the moment, one of the principal instruments of Vieira's missionary vocation: the preaching at which he has made himself a master. Vieira therefore places himself in the role of a puppet: in approaching the Epiphany lesson, he will repeat by rote the words of Scripture to carry out his ministry to the Portuguese.

Vieira's rhetorical insistence on his own muteness leads seamlessly into the substance of his argument, which is that the New World reveals the mysteries of the Old and particularly the mysteries of Epiphany, the feast of light. Here and throughout the sermon, Vieira ex-

---

[18] Vieira, *Sermão da Epiphania*, in *Sermões*, 4: 491.
[19] Ibid., 491–92.

pands the claims for the religious significance of the New World that he made in his Maranhão and Lisbon sermons of the 1650s. He interprets the meaning of the feast day under the present "most novel circumstances": with the return of the religious from the mission field, the feast can be properly celebrated in the royal chapel for the first time in history. "The true mystery of this day is the call [*vocação*] and conversion of the gentiles to the Faith. Until today the Church has celebrated the Birth of Christ; today it celebrates the birth of Christianity."[20]

This is a crucial statement of Vieira's theory of mission as it developed in Maranhão. It prefigures the central points of contention between Vieira and the Inquisition during the six years following his return to Portugal. For Vieira, the history of the Portuguese church is marked by two distinct epochs: the one that preceded the Portuguese discoveries and the one that followed them. This periodization expresses the unique apostolic destiny of the Portuguese nation. In the past, the church—the Christian faithful—celebrated the birth of Christ, and the church hierarchy celebrated his divinity. Now, with the incorporation into the missionary church of the New World that the Portuguese discovered, the church celebrates the birth of Christianity. Vieira, in turn, celebrates the humanity of Christ. He argues for a literal interpretation of the parallel between the Three Kings and their Portuguese successors.

The lands of the Magi lay in the East, while America is in the West. This presents a problem, for the recalcitrant text's account of the number of kings and their place of origin "totally excludes America, which is the part of the world from which I come." The latter phrase may be read in two ways. Vieira is making a straightforward statement concerning his return from Brazil; he is also declaring his own origins to be in America. No comparable declaration is to be found in his other sermons on the New World. Vieira concludes (following Bede and Rupert) that the Three Kings represented only the three parts of the world that were known to the ancients: Asia, Africa, and Europe. America is the fourth land that was prophesied by Isaiah and Matthew and grasped instinctively by Jerome.[21] The fourth king who will bring America into the Christian fold, furthermore, is a composite figure

[20] Ibid., 492.
[21] Ibid., 492–93; cf. Is 43.5; Mt 8.11.

made up of the first builders of the Portuguese Empire: D. João II, D. Manuel, and D. João III.

In making this argument, Vieira provides one of the first glimpses in his sermons of the interpretation of postbiblical history he will develop in the prophetic writings of the 1660s. He refines his opening claim about Scripture speaking for his own experience by stating that he is able to identify the modern successors to the Magi not because of his gifts of interpretation but rather because of his fortuitous placement in history. "Time, which is the clearest interpreter of things to come," has revealed to him the apostolic mission of the three Portuguese kings, "because the first began, the second pursued, and the third perfected the discovery of our Conquests, and all three brought those new lands of the gentiles to the knowledge of Christ, just as the three Magi did with the old lands."[22] Vieira avers throughout the sermon that anyone who reads Scripture with an understanding of the deeds of the Portuguese navigators must inevitably conclude that the Portuguese have been chosen to complete the work of the Magi.

One of the central linguistic conceits Vieira employs in reaching this conclusion is his methodical use of the term *vocação* to suggest the responsibilities that Epiphany imposes on Christians and non-Christians alike. The sermon plays on the many meanings of *vocação* to present Epiphany as both a "calling forth" and a vocation. Vieira's multiple interpretations of the Epiphany *vocação* in the first part of the sermon creates a kind of ripple effect: the *vocação* becomes interchangeable with Epiphany itself because it represents the entire history of the missionary church.

> The better to understand these two *vocações*, or these two Epiphanies, we must suppose that in this very world there have existed in different epochs two worlds: the Old World that the Ancients knew, and the New World that they and the rest of the world did not know until the Portuguese discovered it.[23]

The link in this passage between geographical knowledge and progressive revelation expresses again the sermon's fundamental tension between disillusionment and expectation. Despite the destruction of the Jesuit mission system in Maranhão, Vieira continues to insist on the

---

[22] Ibid., 496.
[23] Ibid., 495.

singular apostolic role that has been reserved for the Portuguese in the postprimitive church.

Another meaning of the *vocação* is the temporal dimension, which is at the heart of Vieira's initial discussion of the dual call. The first call was to the nations (*gentes*) of Herod's time; the second call is to those of the time of D. João and his Portuguese successors. The second call, however, carries with it a range of corollaries that are as important as the historical *vocação* that Vieira emphasizes. Some are stated explicitly in the sermon; others must be gleaned from a knowledge of Vieira's missionary career. The most important is the unique responsibility that this second *vocação* has placed on the Portuguese. For Vieira, the discovery and settlement of the New World has irrevocably transformed the nature of Epiphany. The feast is now invested with a social burden that it lacked in the time of Herod.

The wisdom that led the Magi to heed the call of the star came partly from their study of astrology. They could understand what they saw in the heavens. Vieira's contemporaries, in contrast, are a people blessed with a divine covenant. They must heed the second call of God not because they possess the instruments of the astrologers but because they possess an old faith that the discovery of the empire has infused with a new meaning.

With his "two Epiphanies" conceit, Vieira refines the equivocal view of Portuguese apostleship he began to develop only after his return to the Amazon in 1655. Without ever mentioning the Brazilian Indians, he makes clear that the Epiphany *vocação* is a call to the Portuguese nation as much as to the non-Christians of the New World. This rhetorical strategy is by now a familiar one in Vieira's sermons. Yet just when he appears to invite complacency by celebrating the apostolic mission for which divine providence has chosen the Portuguese, he preaches that the call to the non-Christian world is much more than a traditional invitation to *communicatio*. Such invitations were a foundation block of Iberian justifications of empire.[24] Vieira accepted these justifications, but his experience in the New World showed him that the Portuguese, too, would need to be converted. The *Sermão da Epiphania* constitutes Vieira's last attempt as a member of D. Luísa's inner circle to engage the increasingly polarized political and religious factions of the Portu-

[24] For an analysis of the idea of *communicatio* in the Iberian world, see Anthony Pagden, *The Fall of Natural Man*, especially chap. 1.

guese court in a Jesuit missionary enterprise that the expulsion had thrown into crisis. By the time he developed similar arguments in the *História do futuro* (1664–65), he was a prisoner of the Inquisition and his enemies were installed in the palace.

The *Sermão da Epiphania* contains a series of carefully placed rhetorical signposts, which Vieira uses to help make his argument easier to follow. Although such signposts may also be found elsewhere in his writings, they are rarely inserted as methodically as they are here.[25] The prologue anticipates the objections of the audience and defends Vieira's preoccupation with the sins of the Portuguese. He begins by making a distinction between what he chose to say about Brazil while he was still in the colony and what he is compelled to say now that he has been forcibly returned to Lisbon. This distinction is crucial to understanding Vieira's missionary strategy between 1653 (when he arrived in Maranhão) and 1669 (when he went to Rome following his release from prison). His sense of obligation to criticize and warn the Portuguese prevails over his wish to emphasize the imperial achievements that they too often ignore.

Vieira's self-consciousness about his rhetorical strategy is inspired in large measure by his familiarity with the palace audience. Now that he no longer faces the daily challenge of coexisting with the settlers of Maranhão, he wants to take advantage of his first sermon in Lisbon to preach for the queen with the venom he has brought home with him.

> Let them [the members of the palace circle] hear the excesses of an evil that is so strange and new that they cannot but apply the proper remedy. And if they should fail in their obligation (something that one cannot believe will happen), it would not be just, nor would God permit, that I should fail in mine. The responsibility that I had in that place [the Amazon] and that I have in this one (though I am unworthy of both) is one that with an unbreakable hold on my conscience forces me to break the silence I have observed up to this point. This silence was observed in the hope that my cause (being the cause of Christ) would speak and preach for itself without my having to do so. For this reason Divine Providence permitted that I and my fellow priests be returned to the eyes of the Court in this [violent] manner. It did so in order that the Court might see and not hesitate to believe what would otherwise have been unbelievable.[26]

[25] E.g., the third of the sermon's eight sections is no more than a brief instruction to the reader concerning the historical background for section 4, which Vieira states is the most important section.

[26] Vieira, *Sermões*, 4: 501.

Vieira's presentation of himself as a reluctant witness introduces an autobiographical element to his argument for the dual *vocação*, which his listeners could not have mistaken. He himself has made two calls to the Portuguese: the first as the flash of lightning that carried news of the colony in the 1655 *Sermão da sexagésima*, the second as an instrument of Scripture here, allowing the text to speak for him.[27] His appearance in the royal chapel in 1662 is meant to be as illusory as it was in 1655. This conceit is not simply an example of Vieira's *discurso engenhoso*. It marks the sermon's political agenda as much as its rhetorical one, for it introduces into the fabric of the argument Vieira's equivocal response to the apostolic failures of the Portuguese in both the colony and the metropolis.

Vieira distances himself from his words of criticism in the very act of preaching them. In Maranhão, Jorge de Sampaio and the settlers had accused him of making the Portuguese accountable for acts that would otherwise never have been discussed. Vieira was accused, in other words, of inventing Portuguese sin by speaking of it. His response in the *Sermão da sexagésima* was to decorporealize himself by drawing attention away from the immediate drama of his return to Lisbon and the misinterpretations of the Maranhão mission that his return could inspire. He did this to make vivid the suffering of the Brazilian Indians and the vacuousness of the non-Jesuit clergy. In the *Sermão da Epiphania*, he decorporealizes himself again, by making himself a passive carrier of the words of Scripture, to pursue a larger missionary agenda. In both cases, Vieira places supreme importance on the work of the Jesuits, who must convert the non-Christians of the New World without the gifts that Jesus bestowed on the Magi.[28]

With his allusion to the privileged position of the Jesuits in the missionary enterprise, Vieira reaches the heart of his argument. He defends the Society's conduct in Maranhão against the accusations of its enemies in both the colony and the court. The defense refines the sermon's comparison of the Magi with the contemporary Portuguese missionary church. Vieira identifies the Jesuits as stars—successors to the star that guided the Magi. That star was unique in history, Vieira declares, for it was the star of Christ.[29] The stars that guide the modern non-Christian

[27] See ibid., 1: 11.
[28] Ibid., 4: 544.
[29] See Mt 2.2.

world to the missionary church are the Jesuits. This identification allows the text to continue to speak for Vieira, even as he makes a series of specific references to the circumstances of the Brazilian missions.

The Magi traveled for only three days, Vieira continues, while the Jesuits must cross the ocean and then navigate the Amazon River (the sermon contains few such direct references to the river and to the other terrors of the New World landscape). Vieira compares the relative ease of the Magi's journey through familiar lands to the hardships of the missionaries' journey halfway around the world. Yet he concludes that these physical trials are not the greatest hardship the Jesuits face. This recitation creates the dramatic pitch Vieira seeks, to deliver what he states is the central message of his sermon. And he suspends the answer to the question his audience is waiting for in favor of a new set of questions.

First, he asks why Christ sent a star to the Magi, rather than an angel or a prophet. The reason is that the Magi were astrologers who understood "the language of heaven." They possessed a scientific vocabulary, which is unavailable to the Jesuits seeking to convert the New World. Vieira and his companions have had to create their own vocabulary using nothing but their own resourcefulness. The language of heaven that was clearly recognizable to the Magi had been replaced by the tentative speech of their successors.

> This is why we have embraced a rule and a Constitution that oblige each of us to learn the language or languages of the land where we go to preach; and this is the greatest difficulty and the greatest labor of that work of spiritual conquest, one in which our Stars exceed by far the Star of the Magi.[30]

This comparison is consistent with Vieira's lifelong argument that through experience the missionary gains unique insights into the postprimitive church. The Magi were comparatively passive followers of a star that they could study; but the Jesuits must transform themselves into stars to guide the non-Christians. Yet this transformation signifies only the beginning of the Society's work. The Jesuits must then master the languages of the non-Christian world, or the light they shed will be invisible. Although their goals are the same, the Magi and the Jesuits must work in opposite directions.

[30] *Sermões*, 4: 512–13. The allusion here is to the emphasis in the *Formula* and the *Constitutions* on language study.

There the Magi studied to understand the Star; here the Stars must study. We who seek the gentiles must study and know their languages. Only one who suffers this trial, and God, for whom he suffers it, can know the great difficulty and labor it costs a European to learn not with teachers and books (as the Magi did) but without a book, without a teacher, and without any documents or basic tools, and to learn not one but many barbarous, primitive, and horrible tongues.[31]

For Vieira, the Epiphany sermon's two *vocações* are both complementary and at odds with each other. Vieira had struggled since he was a novice with the problem of linking learning to apostleship. More than any other event in Vieira's life, the expulsion expressed the limits of both learning and mission work. The settlers in Maranhão were amenable neither to reasoned arguments nor to apostolic zeal. When crises such as the expulsion forced him to choose between the two, however, Vieira invariably chose apostleship. His Epiphany reckoning of the two *vocações* thus ties together a series of sermons on Brazil, beginning with the sermons in the Amazon in the 1650s, that were designed to heighten the importance of the Jesuits' unique vocation (a vocation that Vieira commends explicitly here in his reference to the Jesuit *Formula* and *Constitutions*) and of the Society's partnership with the Portuguese crown. D. João III had institutionalized this partnership when the Society was created in 1540, and his successors had maintained it.

Only after setting the historical record straight concerning the conduct of the Jesuits in the Amazon does Vieira begin to put forward the policy recommendations that will attempt to reestablish the Society's presence in the region. After reciting his litany of Portuguese sins, he abruptly shifts direction, in a kind of reminder to himself and to the audience: "Let us follow the star."[32] Vieira develops his analysis of the relative merits of the Jesuits and the Magi without losing sight of their shared apostleship. This analysis, which completes the first half of the sermon, culminates in Vieira's exegesis of Matthew's account of the star that led the Magi to the child.[33]

Throughout these passages, Vieira refines his identification of the Jesuits as the stars that succeeded the star of Jesus. Repeating the rhetorical strategy of his discussion of languages earlier in the sermon,

[31] Ibid., 513.
[32] Ibid., 515.
[33] "And lo, the star which they had seen in the East went before them" (Mt 2.9).

Vieira imagines his way into the physical circumstances of the star of Jesus and its Jesuit successors. The first star and the Jesuits are similar in that both must overcome the forces of nature to guide the Jews and the rest of the non-Christian world to Christ.

> And did [the star] not do herself great violence in going against her own natural velocity, now moving slowly and late, now stopping and remaining immobile, as if she were accommodating in all ways the condition and weakness of those whom she guided, and measuring in all ways how much, when, and in what way they could advance? . . . But this is what one who has the responsibility for bringing Souls to Christ does and must do. . . . This is the work of one who is an Evangelist, this is the work of one who brings strange nations to the Gospel, and this is what the Star did: *Antecebat eos.*[34]

Accommodation is a concept that is characteristic of the Society's theory and practice of ministry.[35] The word appears only rarely in Vieira's writings, however, and its appearance in the context of a comparison of peoples who are widely separated by time and culture is fitting. Both the star of Christ and its successors accommodate themselves to those they have been sent to serve. The difference between the first star and the Jesuits lies in the respective referents of the evangelist's words, *antecebat eos*. The first star was sent to the Wise Men—that is, the learned men (*doutos*), whom Vieira variously demythologizes or scorns throughout his sermons and prophetic writings. The Jesuit order contains a multitude of learned stars, but the truest measure of the stars' achievement is that they have willingly left the scene of their successes to convert the non-Christian world.

Vieira sets forth as complete a statement of the tension between learning and mission work as may be found in the sermons when he picks up Matthew's *antecebat eos*, like a found object, and addresses the two referents for it that the two *vocações* have produced.

> Here is the difference between that Star and our own. The Star of the Magi accommodated itself to the gentiles whom it guided; but these gentiles were the Magi of the East, the wisest men of Chaldea, and the most learned in the world. Our stars, after leaving the chairs of the most illustrious Uni-

[34] Vieira, *Sermões*, 4: 516.
[35] On accommodation in the New World context, see MacCormack, *Religion in the Andes*, especially 249–81; and James Axtell, *The Invasion Within*.

versities of Europe (as many of them did), accommodated themselves to a people more lacking in reason and understanding than any that nature has created (or aborted), and to men who caused them to wonder whether they were men, such that it was necessary that the Popes determine that they were rational creatures and not brutes. The Star of the Magi stopped, yes; but it never turned to go back. Our Stars go back one time and a thousand times in order to walk what has already been walked, to teach what has already been learned, because the rude and primitive barbarian, the undeveloped and brutish Tapuya (since he cannot understand things completely) neither stamps nor retains anything in his memory.[36]

Following this summation, Vieira turns, in the second half of the sermon, to the political reforms he hopes to persuade the queen to introduce in the Amazon. In comparison with the rhetorical and exegetical novelties of the first four sections, the style and substance of his argument in the next four sections have a familiar feel. What is not familiar is the impression of irredeemable disorder that Vieira sustains throughout his discussion of colonial society. The Lenten sermons of 1655 and other texts from Vieira's years in Maranhão provide a critical view of Brazil, but one of the distinguishing marks of those texts was the care Vieira took to temper his criticism with encouragement. When he could not find anything to praise in the colonial administration, he always found heroism among the settlers. The characteristic balance of criticism and praise in Vieira's Brazilian sermons undergoes an unmistakable shift here.

The second half of the sermon opens with a review of the main developments in Vieira's thought since his 1653 *Sermão das tentações* in São Luiz. Vieira also addresses, for the first time, the particular circumstances of the Jesuit expulsion from Maranhão. These passages are striking from a rhetorical standpoint because Vieira shifts his analysis of the Jesuits from the intimate style of the previous passages to a more dispassionate exposition (marked by a shift from first-person to third-person narration) of the dispute over the control of Indian labor in the Amazon. In one of the most closely reasoned arguments to be found in his writings, Vieira provides a point-by-point refutation of the idea that the Portuguese lay administration in Brazil is capable of protecting the Indians as the law demands. Vieira could not have made the argument

[36] Vieira, *Sermões*, 4: 516–17.

for the indivisibility of temporal and spiritual power as forcefully in 1653, or even in 1659.

Once again, his argument hinges on identifying the experience of the Jesuits with that of the Magi. Vieira notes that the star not only guided the Magi to the Child but also guided them away from Herod, ensuring that they could complete their mission. The second path was as important as the first. The Jesuits, however, have been condemned (in both Brazil and Portugal) for refusing to turn the Brazilian Indians over to Portuguese whom Vieira likens to Herod.

> May Portugal finally understand that there can be no Christianity nor Christianities in the Conquests without the Ministers of the Gospel keeping open and free the two paths that Christ today showed the Magi. There must be one path to bring the Magi to worship, and another to deliver them from persecution.[37]

At stake here is not merely a new way of understanding the relationship between church and state. Vieira is giving voice to a view of human nature—especially the power of evil—that is not new in his writings, but that now receives its most complete expression to date.

Like the first *vocação*, the second one includes a second path and its attendant temptation. Throughout most of his previous sermons, Vieira has navigated between the spiritual needs of the Indians and the material requirements of the Portuguese. In the latter sections of the Epiphany sermon, he comes as close to abandoning this effort as he has ever done. It is the second path (the one that leads away from the rulers) that Vieira sees as particularly fraught with difficulties at the present stage of church history, "because on [the second path] lies all the temptation."[38] Only a few months earlier, Vieira would have been concerned with the implications of this temptation for the Portuguese as well as for the Indians, and with ensuring that the Jesuits not separate themselves from the Portuguese. The problems he addressed in the sermons of the 1650s have by now proven so intractable, however, that separation—and therefore sin—appear to be inevitable.[39]

---

[37] Ibid., 521.

[38] Ibid.

[39] See John Drury's fine commentary on the temptation of Jesus in the wilderness. The devil, Drury writes, is one who pries things apart; and sin is "whatever it is that cuts us off . . . from God" (*Luke*, 52).

The devil became a living reality for Vieira in Brazil in a way that even the *Sermão das tentações* had not suggested would occur. The failure of the Maranhão mission fundamentally altered Vieira's understanding of man's ability to resist evil. The second half of the *Sermão da Epiphania* constructs a model for organizing colonial society that advocates the temporal jurisdiction of the missionary church with a more pronounced sense of foreboding than in any of Vieira's previous writings on this subject. The sermon expresses the Augustinian view that society must be oriented primarily toward combating human evil. The society of apostles gives way in these pages to the society of self-seeking frontiersmen who must be controlled by the religious. Vieira makes no effort to disguise his intention that the religious who should exercise this control are the Jesuits, and he preaches that any attempt to separate temporal and spiritual power is the work of the devil.

In previous sermons, Vieira's interpretation of the traditional partnership between the Jesuits and the crown had been subject to the vagaries of imperial politics. When D. João IV was on the throne and the position of the Jesuits seemed secure, Vieira chose to leave aside, whenever possible, the problem of specifying the Society's political jurisdiction. In the present context, however, securing D. Luísa's affirmation of this jurisdiction is essential. The queen has come to be known as the Protectress of the Missions, but she will be succeeded by her son, D. Afonso VI, whom Vieira and many others believe to be intellectually and physically unfit to rule. Viera therefore hopes to institutionalize as much of the Jesuit program as possible, using recent events in Maranhão as a catalyst. He seeks, above all, to make sure that the Jesuits regain sole authority over the distribution of Indian labor in the Amazon, arguing that without such authority Belém will literally be bathed in blood.

Vieira makes no direct reference to the city from which he has recently been expelled. In keeping with his intention of allowing Scripture to speak for him, the Bethlehem of Jesus' birth here represents Belém do Pará and, by extension, the rest of the colony. Following his warning about Bethlehem, however, Vieira momentarily abandons the conceit of being a passive carrier of the words of Scripture and takes up an argument about the relationship between the pastor and his flock, in an effort to warn the queen and her advisers against those who are bent on destroying the flock they have been entrusted to protect. Citing Amos and John as examples, he argues that the pastor must use his staff both for nurturing the flock and for defending it.[40] To abandon the latter function is to betray the flock.

> So that some Politician who is a poor grammarian and a worse Christian not suppose that the duty of the Shepherd (as his name suggests) is only to herd the flock, let him know that only one who herds and defends the flock is a Shepherd, and one who does not defend the flock, even if he herds it, is not a Shepherd.[41]

Vieira's opponents, he argues, have exceeded the bounds of cunning in Scripture or traditional fables—they make their appeal not to the sheep-dogs but directly to the shepherds. He underlines his own ability to discern the lesson that has eluded those who preceded him: "The fables have not spoken of this [deceitfulness]; but our own stories will speak of it."[42] Vieira's scorn for pastors who silence the truth represents in this context an unmistakable attack on his enemies among the clergy of São Luiz and Lisbon.

The *Sermão da Epiphania* has a fuguelike quality, achieved partly through its tight organization and partly through its length, which gives its arguments a cumulative weight. Throughout the last part of the sermon, Vieira focuses on the Jesuits' achievements and the need to institutionalize and strengthen the Society's authority.[43] He provides a new gloss on his earlier discussion of the Jesuits as stars by arguing that the Magi "also were Indians"—turning the *doutos* themselves into *barbaros*. The missionaries' nonacademic training, by contrast, allows them to act on the second *vocação* and transforms them into stars. The Magi, despite all their learning, were dependent on the *vocação* of Jesus, whose star guided them.

As the successors to that star, the Jesuits operate under a different kind of constraint; namely, their partnership with the Portuguese kings. Here, Vieira describes the Society's temporal and spiritual partnership with the crown—which gave the order a privileged position in Portuguese society—with a combative edge that was missing from the sermons of the 1650s. Those sermons (with the notable exception of the *Sermão da sexagésima*) looked at non-Jesuit clergy with a semblance of col-

[40] He cites Am 3.12 and Jn 10.12 in support of his argument.
[41] Vieira, *Sermões*, 4: 525.
[42] Ibid., 526.
[43] These arguments make up sections 6 and 7, followed by a brief peroration in section 8.

legiality. But when Vieira cites the Gospel of Matthew in the *Sermão da Epiphania*, he excludes the possibility that any other group in the church might live up to the gospel's apostolic ideal.[44] Echoing Nóbrega's criticisms of a century earlier, Vieira suggests that not only the secular administration but also his fellow clergy have come to the New World to be served. The admonitions Vieira put forward somewhat tentatively at the beginning of the sermon he now states with no conciliatory gloss. Vieira characterizes the Jesuit policy of compromising with the Portuguese as a farce that should never have been tried.

The single fault that Vieira finds in his own conduct and that of the Society as a whole is the failure to recognize earlier the true nature of the conflict with the settlers. The Jesuits were not mere witnesses to the Indians' losses: the missionaries helped persuade the Indians to surrender by entering the aldeia system. This is a criticism Vieira has not voiced before, and he repeats it throughout the last section of this sermon. Another novel criticism reflects the transformation of his view of Portuguese society. Vieira had long argued that public misfortunes constituted divine punishment for the sins of the Portuguese. In making this argument, he had focused on the internal dynamics of Portuguese society, particularly the church's relatively weak penetration among the Portuguese in Brazil. Now, however, he focuses on the settlers' treatment of the Indians. He links the punishments of divine providence specifically to Portuguese racism, preaching that because the comparatively light-skinned Portuguese had subjected the Indians, the lighter-skinned Dutch were chosen to subject the Portuguese.[45]

The force of this statement is best understood not by comparing Vieira's analysis of the workings of divine providence in the 1660s to his analysis in the 1640s, but by comparing the present sermon's call for expunging Portuguese racism to his previous emphasis on individual conversion; for example, in his address to a black brotherhood in the 1633 Rosary sermon.[46] In the Epiphany Sermon, Vieira pushes the limits of what Luís Palacin calls the *consciencia possível* of the Luso-Brazilian world. Vieira stays strictly within those limits, however, by immediately hedging his argument. Once again, he strays from his declared intention of allowing Scripture to speak for his own experi-

[44] "The Son of Man came not to be served but to serve, and to give his life as a ransom for many" (Mt 20.28).

[45] Vieira, *Sermões*, 4: 532–34.

[46] Vieira, *Sermão XIV do Rosário*, in *Sermões*, 5: 484–521.

ence. His analysis rests squarely on the evidence of the Jesuit experience in Maranhão.

> It is not my intention that there be no slaves. Rather I have asked ... that this Court form a Junta (as has been done) and that this Junta declare the criteria for legal enslavement, as it has done in the Law it has issued.[47]

Under the present circumstances, this distinction is more technical than substantive. But the passage shows that Vieira contemplated a broader criticism of the assumptions of the missionary and imperial enterprises than he ever systematically developed. The reasons for this omission lie partly in the limitations emphasized by Palacín. The *Sermão da Epiphania*, however, establishes the foundations for Vieira's critical analysis (in his Inquisition defense) of religious authority and of the future of the missionary church. In the Inquisition defense, he will surpass some of the contemporary limits on debate about the missionary and imperial enterprises, albeit not in the context of an analysis of specific policies. Meanwhile, in the Epiphany sermon, although Vieira holds out the possibility that slavery might yet become a viable institution in Brazil, his underlying message is that human greed makes the defense of slavery in its present form an untenable position for Christians.

These closing sections of the Epiphany sermon provide the sermon's first reference to Luke, with the story of the slave girl who was possessed by the devil.[48] Vieira's exegesis suggests the fundamental shift taking place in his missionary strategy. It posits an irreducible opposition between temporal gain and Christian apostleship. Here Vieira abandons his attempt (made most forcefully in the *Sermão das tentações*) to reconcile the conflicting demands of the settlers and the missionary church. Vieira preaches that the story of Paul's Philippian persecutors is identical to that of the Jesuits' Portuguese persecutors.

> Because in holding the slave girl without the Devil, [the settlers] lost all their hope of gain. Those slaves who are legal and without the Devil [*sem*

---

[47] Vieira, *Sermões*, 4: 534; cf. Palacin, *Vieira e a visão trágica do barroco*. Vieira's argument here recalls Nóbrega's demand that the crown name a Protector of the Indians to deal with the settlers' abuses.

[48] When the girl followed him, Paul "turned and said to the spirit, 'I charge you in the name of Jesus Christ to come out of her.' And it came out that very hour. But when her owners saw that their hope of gain was gone, they seized Paul and Silas and dragged them into the market place before the rulers" (Acts 16.18–19).

Demonio] are few, while those who are illegal and with the Devil [*com o Demonio*] are as many as they wish to capture and do capture. And as their profit (though it be the profit of hell) depends on their having slaves with the Devil, they prefer the Devil to the Apostles and expel the Apostles from their midst.[49]

These words provide a glimpse of how, beginning with the expulsion, Vieira felt compelled to redefine his mission to the Portuguese. When he preaches about *escravos com o demonio* he is also preaching about Portuguese who join with the devil to destroy the missionary church.

Following in Nóbrega's path, Vieira had begun his work in the Amazon with the expectation that the missionary church would find a way to coexist with the institution of slavery. Now Vieira declares that the two are irreducibly opposed, not because of slavery's inherent evils but because of human greed. In criticizing the practice of slavery rather than the institution itself, these passages recall José de Acosta's criticisms of the Spanish American encomienda system. Acosta, however, never argued that the clergy should separate itself from the slave system, as Vieira does for the first time here.[50] Because individual souls are at stake, it is ultimately impossible to legitimate the institution apart from the acts men perform within it.

Brazil has transformed Vieira's reading of Luke. He continues to develop this new reading throughout his sermons and prophetic texts. The exegesis of Luke that emerges from Vieira's later writings is characterized above all by an attentiveness to individual conversion. Aware of the limits of the society of apostles, Vieira still affirms the social side of Lukan theology in an effort to salvage Jesuit apostleship in the New World. Like Jesus in Luke's gospel, Vieira retreats not into a desert but into a world of souls waiting to be saved.[51] His de-emphasis of Jesuit ministry among the Portuguese is, at its root, a strategic shift that (in good Lukan fashion) takes into account the experience of the missionary church in this world.

[49] Vieira, *Sermões*, 4: 535.

[50] See Acosta, *De procuranda indorum salute*, especially books 1–3.

[51] "Luke was in a sense the first Christian politician, in that he seems to have been the first consciously to think through the fact that the world is here to stay; Christianity must make its way in the world and do so on the world's terms. ... Christianity must change with changing times ... anticipating Augustine, [Luke] concerned himself with transforming society into the *civitas Dei*." James M. Robinson, "Acts," in *The Literary Guide to the Bible*, ed. Alter and Kermode, 477–78; cf. Drury, *Luke*, 99–119.

Vieira concludes his discussion of Luke in the Epiphany sermon by turning to the parable of the lost sheep. In one of the most moving exegeses in his sermons, Vieira offers a view of both his hope in the Jesuit partnership with the crown and his sense of the limited ability of the Society—and of the missionary church as a whole—to create in the New World even a precarious signpost of the city of God. The exegesis rests on a comparison between Isaiah and Luke. Isaiah prophesied, "to us a son is given, and the government will be upon his shoulder"; Luke, in turn, wrote of the one who finds the lost sheep: "he lays it on his shoulders, rejoicing."[52] From these two passages Vieira derives a question, for which the souls of the Indians and their persecutors provide the answer.

> An Empire, then, on one shoulder, and a sheep on both shoulders? Yes. Because a sheep requires more shoulders than an Empire. An Empire does not weigh as much as one sheep. For an Empire half a King is enough: for a sheep the whole is necessary.[53]

Though the salvation of the Indians is the piece of Vieira's own experience that speaks through Luke's text, Vieira's reading cannot but speak as well to the salvation of the Portuguese themselves. The discovery and continual reinterpretation of this intersection between the sin and the redemption of the Portuguese is the defining characteristic of Vieira's later missionary exegesis.

Before the concluding passages, another reference to Luke reveals the depth of Vieira's personal response to the expulsion. Here the evangelist records Paul's instruction to the apostles should they be spurned: "And wherever they do not receive you, when you leave that town shake off the dust from your feet as a testimony against them."[54] Vieira's scorn for the settlers so animates this passage that he combines a correct citation of Matthew with a reference to a *testimonium* that appears only in Luke and Mark. The addition is revealing: in his despair over the expulsion, Vieira has misread Luke. The *testimonium* the gospel invokes is an act of apostleship rather than of anger. The kind of anger that Vieira invokes is as uncharacteristic of Luke as it is of Vieira himself, even the Vieira of the *Sermão da Epiphania*.[55]

---

[52] Is 6.9; Lk 15.5.

[53] Vieira, *Sermões*, 4: 547.

[54] Vieira's citation actually conflates Lk 9.5, Mt 10.14, and Mk 6.11.

[55] Vieira reinforces the apparent anger by referring to the words of Jesus in the contiguous verse from Matthew: "Truly, I say to you, it shall be more tolerable on

In Luke it is the tenderness of the parable of the lost sheep rather than the anger (albeit equivocal anger) of the *testimonium* that finally triumphs, and in this triumph lies much of what makes Luke's gospel so different from that of Matthew.[56] Vieira, for a moment, cannot see that the story of the slave girl is continuous with that of the lost sheep and, furthermore, with that of the Prodigal Son. Yet Vieira's continued preoccupation with the Society's ministry to the Portuguese in Brazil asserts itself, even as he preaches that he has abandoned that ministry. He is unconvincing when he concludes his reference to Paul shaking the dust from his feet by defiantly telling his Lisbon audience: "I did the same thing."[57]

Had Vieira been able to shake the dust from his feet the way he says he did, his missionary career would have been very different. His interpretation of the history of Brazil and his theory and methodology of conversion would have reflected Matthew's stark view of the choice between good and evil instead of the continuous hope for renewal that characterizes Luke. The parables of the lost sheep and the Prodigal Son differ strikingly in Luke and Matthew. Luke infuses both parables with a hope for individual and collective redemption that is difficult to discern in the gospel of Matthew. Vieira has preached in the Epiphany sermon that the Portuguese have committed an unprecedented sin. It is not that they concealed their evil intentions, but that they successfully lured the shepherds (that is, the Jesuits) into complicity to destroy the flock. Consistent with Vieira's Lukan theology, however, the perpetrators of this sin are redeemable.[58] Despite the evil he has seen,

the day of judgment for the land of Sodom and Gomorrah than for that town" (Mt 10.15).

[56] Drury's discussion of the slave girl and the other parables in Lk 9 emphasizes that Luke is the only evangelist who describes Jesus sending the apostles out to the nations twice rather than just once.

We can be sure that [Luke] is up to something. What? Time and again we have noticed his interest in historical progression, his way of linking one thing to another. Here he is tying the history of the church, represented by the twelve and the seventy, into the history of Jesus. It is not only Jesus' story that he is telling but the church's too, and in this way the Christian community is linked to the splendor and the suffering of the gospel (*Luke*, 99; cf. Drury, "Luke," in *Literary Guide to the Bible*, ed. Alter and Kermode, 427).

[57] Vieira, *Sermões*, 4: 536.

[58] Luke's addition of the homecoming party and its attendant repentance to the Prodigal Son parable "changes the structure from Matthew's twofold pattern (lost-

Vieira reaffirms once more his mission to the Portuguese in Brazil. He leaves open the possibility of repentance and transformation by the Portuguese even as he preaches one of the most uncompromising prophecies of damnation in all his sermons.

> Divine Justice has decreed against the misguided people for whose good and help I have crossed so many seas and braved so many dangers. May it please God to forgive them, for they know not what they do. And that they should not lack another pardon (since I and my Companions have already pardoned them with all our hearts), I here and now state again before God and men our forgiveness, in the name of us all.[59]

Whenever in Vieira's writings on Brazil it appears that his pastoral ties to the Portuguese may be severed, he always reaches a further moment of reflection in which those ties are reaffirmed. Over time, as Chapters 4 and 5 will show, he reached many points when such reaffirmations became necessary, and he refined them in various ways. Throughout the Epiphany Sermon, moreover, Vieira interprets the history of the missionary church as continuous with the lives of Jesus and the Apostles. His juxtaposition of the lost sheep and the spurned missionary at the end of the sermon suggests the full range of both the apostolic confidence and the anger that would inform Vieira's prophetic writings in the coming years of prison and exile.

---

found) to Luke's threefold pattern (lost-found-social consequence). . . . [Luke] has ambiguously good-cum-bad people whose actions are not so much moral achievements to be marked by the ultimate censor on Doomsday, as rescue operations which result in survival" (Drury, "Luke," 433, 436).

[59] Vieira, *Sermões*, 4: 537. The "misguided people" is a reference to Sodom and Gomorrah (Mt 10.15).

CHAPTER FOUR

Vieira and the Inquisition

VIEIRA'S PROPHETIC writings of the 1660s constitute the most important attempt of his career to link his missionary experience in Brazil to his larger interests—the apostolic role of the Portuguese nation and the nature of prophecy. In the *Esperanças de Portugal* (*Hopes of Portugal*), Vieira makes a preliminary attempt, while still in Brazil, to address the prophetic themes of the four texts he later wrote while in the custody of the Inquisition: the *Livro anteprimeiro da história do futuro*, the *História do futuro* proper, and the two *Representations* that comprised his Inquisition defense.[1]

This chapter and the following one focus on the immediate circumstances that led to Vieira's Inquisition trial, and on the ideas about prophecy and Portuguese history he developed following his arrest. This chapter is organized chronologically, and it analyzes the texts associated with Vieira's missionary work in the Amazon, his imprisonment, his years in Italy, and his return to Brazil. Chapter 5 is organized thematically, and it analyzes the *História do futuro* and the *Representations*.

Why did Vieira's ideas provoke a conflict with the Inquisition?[2] The

---

[1] Vieira, *Esperanças de Portugal, Quinto Império do Mundo. Primeira e segunda vida de El-Rei Dom João IV, escritas por Gonçalo Eannes Bandarra e comentadas por Vieira, em carta ao bispo do Japão, D. André Fernandes*, in *Obras escolhidas*, 6: 1–66; *Livro anteprimeiro da história do futuro*, ed. Besselaar; *História do futuro*, ed. Maria Leonor Carvalhão Buescu. The two *Representations* (*Representações*) have been published as *Defesa perante o tribunal do santo ofício*, ed. Cidade, two vols. Unless otherwise noted, the *História do futuro* will hereafter refer to both the *Livro anteprimeiro* and the *História do futuro* proper, neither of which was ever completed.

[2] This is a question the critical literature has addressed inadequately, if not entirely ignored. Azevedo emphasizes the sociopolitical implications of Vieira's In-

answer lies in the interpretation of political and ecclesiastical authority that Vieira developed in the *Esperanças* and refined in the *História do futuro* and particularly in the *Representations*. Vieira's prophetic writings expressed the interconnectedness of metropolitan and colonial society. In addition, they set forth a distinctive theology, focusing on Jesus' temporal mission as much as on his spiritual one. Vieira posited a Christological engagement with Luso-Brazilian reality by those who held religious and political authority. His Christology placed the highest value on the work of the missionaries in the field. With the exception of veterans of the missions, the church hierarchy in Lisbon and Rome had no place in Vieira's prophetic schema. The Inquisitors' preoccupation with the metropolitan church, moreover, symbolized the larger failure of the Portuguese to recognize the religious and historical significance of the New World.

Analyzing the gift of prophecy, Vieira argued that every member of society was a potential prophet. This affirmation had a temporal corollary in Vieira's interpretation of the gift of apostleship. Every group that participated in the imperial project—the crown and the settlers, the missionaries and the Indians, the Inquisitors themselves—had a role to play in the schema of progressive revelation that Vieira drew from Scripture and then read into Portuguese history and the history of the missionary church. Vieira assigned no special status to the ecclesiastical hierarchy in the interpretation of Scripture; and he claimed that lived experience is a more valuable guide than scholarship for understanding the accidents and contingencies that mark the pilgrimage of the missionary church.

The prophetic texts are unsurpassed in Vieira's writings for demonstrating his particular genius; namely, his ability to articulate an inclusive vision of Christian mission that invites the participation of all sectors of Luso-Brazilian society. The missionary enterprise, with all its hardships, should be broadened rather than narrowed, Vieira insists. The New World represents for Vieira a locus of prophecies that the

---

quisition trial but pays little attention to the doctrinal and exegetical issues at stake (*HAV*, 2: 5–95). Cidade provides an excellent analysis of the importance of Brazil in Vieira's interpretive schema, but like Azevedo, he is not primarily concerned with the specific interpretive strategies to which the Inquisitors objected (*Representação primeira*, 1: *Prefácio*). Besselaar is an indispensable guide to the prophetic texts up to, but not including, the defense; he underlines the need for an analysis of the *Representations* (*O sebastianismo*, 137).

Portuguese have been uniquely chosen to reveal. The process of revelation, however, works two ways: in revealing the New World to Europe, the Portuguese will also engage in self-revelation.

It was his uncompromising identification of the failings of the
church hierarchy that made Vieira's views objectionable to the Inquisition. The Spanish preacher Diego Murillo aptly called the Inquisitors
clockmakers, "who set all the clocks of Christendom to Rome time and
correct them when they deviate."[3] Vieira sought to change the terms of
the relationship between Rome and the rest of Christendom, especially
the New World. His prophetic writings demanded the integration of
the New World ("the exotic and the marginalized," in Eduardo Lourenço's phrase) into the consciousness of the Old.[4]

The conflict between Vieira and the Inquisition may thus be understood as a conflict between a missionary from Brazil who viewed the
conversion of the New World as the culminating event in the history of
the Portuguese church, and a tribunal in Lisbon that viewed the missionary church as a mere appendage of the metropolitan church. The
texts in which this conflict is played out convey the tension resulting
from Vieira's insistence on his right to draw on lived experience in interpreting the progress of the missionary church, while at the same
time he is developing an interpretation of empire based on the eschatological orientation of the Book of Daniel. Vieira, however, was not an
isolated visionary but a missionary, who sought to interpret the signs
of the times and contribute to the incremental progress of the church
during his lifetime. It is this effort that drives the most powerful passages in his prophetic writings and invests those writings with an animus against the metropolitan church.

Text and context are finally inseparable in Vieira's writings on the
missionary enterprise. Confronted with the realities of the conversion
process in Brazil, Vieira developed the inclusive exegetical style that
defines his later missionary exegesis and pastoral thought.[5] By chal-

---

[3] Quoted in Smith, *Preaching in the Spanish Golden Age*, 152.

[4] Eduardo Lourenço, *O labirinto da saudade*, 40. Even when Vieira did refer to the
so-called exoticism of the New World and Brazil, his purpose was to invert common perceptions of the very practices he was describing. Thus his emphasis on
cannibalism in the *História do futuro* appears in the context of an attempt to identify
the Indians of Maranhão as the referents of Isaiah's prophecies. See *Livro anteprimeiro* 12, and Chapter 6.

[5] This style of exegesis corresponds roughly to the "new exegesis" identified by
Besselaar, who emphasizes the larger exegetical current of which Vieira was a part

lenging the exegetical assumptions of the metropolitan church, Vieira incorporated the New World, and especially Brazil, into a traditional Christian interpretation of history, and thereby achieved a resolution (albeit an uneasy one, given the volatile nature of the missionary church) of the tension between eschatology and lived experience.

The discussion of Vieira's prophetic writings begins with the *Esperanças* (1659), which constitutes his first extended treatment of the *Trovas* of Gonçalo Bandarra (fl. ca. 1540) and his first attempt to present in court circles his ideas about the resurrection of D. João IV.[6] The *Trovas*, doggerel composed by an uneducated cobbler, predicted the return of the *Encoberto*, or hidden king, of Portuguese legend. They gained wide popularity and authority among the Portuguese, especially after the death of D. Sebastião. Vieira drew on the *Trovas* uncritically in developing his own prophetic interpretation of Portuguese history. In the *História do futuro* (1663–65) and the *Representations* (1665–66), Vieira reformulated his discussion of Bandarra, as well as his criticisms of the Inquisition. In the *História do futuro*, Vieira provided a more formal analysis of the nature of prophecy and the gift of interpretation than he did in the *Esperanças*. This analysis, in turn, anticipated Vieira's attempt in his Inquisition defense to weave together all the major strands of his prophetic writings. This chapter concludes with an analysis of Vieira's continuing preoccupation with the missionary enterprise during his years in Rome and Lisbon following his release from prison.

The *Esperanças de Portugal*

Vieira began writing the *Esperanças de Portugal* in 1659, while traveling in a canoe on one of his last journeys into the Amazon backlands. The expulsion two years later dealt the Society a blow from which it took a generation to recover. The violent resolution of the struggle with the settlers marked the turning point in Vieira's reassessment of his inclusive vision of colonial society and the missionary church, the vision with which he had begun his work as Superior in São Luiz in

---

(*Livro anteprimeiro*, 2: *Comentário*, 12: 586, 587, 1040). The specifically Brazilian elements of this exegesis, however, fall outside the scope of Besselaar's editorial project.

[6] Gonçalo Bandarra, *Trovas do Bandarra*.

1653. The reassessment process would continue until well after Vieira's final return to Brazil in 1681. But his writings offer clear evidence that his early vision had begun to break down while he was still in Maranhão—that is, three years before he preached the Epiphany sermon of 1662. That evidence may be found in the *Esperanças*.

The text was presented in the form of a letter to Vieira's fellow Jesuit D. André Fernandes, bishop of Japan and confessor of D. João and D. Luísa. As he often did, especially when he was in the mission field, Vieira wrote quickly and without recourse to supporting documents. The physical circumstances in which the letter was composed were to become a central element of his Inquisition defense. Addressing D. André, Vieira notes, "The subject [the resurrection of D. João] needs to be addressed at length, and not written en route as I am doing, in a canoe in which I am traveling down the Amazon River in order to send this paper by another canoe that will reach the ship that is in Maranhão preparing to sail for Lisbon."[7] Later, Vieira would emphasize in his defense that the unsystematic and conjectural nature of the *Esperanças* resulted not only from the limited audience he professed to be addressing but also from the limitations imposed by the Brazilian environment. (Vieira gradually came to see these limitations as contributing to the force of his own arguments.[8])

Like Augustine (to whom his philosophy of history constantly refers), Vieira was acutely aware of the limitations of postbiblical prophecy. Yet he abandoned all caution in his assessment of Bandarra. He assigned canonical status to the *Trovas* throughout his writings, but especially in the *Esperanças* and the *Representations*.[9] The text of the *Esperanças* contains the specific arguments—concerning the resurrection of the *Encoberto*—for which Vieira was arrested. The *Esperanças* also suggests some of the broader issues that brought him into conflict with the Inquisition.[10]

---

[7] Vieira, *Esperanças*, in *Obras escolhidas*, 6: 1–2.

[8] See Vieira, *Representação primeira*, 1: 5–6.

[9] Saraiva writes, "for Vieira, Bandarra was a prophet with the same authority as those of the Old Testament" ("António Vieira et Menasseh ben Israel," 27).

[10] With the exception of Cidade's introduction to the *Obras escolhidas*, vol. 6, the literature on Vieira's ideas about the Fifth Empire ignores the *Esperanças*. The *Representations* have been similarly neglected, with Cidade again providing the most important study of these texts. See *Representação primeira*, vol. 1, *Prefácio*, and *Representação segunda*, vol. 2, *Posfácio*. Besselaar's useful survey of the literature calls the *Esperanças* "an oasis in the generally tiresome literature of the Sebastianists" (*O se-*

Perhaps no single strand of Vieira's thought has received more dismissive treatment from critics than his unshakeable belief in the prophecies of the uneducated Bandarra.[11] Yet Bandarra's humble origins and lack of education were an asset, in Vieira's view; and modern scholars' charges of dishonesty and madness reflect an assessment Vieira and the majority of his contemporaries rejected. Although Vieira was committed to the literal truth of the prophecies, furthermore, his interpretive framework would lead him to argue in the *Representations* that belief in the prophecies, unsupported by any evidence, was enough to ensure their fulfillment in ways people were unable to discern.[12] The *Representations* placed ever greater emphasis on belief without evidence as the highest form of faith; and the Jesuit order as a whole took the lead in transferring the messianic hopes of the Portuguese from D. Sebastião to D. João IV.[13]

---

bastianismo, 120). He also calls the *Representations* "the most important document of Portuguese messianism" and the last significant example of Joannism (devotion to D. João IV) in the literature (ibid., 139).

[11] Azevedo characterizes Bandarra as a "deceiver by inclination," a "charlatan," and a "maniac," and concludes that Vieira's fascination with him was a "singular aberration of an elevated spirit" (*A evolução do sebastianismo*, 28). Besselaar has refuted the popular belief that Bandarra was illiterate (*O sebastianismo*, 49). Bandarra and Sebastianism have inspired some of the most visceral passages in Azevedo's writings. Although he has made a central contribution to the literature on both Vieira and Sebastianism, however, Azevedo has shown little interest in systematically analyzing Vieira's ideas about Bandarra in the *Esperanças* and the *Representations* (both of which remained unpublished during Azevedo's lifetime). He has cited both texts in passing but has focused on the interpretation of Bandarra in the *História do futuro*, noting that this text "grew directly out of that same absurd vision"; i.e., the *Esperanças* (see *História do futuro*, ed. Azevedo, 114).

[12] Azevedo, after clearly expressing his distaste for the *Trovas*, introduces a variation on Vieira's argument by admitting that Bandarra might be considered "truly a prophet, not because he was correct in his prophecies but because of the intense activity that he inspired in his people" (*A evolução do sebastianismo*, 29).

[13] Azevedo argues that Vieira's Inquisition trial "was also the trial of Sebastianism, an illusion of the simple people during a time when the *Patria*, under foreign rule, hoped for some marvelous event that would relieve it of its suffering. At the present time, however, it was no longer justifiable, and the Jesuits themselves, who had been the principal proponents of this deceit, had to submit to the proof of its absurdity" (*Os jesuítas*, 114). Cidade shares Azevedo's view of Vieira's adherence to ideas that "we reject today as absurd" and of Bandarrism as a "collective psychosis, a morbid reaction of discoverers and conquerors of worlds in the face of the humiliation of the *Patria* under foreign rule" (Preface to *Representação primeira*, 1: xxi). Elsewhere Cidade observes that in Vieira's ideas about Bandarra and about Portugal's role in the universal conversion may be found "if not the point of departure,

The most famous fellow Jesuit to share Vieira's readiness to accommodate prophecy to contemporary politics was Gregorio de Almeida.[14] Like Vieira, Almeida drew on a wide range of biblical and domestic Portuguese prophecies to support his interpretation of the nation's destiny. His text achieved an unparalleled degree of authority during the decade following the Restoration.[15]

The *Esperanças* begins with a rhetorical flourish that may have been an attempt to guard against the controversy that the text, once circulated, was sure to inspire. Vieira is responding, he writes, to D. André's request for a more detailed exposition of the ideas about D. João IV that he had previously communicated (presumably in conversation). Vieira thus begins by implying that had it not been for this request from one of his superiors in the Society, he would have been content to keep to himself his belief in the resurrection of the king. Vieira would later employ this rhetorical strategy again in the *Representations*.[16]

---

at least the supporting pillar of the missionary's grand illusion" (Introduction to *Obras escolhidas*, 6: xli). Besselaar states, "Bandarra was included among the ranks of the prophets who had prophesied the Restoration and the future glories of Portugal. . . . The restored country was enthralled by the Joannine Bandarrism for which António Vieira became the great spokesman. Spokesman, but not inventor. Enthusiasm for Bandarra was general and would endure for another decade" (*O sebastianismo*, 95).

[14] Almeida, *Restauração*. Vieira's *Cartas* definitively established that Almeida was the pseudonym of João de Vasconcelos (1592–1661), who served as rector of the Jesuit colleges in Braga, Santarem, Porto, and Coimbra (2: 38; see also Besselaar, *O sebastianismo*, 97; and Azevedo, *A evolução do sebastianismo*, 72). The Portuguese New Christian Manoel Bocarro Francês identified D. João IV as the *Encoberto* before the Restoration of 1640. Raymond Cantel states that Bocarro Francês was the only writer to have identified the king in this manner (*Prophétisme et messianisme dans l'oeuvre d'António Vieira*, 37).

[15] Azevedo calls Almeida the "doctor par excellence of Restoration messianism" (*A evolução do sebastianismo*, 72).

[16] Vieira begins the *Representations* by disavowing any intention of defending his ideas; he claims that his sole purpose is to restate for his accusers the propositions of the *Esperanças* (*Representação primeira*, 1: 3–6). In the concluding pages of the *First Representation*, Vieira will insist again on the violated secrecy of the *Esperanças*. The passage includes the text's first hint of resentment against D. André, who had died by the time Vieira was imprisoned. D. André was forced to deliver Vieira's private letter into the hands of the Inquisition; the letter, Vieira argues, "was not a public paper but rather an extremely secret one, and sent to one person alone (and such an important person) by the most secret channels, which were those of the confessor himself. And if that same confessor passed the paper to others and made it

The main arguments of the *Esperanças* are constructed around the following proposition.

> Bandarra is a true prophet; Bandarra prophesied that El-rei Dom João IV shall do many things that he has not yet done and cannot do without being resurrected; therefore, El-rei Dom João IV shall be resurrected.[17]

The proposition is rooted in Vieira's assumption that Bandarra's status as a true prophet had been proven, because Portuguese history has unfolded exactly as Bandarra prophesied. Those prophecies in the *Trovas* that remain to be fulfilled reflect the limitations of Bandarra's interpreters rather than a flaw in the prophecies themselves. Vieira here introduces an interpretive strategy he will employ frequently in the *História do futuro* and the defense. He argues that the veracity of the prophecies is confirmed because they have not yet been fulfilled. The argument demonstrates Vieira's ability to reformulate the meaning of specific prophecies; it also reveals his penchant for conducting preemptive strikes against his critics, particularly when controversial questions of interpretation are at stake.

Vieira states that he himself predicted (at an unspecified time before his departure for Brazil) that the frontier that appeared in one of Bandarra's visions was Badajoz, where Joane Mendes de Vasconcelos led a siege in 1658.[18] Vasconcelos failed to achieve the hoped-for victory, and was standing trial in Lisbon for treason when the *Esperanças* were being written. Nevertheless, these circumstances did not alter Vieira's belief in the truth of Bandarra's prophecy or in his own interpretive method. "I will readily concede this error," Vieira writes, "and admit that Bandarra speaks of another Frontier"—and most likely of another war hero. After

---

public, the fault lies with him and not with the one who wrote it" (ibid., 217). Cidade summarizes the circulation of the *Esperanças* as follows:

> Vieira sent it [the text of the *Esperanças*] to the Queen through an intermediary (the bishop who was her confessor). It was delivered by Captain Paulo Martins Garro, a secular brother of the Society, who kept a copy. Other copies were made by the emissary, with the consent of Vieira, who might well be expected to have been interested in keeping the light of that great hope from remaining concealed. In this way the diffusion of his utopian text was not delayed" (Preface, ibid., xv).

[17] Vieira, *Obras escolhidas*, 6: 2.
[18] "Vejo subir um Fronteiro/Do Reino de trás da serra,/Desejoso de pôr guerra,/Esforçado cavaleiro" (Bandarra, *Trovas*, 152). All quotations from the *Trovas* are taken from the Porto edition of 1866.

examining the particular events of the siege, however, Vieira perceives a second explanation: his admission of error is unnecessary because the prophecy will be fulfilled in a manner he has ignored in his initial enthusiasm over Vasconcelos's prospects on the battlefield. Bandarra's verses might yet be proven to refer to the very failure of the siege and the hopes invested in it. Here Vieira suggests that prophecy and its fulfillment are linked the same way as hope and the objects of hope in history.

> Should someone wish to insist on the first meaning which we assigned to the verses he will be able to draw from them the same solution and to state what I stated before the retreat from the Badajoz siege was known here [in Maranhão]. I said (and I have many witnesses) that should entry to the site not be won, the application and aptness of the verses would not for this reason be undone; rather the verses might in this way be seen to have been still better crafted, because the words "desiring to make war" [*desejoso de pôr guerra*] do not signify effects but rather desires; so that in a certain manner it appears that the verses prophesied that the effort would end only in desires, though desires gallantly expressed.[19]

Addressing his potential critics concerning his prediction, Vieira cedes no ground. Prophecy, like human hopes, is rarely fulfilled in the way people expect. Interpreters are fallible, but their failure to discern how prophecies are fulfilled in history reflects their own limitations rather than those of the prophet.

Bandarra, Vieira affirms, prophesied the unfolding of Portuguese history with unerring specificity. Vieira, in turn, wishes to defend not the accuracy of his interpretations of Bandarra but the unassailable truths of the *Trovas* themselves. He therefore assigns to Bandarra's visions a reality that supersedes the reality of the historical events Bandarra prophesied. Thus, Vieira writes, "certainly it seems that [Bandarra] saw the events he foretold with a clearer light than that of the very eyes that afterward witnessed them."[20] That light, Vieira continues, il-

---

[19] Vieira, *Obras escolhidas*, 6: 15. In a further reversal that fits neatly with the interpretive schema of the *Esperanças*, Vasconcelos was found not guilty by the Lisbon court and was rewarded by D. Afonso VI to make up for the libel to which he had been subjected. "It seemed to the Junta that His Majesty not only should free Joane Mendes de Vasconcelos but also should honor him and grant him favor in compensation for the discredit that he suffered in prison as an innocent man" (Luis de Meneses [Conde da Ericeira], *História de Portugal restaurado*, 3: 229; see also 131 for an account of the failed siege at Badajoz).

[20] Writing about D. João's destiny, Almeida assigned a similar power to texts, both prophetic and historical. He placed greater emphasis than did Vieira on the

luminated Portuguese history and placed a singular blessing on that history by permitting it to be prophesied by an ignorant man.

> It was thus a supernatural light, prophetic and divine, that illuminated the understanding of this simple and humble man, in order that the wonders of God that the world was to see in Portugal in recent times might also have that preeminent quality of all great divine mysteries, which is to be prophesied long before.[21]

This passage represents the most unequivocal claim in the *Esperanças* for the divine inspiration of the *Trovas*. It also suggests the main points of conflict between Vieira and the Inquisition. The first and simplest problem stemmed from the historical context in which Vieira made his claim. Vieira's patron, D. João IV, was posthumously investigated by the Inquisition because of his hostility to the tribunal in general and his efforts on behalf of the New Christians in particular.[22] The king's opposition, in turn, was a direct result of Vieira's influence. Thus when Vieira interpreted the *Trovas* as prophesying the resurrection of D. João, he revived a series of social and political debates that assumed a particular delicacy following the king's death in 1656. During these years, moreover, the ability of D. João's son, D. Afonso VI, to rule was actively challenged. Vieira himself was numbered among the supporters of the new king's younger brother, the future D. Pedro II.

Had Vieira limited himself to calling Bandarra a true prophet whose

---

intrinsic importance of reliable historiography; he even argued that the accurate preservation of the historical record is the reason books are written. "The composition of books was invented as a remedy for forgetfulness and as an antidote to the malice and strength of time, which uses up and consumes everything with the power and violence of its course. Quintilianus said that truth is the inseparable companion of history, for without truth nothing of what we have said exists, because, being unable, without the truth, to survive in its being and true nature, history transforms itself (for the very reason that it is lacking truth) into pure pretense and vain and poetic plots" (*Restauração*, 1: 24).

[21] Vieira, *Obras escolhidas*, 6: 17. Almeida was somewhat more careful than Vieira (in theory if not always in practice) in his attribution of the gift of prophecy. "I strove hard not to use words such as *prophecies, miracles, revelations,* and *visions*, except those that were used by the canonized Saints and that have been accepted by the Catholic Church ... and if some of these words should fall from my pen it is not my purpose to use them in anything other than their popular sense, and in the common way of speaking, without seeking to invest them with more credit than we commonly give to purely human utterances by wise people who speak the truth" (*Restauração*, 1: 9–10).

[22] João Lúcio de Azevedo, *História dos cristãos novos portuguêses*, 263–64.

Trovas foretold D. João's resurrection, it is unlikely that he would have entered into an extended conflict with the Inquisition. But Vieira viewed Bandarra's lack of education and low social status as a sign of being chosen by God, and this created a second point of conflict. In the passage about divine light, Vieira's invocation of that "simple and humble man" is a call to the Portuguese to recognize the knowledge that comes from God alone. Such knowledge symbolizes the singular blessing God has placed on the Portuguese nation by revealing its future to the cobbler Bandarra. This passage looks ahead to the extended treatment of Bandarra in the *First Representation*, when Vieira will again celebrate Bandarra's simplicity (this time with the Inquisitors as his audience). Comparing Bandarra to Amos, whose simplicity made him particularly blessed among his people, Vieira suggests his own preferences for the Portuguese, whom he identifies throughout both the *Esperanças* and the *Representations* as the successors to the Israelites.[23]

In making his claims for Bandarra's status as a prophet, Vieira draws on his own experience as a missionary in a way that challenges the Inquisitors' authority. The challenge is posed indirectly in the *Esperanças* and directly in the *Representations*. The supporting texts with which Vieira develops his claims for Bandarra's status themselves reveal the contrast between the speculative missionary in the Brazilian backlands and the beleaguered defendant in the Coimbra prison.

In the *Esperanças*, Vieira argues that D. João will be proven to be the true restorer of the faith, gathering in the ten lost tribes of Israel and ridding the world of the Muslim threat to Christianity. Notably absent from his commentary on the *Trovas* is any discussion of the Fifth Empire prophecies of Daniel, which Bandarra interpreted and which Vieira himself will examine in the *Representations*. Instead of focusing on Scripture and its learned interpreters, the *Esperanças* focus on the *Trovas* alone. Vieira laces his text with gently ironic admonitions to Portugal's learned men to try to understand the meaning of these verses.[24]

---

[23] Vieira, *Representação primeira*, 1: 123.

[24] E.g., Vieira begins his interpretation of Bandarra's vision of the ten tribes with the admonition "Let the learned take note" (*Esperanças*, 31). Later in the same passage, Vieira draws on Bandarra to advance another warning to learned men who doubt the destiny of D. João: "Bandarra said, as a great interpreter of the Scriptures, that there are many who are taken to be wise men who fear the coming of the ten

The *Esperanças* argues that we are able to gain only glimpses of the light that is contained in Scripture. God gives knowledge of the mysteries of divine providence even to His most humble servants; this is true not only of the Hebrew prophets but also of the postbiblical interpreters of prophecy and the domestic prophets of Portugal, among whom Bandarra possesses unique authority. The meaning of Bandarra's humble status to Vieira in the Brazilian missions cannot be overstated. Maranhão had transformed Vieira's understanding of the apostolic purpose of the missionary vocation's isolation and hardship. The subtext of the *Esperanças* is that the church hierarchy is useful only insofar as it furthers the work of mission and allows God's chosen prophets to make themselves heard.[25]

Attacking those who refuse to recognize the imminent resurrection of D. João, Vieira alludes to the arguments of Augustine that he will cite directly in the *História do futuro* and the defense.

> It is clearly shown and demonstrated that Senhor Rei Dom João IV, who is in the sepulchre, is the fateful King of whom Bandarra speaks in all his prophecies, both those that have already been fulfilled and those that have not yet been fulfilled. And if this same king Dom João is today dead and buried, it is not mere love and *saudade* [longing], but reason, duty, and understanding that force us to believe and to hope that he shall be resurrected. To believe the contrary would be to be stupid and ignorant men, as St. Augustine calls those who, having seen one part of the prophecies fulfilled, do not believe the other part. It pains me not to be able to cite [Augustine's] words, which are excellent.[26]

This passage is at once a tribute to Augustine and Bandarra, a reminder of Vieira's limiting circumstances in the Brazilian backlands, and a

---

tribes and the conversion of the Jews because they believe that when this happens the end of the World will have arrived" (ibid., 33).

[25] The most important of those prophets for the Portuguese (in addition to the Hebrew prophets) were Bandarra and S. Frei Gil. Vieira also frequently cites the Juramento d'Ourique. See Chap. 6.

[26] Vieira, *Esperanças*, 46. Vieira refers often in the *História do futuro* to those who refuse to believe the prophecies and to the punishments that await the unbelievers. Cf. Augustine of Hippo, *City of God*, especially book 10, in which Augustine attacks the neo-Platonists who refuse to recognize "the right road which leads to the vision of God and to eternal union with him; it is proclaimed and asserted in the truth of the holy Scriptures. And all those who do not believe in it, and therefore fail to understand it, may attack it; they cannot overthrow it" (32).

swipe at his learned adversaries. It is particularly important, however, because it sets forth the pastoral ideal that the Inquisition will investigate. Vieira interprets the prophecies in a defiant tone that will generally be absent from the prison writings. There, he will be circumspect about his allusions, however indirect, to the Inquisitors and their kind. But here, Vieira makes no effort to reassure his future accusers or others he knows will object to the *Esperanças*. Instead, he warns repeatedly that Christians who do not act on their faith are undermining the missionary enterprise and preventing Portugal from fulfilling its destiny. The *Esperanças* prepares the ground for Vieira's later pastoral thought by making a learned argument against learning itself.

The Brazilian context is essential to this argument. Vieira invests the isolation of the backlands with an instructional purpose. Thus, even as he notes that he is unable to support his arguments with specific citations, he undermines his lament and makes a virtue out of his lack of sources. This internal undermining parallels Vieira's effort to show that D. João will be resurrected because of his limitations rather than in spite of them. By turning the king's limitations into virtues, Vieira focuses on the imminent fulfillment of the prophecy, implying that to enlist supporting scholarship is at best of secondary importance and at worst impious. He thus shows the physical circumstances and spiritual purposes of his mission in the Amazon to be precisely suited to the interpretation of the prophecies of Bandarra.

Vieira holds his text up as much to the standard of the uneducated cobbler as to that of the church fathers, and his lack of books during the years in the Amazon and in the Inquisition prison strengthens his affinities with Bandarra. Vieira, who read widely but unsystematically, characteristically valued faith over learning and never pretended to have a thorough command of the patristic literature.[27] Instead, he drew on experience and the texts available to him, much like Bandarra, who borrowed a Bible from the New Christians of Trancoso.[28] The light of

[27] Cidade writes of the Inquisition defense: "the surprising erudition of the theologian shows itself clearly" (*Representação segunda*, 2: vi). This assessment credits Vieira with more learning than he possessed. The defense (and Vieira's other prophetic writings) are striking not for the depth of Vieira's learning but for his ability to draw on memory and his breviary in enlisting the works he does know in support of his arguments. See Besselaar, "Erudição."

[28] Theophilo Braga, *História de Camões*, 1: 412.

scholarship, Vieira would argue before the Inquisition, can blind as much as shadows can.[29] Here, he makes a similar argument by offering his equivocal lament over not being able to provide the supporting commentary by Augustine. Bandarra needed only Scripture and the domestic prophecies of Portugal to exercise his prophetic gift; Vieira, claiming a lesser gift, relies for now on Scripture, the *Trovas*, and memory.

That the true object of Bandarra's prophecies remains hidden is a reflection of the workings of divine providence, which never imperils those for whom it has reserved a singular destiny. To potential critics who suggest that the vacillating D. João could not be the perfect king of whom the prophets spoke, Vieira recalls the prophecy that the *Encoberto* must remain hidden until his resurrection.

> And who can doubt that after El-rei Dom João IV is resurrected he shall be a perfect knight and shall show himself to have been made perfect by God? This will be all the more evident because a man without any imperfection cannot be a man of this world but rather must be of the other world. In the same manner Bandarra says that this king is a good hidden king, because in El-rei Dom João God placed to the highest degree many parts and qualities of a good king which have until now been hidden and which afterward will be discovered. . . . Oh! how much was hidden in that man, El-rei Dom João! El-rei Dom João was hidden within himself; and certain imperfections of the king that were most widely commented on were a natural covering and mask with which God had hidden in the king what He wanted to bring about through him, in order that the king's wonders might be more wondrous.[30]

It was finally D. João's humility and simple faith that made him an instrument of divine providence. Humility is "the quality that God seeks more than any other in those he wishes to make an instrument of his wonders, without dwelling on their other imperfections and human weaknesses."[31] God transforms those imperfections and weaknesses into agents for the fulfillment of prophecy. This passage provides the most complete statement before the *História do futuro* of Vieira's interpretation of how prophecy is fulfilled.

Vieira here subverts the categories with which we define heroism and its manifestations in history. His text recalls the Maundy Thursday

---

[29] Vieira, *Representação segunda*, 1: 234.
[30] Vieira, *Obras escolhidas*, 6: 46.
[31] Ibid., 47.

sermons of 1655. Preaching on the humanity of Jesus, Vieira affirmed that the washing of the feet was a more important manifestation of God's love than the Incarnation. In the *Esperanças*, he focuses on D. João's humility as an example of *imitatio Christi* and the hidden workings of divine providence.

José van den Besselaar, assessing Vieira's various writings on D. João, concludes that the *Esperanças* praised D. João excessively, and that by the time Vieira wrote the *Representations*, he had arrived at a more realistic view of the king.[32] It might be more accurate, however, to place the *Esperanças* and the *Representations* in a continuum. During the years that elapsed between the writing of these two texts, Vieira refined, but never abandoned, his interpretation of D. João. In the *Representations*, he would focus on the difference between kings who have been seen and kings who have been read (*reys vistos* and *reys lidos*). The years in prison simply made this difference more apparent, as Vieira placed increasing emphasis on the mysterious relationship between history and the prophetic text. Over the course of his prophetic writings, Vieira transferred the focus of his hope in the *Encoberto* successively from D. Sebastião to D. João IV, D. Afonso VI, D. Pedro II, and finally to D. Pedro's two sons, the first of whom died in infancy and the second of whom became D. João V. This continuous transfer, rather than reflecting the inconsistencies in Vieira's interpretation of the Fifth Empire, obeys the logic of prophecy that he develops for the first time in the *Esperanças*.[33]

Vieira follows up his long attack on the Portuguese (particularly the learned Portuguese) who refuse to recognize the prophecies with a passage in which he compares the imminent resurrection of D. João to the raising of Lazarus. His purpose runs deeper than merely equating

[32] "Specious argument: Dom João, precisely because he is an antihero, will be chosen by God to be the hero of the last times!" (Besselaar, *O sebastianismo*, 124; cf. Vieira, *Representação primeira*, 1: 198).

[33] Azevedo recognizes the internal logic of Vieira's thought but continues to dismiss his preoccupation with the Fifth Empire as an aberration. "Like all superior intellects, António Vieira, tenacious in his ideas and driven by a tyrannical desire to impose them, was able to abandon these ideas and pass on to other ones through a process of evolution that was both easy and in the end absolutely logical. Those who are inclined to oppose him might suggest that this shows him to be inconsistent. The fact is that little by little he was abandoning the idea of the resurrection of D. João IV, which he saw was not coming to pass, and placing in other kings his hopes for the Fifth Empire" (*A evolução de sebastianismo*, 93–94).

two miraculous events. Casting himself in the role not of a prophet but of a venturesome apostle, he draws on the story of Thomas's exhortation to the apostles after they learned of Jesus' plan to return to Jerusalem.[34] This story of fear, hesitation, and resolve is a call to action based on faith alone. Vieira makes this same call to the Portuguese. Like his direct references to Bandarra, Vieira's evocation of the primitive church deemphasizes erudition in favor of the simple piety he would emphasize more and more in the course of his imprisonment and trial.

The closing lines of the *Esperanças* were written for the wide Portuguese audience Vieira hoped to reach with his avowedly secret letter. Like Bandarra, Vieira suggests that those who dispute his conclusions have misunderstood his text. He stops short, however, of claiming the kind of authority for the *Esperanças* that he asserts for the *Trovas*. Despite the attention he expects his commentary to receive, he declines to liken himself to Bandarra, who wrote in his dedication of the *Trovas* to D. João de Portugal: "Indaque estem remoendo,/Não me toquem no calçado." Bandarra predicted that he would have many critics (*glosadores*); Vieira suggests that his gloss on Bandarra will attract even more attention than the *Trovas* themselves. He concludes by quoting Bandarra, who claimed to have concealed more than he revealed.

> Sei medir, sei talhar,
> Sempre [sem que] vos assim pareça;
> Tudo tenho na cabeça,
> Se eu o quiser usar;
> E quem o quiser grozar,
> Olhe bem a minha obra,
> E verá que ainda me sobra
> Dois cabos para ajuntar.[35]

---

[34] "'Rabbi, the Jews were but now seeking to stone you, and are you going there again?' . . . 'Let us also go, that we may die with him'" (Jn 11.8, 16). Vieira also refers to this passage in a letter to his friend D. Rodrigo de Meneses, to show that he is as much concerned with evangelical resolve as with miracles. Resisting D. Rodrigo's efforts to obtain his release from prison, Vieira wrote, "I wish to be resurrected not with Lazarus but with the universal resurrection of humanity, because I believe it is certain that our day of judgment shall come soon" (*Cartas*, 2: 25).

[35] Bandarra, *Trovas*, Dedicatória, quoted in Vieira, *Esperanças*, 66. Besselaar wrily notes that these verses "do not reveal any inferiority complex" on the part of the cobbler (*O sebastianismo*, 54).

In Maranhão, Vieira could not have envisioned the resonance these words—half invitation, half taunt—would soon possess for him. Between his purposeful affirmation of Bandarra in the *Esperanças* and his meandering and often evasive defense in the *Representations* lay seven years of defeat that proved to be the decisive influence in shaping Vieira's later pastoral and prophetic thought.

From Maranhão to Coimbra, 1661-1667

The writing of the defense was only one of the many dramas of the years Vieira spent in the Inquisition's custody. Vieira repeatedly delayed submitting the two *Representations* to the Inquisitors, ostensibly for reasons of health (he suffered bouts of malaria throughout the years he spent under house arrest and in prison, and may also have had tuberculosis).[36] Besides illness, Vieira had some strategic reasons for delaying the conclusion of the trial as long as possible. First, D. Afonso's grip on power was precarious at best, and with each delay the probability increased that D. Pedro (to whose faction Vieira belonged) would become prince regent. Second, Vieira was working on a prophetic treatise—the *História do futuro*—which he hoped would find a warm reception from the Inquisition and the crown, regardless of who the king might be. The audience—particularly the royal audience— figures prominently in the *História do futuro*. The text is suffused with the inflections of the preacher who seeks both to revitalize Portuguese religious and political life and to free himself from the grasp of the Inquisition.[37]

[36] See Cidade's speculations about Vieira's possible bout with tuberculosis in the preface to *Representação primeira*, 1: viii. For references to Vieira's illnesses see also Vieira, *Cartas*, 2, especially the Christmas letter of 1663 to D. Rodrigo de Meneses, in which Vieira writes of "this frozen Coimbra backland, where I have already been three times dead; and I do not know how I will be able to sustain even these weak breaths that keep me more in an absence of illness than in a state of health" (18).

[37] See Azevedo, *HAV*, 2: 31. Azevedo discounts the possibility that the *História do futuro* might ever have made its way to the councils of D. Afonso; Vieira's belief that the text might improve his standing with the Inquisition, furthermore, was an example of his self-deception.

> Supposing ... despite the immensity of the project, the text's lack of organization, and the author's continual diversions, that Vieira had been able to appear before the Holy Office with the *História do futuro* completed, his position would not thereby have changed. It is certain that the Inquisitors would not have seen

Vieira's dealings with the tribunal during his first two years of imprisonment appear in many ways to have been marked by a certain insouciance, particularly with regard to the deadlines he had been handed for the submission of his defense. As late as the waning months of 1665, Vieira showed relatively little outward concern with its progress. After a combative session with the Inquisitor Alexandre da Silva, he continued to be more preoccupied with interpreting the recent appearance of a comet in Coimbra than with presenting to his accusers the document he had promised them. This, furthermore, was the period during which Vieira (along with his Jesuit colleagues) identified D. Afonso VI as the *Encoberto*. Vieira's apparent lack of regard for the Inquisition proceedings is misleading, however. He had sworn to maintain secrecy concerning the trial, and was therefore not permitted to leave any written evidence of his preoccupation with his defense other than the documents that he later submitted to the tribunal.

While it has been clearly determined that the *Representations* were written in 1665–66, the precise period when the *História do futuro* was written has been one of the central points of controversy concerning the text.[38] With the notable exception of Marcel Bataillon, readers have attached merely a biographical interest to dating the text.[39] Internal

---

in the glorious book anything but matter for new accusations. The hope that Vieira placed in the book was one more of his illusions (*HAV* 2: 53–54).

[38] The final page of the *Second Representation* is dated July 23, 1666. From examining the original manuscript of the *História do futuro*, Azevedo concludes that after writing the opening passages in 1649, Vieira abandoned the project until 1663, when he could devote himself to it while under house arrest (*História do futuro*, ed. Azevedo, 114). Cantel rejects this conclusion and argues that much of the work was done in Brazil, where, with the natural and human obstacles to conversion Vieira faced daily, "his thinking was opened up" ("L'*História do futuro* du père António Vieira," 35). Besselaar, who offers the soundest argument for the composition dates, takes it as a given that much of the thinking took place in Brazil, but concludes that the text was written mainly in Coimbra (*Livro anteprimeiro*, Introduction, 7).

[39] Marcel Bataillon, in his excellent essay on the *História do futuro*, does not address this question but assumes that Vieira composed the text after returning from Maranhão. See "Le Brésil dans une vision d'Isaie selon le père António Vieira." Bataillon's discussion of the importance of Brazil in the *História do futuro* also leaves aside several of the specific Amazonian referents that render Vieira's interpretation less mysterious than Bataillon suggests. He takes the text's "astounding Brazilianness" as evidence of both Vieira's eccentricity and his exegetical genius. But Bataillon does not look with any precision at the text's minute examination of Indian life: "What good would it do to enter into more details?" (13). In concentrating on

biographical evidence suggests that sections of the *História do futuro* were drafted before 1664. That evidence becomes relatively unimportant, however, when considered alongside Vieira's interpretive schema. Vieira's missionary experience, his exile from Maranhão, and his imprisonment were the decisive factors in the composition of the *História do futuro* and the transformation of the millenarian vision Vieira had first expressed in the 1640s.[40]

Vieira's "Lusocentric millenarianism," as Besselaar has described it, took early shape from his contact with the Portuguese Jewish community in Amsterdam in 1646 and 1648. A series of conversations with Rabbi Menasseh ben Israel inspired Vieira to forge what proved to be a fateful link between the Jewish belief that the ten lost tribes would be restored to Israel and his own incipient belief in redemption by a Portuguese king who would serve as the temporal vicar of the Fifth Empire.[41] The spiritual vicar of this empire would be the pope. Besselaar underlines the importance of Vieira's eight-month sojourn in Amsterdam in 1648 and suggests that it was there that Vieira experienced his second *estalo*.[42] The months in Amsterdam were decisive, above all, in forming Vieira's conception of the pivotal role of the Jews in the missionary enterprise.

Vieira's larger interpretive schema, however, Bataillon draws a series of suggestive conclusions. Vieira, he argues, "identifies behind the veil of prophetic language a whole complex of Brazilian realities that alone, he believes, provide the key to the text from Isaiah [chap. 18]. Even better, it is the Brazil of Maranhão that alone can explain everything" (12). In his discussion of the role of the Antipodes (of which Maranhão is a part) in the universal conversion, Bataillon introduces the elegant conceit that "one hardly betrays Vieira's thinking in saying that the last days are the temporal 'Antipodes' of the creation of the world" (20).

[40] Several passages in the *Cartas* make it possible to identify the period when Vieira worked on the *História do futuro* (2: 59, 74, 143, 160, 166). Cantel makes effective use of the internal evidence in the text ("L'*História do futuro* du père António Vieira").

[41] "Vieira convinced [the Rabbi] of the truth of the true Messiah who was being awaited [by the Jews], and of the coming of Jesus Christ in whom this truth had been fulfilled; and by this same Rabbi the same Father Vieira was convinced that in the second coming that was hoped for the reign of the king or universal emperor would be both temporal and spiritual" (Lusitanus Anonymus, *Crisis Paradoxa super Tractatu Insignis P. Antonii Vieyrae Lusitani Societatis Iesus: De Regno Christi in Terris consummato*, cited by Besselaar in Vieira, *Livro anteprimeiro*, Introduction, 5).

[42] Vieira's first *estalo* (revelation) occurred during prayer when he was a novice in Bahia; see Introduction.

The factors that led Vieira to recognize the dual Jewish hope were not merely speculative. Essentially a man of action, Vieira saw in this hope a powerful motivation for the renewal of missionary activity: should the Church come to recognize the legitimacy of the aspirations of the people of Israel, it would be a relatively simple task to remove the principal obstacle preventing that people from seeing in Jesus Christ its spiritual Messiah. The Amsterdam discussions held for Vieira an interest that was not only academic but also (and more importantly) existential. These discussions would guide his studies and activities until the end of his life.[43]

Although the importance of these discussions should not be underestimated, it was not in Amsterdam but rather in prison that Vieira experienced a second *estalo*. The defeat in Brazil and two years in prison tested Vieira's certainty about his messianic vision as no previous experiences had. Only through reflection in prison on his own mission work and on the Society's recent history did Vieira cement the link between the conversion of the Jews and the conversion of the New World that he had begun to consider in Amsterdam. Vieira in prison experienced a "revelation of pure suffering" that made him perceive with unprecedented clarity the prophetic themes of the *História do futuro*, and left him more convinced than ever of the truth of his Fifth Empire vision.[44]

In the closing pages of the *Livro anteprimeiro*, in a lyrical passage about the nature of hope, Vieira provides a foretaste of the language and logic with which he will interpret verses from Isaiah to apply to Brazil and the Portuguese missionary vocation.

This world is a theater; men are the players on its stage, and the true history of their fortunes a comedy by God that is wondrously drawn and staged by the ages of His Providence. And just as the excellence and subtlety of the art of comedy consists principally in that suspension of the understanding and sweet confusion of the senses with which the plot carries men along, leaving them hanging from one development to the next, and shielding the end of the story from those who would guess it, so that no one can know where it will end until the moment when that end comes upon him and reveals itself suddenly between the expectation and the applause; in the same way God ... does not permit us to grasp and understand the secrets of His intentions until the ends of those intentions are

---

[43] Besselaar, Introduction to Vieira, *Livro anteprimeiro*, 7.
[44] The phrase is from Iris Murdoch, *The Black Prince*, 349.

upon us, in order that we might be held always suspended in expectation and hanging by His Providence.[45]

Between the expectation and the applause, the mysteries of secular history unfold. Foremost among them is the faltering progress of the missionary church. The church, for Vieira, is a necessarily fragile creation whose future can never be adequately discerned. It is the obligation of those who possess a gift for interpretation to draw on the increments of knowledge from each successive age to understand how the prophecies of Scripture will be fulfilled. Prophecies, however, are like water, "dark . . . however clear they might be."[46]

In anticipation of potential criticisms of his insertion of Brazil into the traditional Christian interpretation of history, Vieira suggests in the *Livro anteprimeiro* that those who have rejected him for the novelty of what he wrote are guilty of the very pride for which they have condemned him. He takes as his point of reference the ideal relationship between writer and reader as described by Augustine.

> We are not obliged to regard the arguments of any writers, however Catholic and estimable they may be, as we do the canonical Scriptures, so that we may not—with all due respect to the deference owed them as men—refute or reject anything we happen to find in their writings wherein their opinions differ from the established truth, or from what has been thought out by others or by us, with divine help. I wish other thinkers to hold the same attitude toward my writings as I hold toward theirs.[47]

Vieira insists throughout the *História do futuro* and the *Representations* that his own texts be read in the manner that Augustine describes. In doing so, he turns Augustine's argument into a more general appeal to the imagination of his audience. In Vieira's hands—especially in the *First Representation*—Augustine's attenuation of the authority of his words and those of other writers prescribes a mode of interpreting not only texts but also lives. For his part, Vieira proposes a two-pronged argument about reading, writing, and interpretation. First, he warns that fear of new ideas ties the living to the dead and thus impedes the progress of the church.[48] Second, he links his warning (with its echoes

[45] *Livro anteprimeiro*, 10: 223.

[46] Ibid., 290.

[47] Ibid., 12: 348, citing Augustine, *Letters*, 148, in *The Fathers of the Church*, vol. 20 (New York, 1953), 235–36.

[48] Vieira had sketched the outlines of this new ecclesiology in an even more

of Jesus' teaching, "Let the dead bury the dead") to his larger interpretation of postbiblical prophecy.

Only by keeping this argument in mind can the *História do futuro* and the *Representations* be understood as more than just arbitrary attempts to validate the controversial prophecies of the *Esperanças*.[49] These texts constitute a sustained argument for human fallibility and for the right of every exegete to interpret the signs of the times. Vieira opens his Inquisition defense by disavowing any intention to defend the truth of the *Esperanças*; instead, he asserts only his right to draw on his experience in Brazil (and the disillusionment that followed) to reformulate his ideas. Although Vieira never refers directly to Brazil in the introductory pages of the *First Representation*, the text bears nevertheless the unmistakable mark of the missionary who set to work on the *Esperanças* while sitting in a canoe and who now insists that his ideas have moved beyond their rudimentary beginnings.

> The propositions [of the *Esperanças*] are today in a very different time and state from those in which they were put forward [in 1659], because the very demonstration to which the author has been subjected [by the Inquisition] is both a tacit and an explicit condemnation of these propositions; [yet] when they were put forward they were under no prohibition, censure, or qualification of any kind other than the truth or natural probability of their foundations. And this is the supposition and reflection with which these propositions should now be seen and examined, or censured, as if they had never been subjected to this scrutiny . . . for having been adopted in such a

---

veiled form in the *Esperanças*; he would develop it at length in the *Second Representation* and the later sermons.

[49] Cidade and Besselaar briefly note that interpretations such as linking Isaiah to Maranhão might appear implausible to the modern reader, but in general they take a sympathetic approach to Vieira's exegetical project, even when they think Vieira overreaches. Besselaar is careful to temper his analysis of Vieira's limitations as a scholar by observing, "the present work might give the impression of coming from the hand of a small-minded critic who is no friend of Vieira. In reality, I love and admire Vieira, in spite of his lack of solid erudition, critical spirit, and precision. It is not difficult for me to admire and love him as he is; I feel no need to embellish him or cover his faults" ("Erudição," 78). For a similar (though less exuberant) admission of affection, see Cidade's tribute to the "vigorous power of [Vieira's] audacious imagination" (*Representação primeira, Prefácio*, 1: xx). Cidade, however, creates a false distinction between "moments in which Vieira's thought moves from the quotidian plane to the transcendent one" (*Representação segunda, Posfácio*, 2: vii). Vieira recognized no firm categories of this kind; in both his writings and his political activities, he insisted on the link between history and Scripture and viewed the apparent inconsistencies between the two as a welcome challenge to the interpreter.

different time and under such different circumstances, these propositions are no longer the same but rather distinctly different from what they were; likewise it is certain that the one who advanced them at that earlier time would not advance them now.[50]

The words of the interpreters, like the Bible itself, must be read in the light of history. The mixture in this passage of confidence and caution sets a tone that is sustained throughout the discussion of Bandarra and D. João in the first part of the defense. The defense suggests that Vieira's modification of his earlier propositions has resulted as much from the evolution of his missionary exegesis in the colony and in prison as from the Inquisition's condemnation of the *Esperanças*. Vieira petitions his accusers to review his ideas as they have evolved since his return from Brazil. And if his avowed submission to the authority of the Inquisition is a procedural nicety, it is also an affirmation of the hope that his defense will demonstrate the orthodoxy of his interpretive method.

The *First Representation* systematically develops one of the arguments Vieira treated in the *Esperanças*: that the gift of prophecy has no necessary connection to wisdom or to virtue. Fortune—which alone gives insight to any individual—may favor children as readily (and as mysteriously) as bishops. Vieira's strategy for presenting this argument undergoes a gradual change over the two parts of the defense. As a result of his experience in Brazil and the reprimands he has received from the Inquisition, Vieira begins the *First Representation* with a series of disclaimers (albeit characteristically equivocal ones) in which he tries to placate the Inquisitors. At this point, moreover, Vieira does not affect to speak to the inaccessible audience outside the prison walls, the way he will in the second part of the defense. In the *Second Representation*, Vieira subtly recasts the apostolic lesson from his composition of the *Esperanças* on the Amazon, showing that his distance from the church hierarchy is not a liability but an integral part of his gift of interpretation. He no longer describes his isolation in Brazil as an impediment to orthodoxy. Instead, he presents it as the raw material with which he instructs—and converts—the guardians of orthodoxy in the metropolis.

As he develops this idea (along with the larger theme of progressive revelation) in the *Second Representation*, Vieira begins to recover some of the contentiousness that is absent from the defense's relatively con-

---

[50] Vieira, *Representação primeira*, 1: 5–6.

ciliatory introduction. His analysis of the incremental steps by which secular history is revealed was stated objectively in the *First Representation*, but here his tone becomes more personal as he moves successively from specific interpretations of the conversion of the Jews and the non-Christians of the New World to a wider-ranging (and more exhortatory) discussion of the Fifth Empire and Portuguese mission.

To accompany this shift in tone, Vieira increasingly emphasizes Brazil's role in the fulfillment of prophecy and the importance of his own missionary experience in demonstrating the intermixing of the temporal and spiritual kingdoms. His experience has convinced Vieira that the Portuguese are more culpable for failing to read "the signs of the times" than preceding Christians were. He compares the church fathers to mariners unable to reach the right destination because of faulty maps; their wisdom gets them to the right place unaided, but they cannot recognize that they have arrived, so they rewrite history, accommodating events of the distant future to events that have already occurred.[51] The Portuguese, likewise, are responsible for historic changes in the missionary church that, out of willful blindness, they do not recognize. The prophecies have been obscure and will remain so, despite the insights of the church fathers. This is partly because in concentrating on the allegorical sense of such mysteries as the Incarnation and the Resurrection, the fathers ignored the literal meaning of Scripture in history. The Portuguese of the present generation, Vieira argues, have been granted unique access to this literal meaning of the truths of Scripture, and his defense to the Inquisition—despite his stated intentions—gradually becomes as impassioned a call to recognize these truths as is the *História do futuro*.

Vieira's most telling demonstration of these ideas occurred during his fifteenth interrogation by the Inquisition, on November 24, 1666. He carried his theory of interpretation further than at any point in the defense or in his other prophetic writings, supporting his argument by pointing to biblical precedents for questioning the fundamental tenets of the faith.

The Inquisitors ordered Vieira to acknowledge that Jesus' self-revelation to the disciples left no room for exegesis. Vieira refused to yield. Throughout the proceedings, the Inquisitors had refused to allow Vieira to consult a Bible; in this interrogation, his request was again de-

---

[51]*Representação segunda*, 1: 228–35.

nied, even as the Inquisitors challenged him to cite the passages from Luke in which Christ's redeeming mission might be subject to different interpretations. Arguing from memory, therefore, Vieira responded,

> the text from the passage cited in St. Luke was about the doubt and despair of the Disciples at Emmaus, when they said, "But we had hoped that he was the one to redeem Israel," and the text from the passage in the Acts of the Apostles was of the same kind: "Lord, will you at this time restore the kingdom to Israel?"
>
> And as for the places in which Christ provided explanations concerning himself or else declined to explain, it likewise seems to him [the prisoner] that these cannot be perfectly understood; for inasmuch as the Evangelists do not refer to these passages, the Church Doctors cannot interpret them with certainty, as they themselves confess; so that for the defendant to say that Christ did not explain all the words that speak of Him but only those pertaining to the passages discussed above, is in conformity with the general rule of all the Expositors of Holy Scripture, which states in such cases that when one speaks about any passages in Scripture one is speaking only about those passages that belong to the particular text that one is interpreting.[52]

With this argument, Vieira turned the Inquisition's own weapons against his accusers. He also demonstrated how much his imprisonment had informed his interpretation of Scripture. The doubt and despair Vieira discerned among the Disciples from his confinement in the prison cell and the interrogation chamber would be wholly absent from his presentation of the same scriptural lesson to the novices in Bahia 25 years later.[53] Then, Vieira would speak from a position of strength; in prison he spoke from a position of weakness. He was weakened by the Inquisitors' assumption of guilt and by the intellectual disadvantage of being denied the texts he needed to mount a thorough defense. Equally important, Vieira was physically weakened by his imprisonment and by the illnesses that had nearly taken his life earlier. Vieira's genius for imagining his way into the literal circumstances of Scripture thus received its quintessential expression in these last sessions with the Inquisitors.

The despair of the imprisoned missionary in Coimbra found its scriptural antecedent in the period of doubt between Jesus' death and the birth of the church militant at Pentecost. Vieira's interpretation of

---

[52] Ibid., 334.
[53] See Vieira, *Exhortação primeira em vespora do Espírito Santo*, in *Sermões*, 8: 514–34.

Luke's narrative demonstrates his view that the exegete can and must intertwine his own history with biblical prophecy and its interpretation. In Jesus' words to the disciples, Vieira found an affirmation that our understanding of Jesus' saving mission is fragile. Vieira sought to reclaim the humanity of Jesus for the missionary church. An unwritten premise of the defense, and particularly of the *Second Representation*, is that in insisting on the purely spiritual nature of Jesus' kingdom, the Inquisitors were suppressing the primary meaning of the Incarnation. Vieira insisted, even in his final confrontations with his accusers, that it was the duty of Christians to discern the signs of Jesus' mission in his works in this world and in the provisional progress of his church.

Exile, 1668-1681

The Inquisitors offered Vieira several opportunities to retract the propositions of the *Esperanças*. His primary reasons for refusing to do so were his belief in the justice of his cause and his sense of personal dignity; but he also refused, he said, to stain the reputation of Portugal by compromising his interpretation of the nation's historic mission, or to stain the honor of the Jesuits with an acknowledgment of guilt. As late as the interrogation of December 1666—five months after submitting the *Representations*—Vieira was still adamant on all these points. A session intended to allow Vieira finally to disavow the propositions that had brought him so much trouble turned into a forum for Vieira's most impassioned confrontation with his accusers.[54]

Besides repeating his refusal to impugn the honor of the nation and the order, Vieira warned of the implications—for the progress of the missionary church in general and for the conversion of the Indians of Brazil in particular—if he were convicted. The theme of apostleship that figures so importantly throughout the *História do futuro* and the defense looms larger than ever in the later interrogations. Once again, Vieira stresses his work as a missionary to the Indians (and the Jews) rather than his position as a religious from the metropolis.

[54] The interrogation appears in the defense under the title, "Eighteenth Examination, and Mediation, for the purpose of concluding once and for all with the many verbal protests, petitions and submissions that the defendant makes, and of forcing him to state clearly whether he wishes to recognize the censures and warnings and desist from his defense and further explanations and philosophical arguments." *Representação segunda*, 2: 357.

From the examinations and warnings that have been made to the deponent concerning these matters he understands that he is suspected of Judaism and of other errors against our Holy Catholic Faith; and that if he were to desist from seeking to dispel this suspicion ... such an action would without doubt not only bring grave discredit to his religious order but would also be a great scandal for this Kingdom and for all Christianity, where he is known not only as a religious but also as a very distinguished teacher for the preaching and defense of the faith, for the truth of which he has had many disputations in the principal Provinces and Cities of Europe against every kind of heretic and against the Jews themselves; and recently in America he has worked for the propagation of this same Faith, bringing about the conversion of thousands of gentiles. Should the deponent be judged and taken for suspect in matters of the Faith, these gentiles (along with the rest of the Infidels) would rightly be most scandalized and would form a very different conception from what they ought to have of the preachers of the Gospel and defenders of the Faith.[55]

Vieira's refusal to yield prolonged the trial by eight months.[56] When he finally capitulated, in August 1667, he submitted to the authority of Pope Alexander VII and not to the arguments of his accusers. After being informed that the pope had personally censured the propositions of the *Esperanças*, Vieira abandoned his attempt to prove his innocence and agreed to be sentenced. By submitting to the pope, Vieira availed himself of an honorable means to end a trial that had become burdensome for the Inquisition as well as for the prisoner. For its part, the Inquisition, facing the imminent removal of D. Afonso VI and the prospect of confronting Vieira's powerful allies from the faction of the future D. Pedro II, was eager to rid itself of one of its most insistent opponents.[57]

The Coimbra tribunal, acknowledging that both the General Council

[55] Ibid., 364. Vieira refers to himself not as a defendant but as one who provides testimony (*declarante*). The link between the conversion of the Jews and the conversion of the Indians is a recurrent theme of the *Representations*. See Chap. 5.

[56] Azevedo singles out this encounter as one of Vieira's finest moments. "Here Vieira revealed all his determination and the extent of his intrepidness. It was no longer the vanity of the unyielding polemicist who was mindful of his reputation but rather an exalted sense of personal dignity that allowed Vieira to endure the prolongation of the present sacrifice [imprisonment] and brave the dangers of the final punishment" (*HAV*, 2: 77).

[57] "The [Inquisition's] prestige was not heightened by the persistent defiance of a defendant whom it sought to humble but against whom it could not easily proceed with extreme violence. ... For both parties, then, the solution was advantageous" (ibid., 79).

in Lisbon and the Sacred Congregation in Rome had been informed of the *Esperanças*, censured Vieira for his arguments, "noting that some of them were against common Catholic interpretation and were presumptuous, dangerous, and scandalous; while others offended the ears of pious and faithful Catholics and were erroneous and injurious to the Holy Fathers and Holy Scripture, and had the flavor of heresy."[58] The tribunal's relatively benign sentence placed only one restriction on Vieira: he had to remain in Portugal. This measure was taken to prevent Vieira from undermining the Inquisition's authority by advancing his ideas outside the country. The General Council, however, overruled the tribunal and issued a sentence that surely wounded Vieira: it permanently barred him from preaching and placed him under house arrest in the Jesuit novitiate in Cotovia, near Lisbon. (The original order to send Vieira to the Jesuit house at Pedroso was commuted before his departure.[59])

The sentence was read to Vieira in a private audience on December 23, 1667, and in a special Jesuit convocation the following morning that inspired the most resounding demonstration of solidarity that Vieira would ever receive from his colleagues in the Society.[60] Vieira, however, never resigned himself to the Council's censure; and with the accession of D. Pedro as prince regent, he quickly gained permission to travel to Rome to overturn the sentence. In addition, the Inquisition in June 1668 lifted the ban it had imposed on Vieira and permitted him to preach freely again, demanding only that he no longer speak of the propositions for which he had been sentenced.

The stated pretext for Vieira's trip was an effort to canonize Luiz Figueira and his companions on the ill-fated 1643 journey to Maranhão; but Vieira's real purpose was to overturn his Inquisition sentence, and this purpose was clear to his friends and fellow Jesuits. After five years in Rome, Vieira was vindicated, in a brief issued by Pope Clement X in April 1675. The brief recognized Vieira's "virtues and good conduct"

[58] *Sentença que no tribunal do Santo Ofício de Coimbra se leu ao Padre António Vieira,* in Vieira, *Obras escolhidas,* 6: 181–82.

[59] Cidade, Preface, *Representação primeira,* 1: xxxvii; Azevedo, *HAV,* 2: 82; Vieira, *Obras escolhidas,* 6: 235–36.

[60] "When the condemned man stood up to have his sentence read, all the religious who had convened in the chapter house stood with him. It was a common protest against an injury that the fathers well knew had been imposed (in its calculated reach) as much on the whole Order as on the colleague who personally suffered it" (Azevedo, *HAV,* 2: 83).

and granted him permanent immunity from the jurisdiction of the Portuguese Inquisition.[61]

Vieira's years in Rome were years of triumph. He was invited to become confessor to Queen Christina of Sweden, and he joined the inner circle of the Jesuit General, Gian Paolo Oliva. Yet Vieira never considered himself anything more than a visitor in Rome. Although he welcomed the honors that came to him, he remained preoccupied with Portugal, his return home, and the progress of the missionary church, from which he was enduring an enforced absence.[62] Oliva's recommendation that Vieira succeed him as preacher at the papal court only provoked Vieira to reaffirm his missionary vocation, in a letter to his friend D. Rodrigo de Meneses in Lisbon.[63] He had learned Italian at Oliva's insistence and had become one of the most celebrated preachers in Rome. The audience he wanted to reach, however, was not the learned audience of the papal court; and he asked D. Rodrigo to find him a position that would take him away from Rome.

> These honors, however gilded they might be, will tie me to Rome in such a way that I will die here, though my life be long (and they will help not a little in abbreviating it). . . . I know the language of Maranhão and the Portuguese language, and it is a great misery that being able to serve my country and my prince with either one of these, I should at this age have to study a foreign language in order to serve foreign tastes, and without fruit.[64]

This complaint carries not only a dramatic burden—Vieira's life is endangered by the niceties of religious life in Rome—but also an evangelical one: his speaking will be cut short by the requirement to speak

---

[61] *Breve de isenção das Inquisições de Portugal e mais reinos. Ao amado filho António Vieira, presbítero da Companhia de Jesus, português*, in *Obras escolhidas*, 6: 246.

[62] Azevedo ignores this continued preoccupation in his discussion of Vieira's thirteen-year interlude in Lisbon and Rome; he focuses instead on Vieira's unfulfilled longing to be reintegrated into Portuguese political life (*HAV*, 2: 97–222).

[63] "With this letter goes a sermon that the Father General obliged me to preach in Italian, something that he has desired for a long time. And despite the defects of pronunciation (for which I apologize in the sermon), it was so well received by the cardinals and other important men of this court that the Father General directed me to preach (at the insistence of these same Eminences) to two assemblies that the whole Sacred College [of Cardinals] attends. The Father General is the Pope's only preacher. He is the greatest preacher in Italy, and he and many others wish that I might succeed him in the office." It had also been suggested that Vieira become the Jesuit Assistant in Rome for the Portuguese province (Vieira, *Cartas*, 2: 515).

[64] Ibid.

in Italian and by the accumulated weight of the honors that his preaching in Rome will bring. Vieira sent his first sermon in Italian to the Marquês de Gouveia on the same day he complained to D. Rodrigo,

> The worst of it is that with this sermon being the first one, their Eminences do not wish it to be the last, and have already chosen me for two chapels [assemblies] at which the Sacred College comes together. And they are able to interpret as an omen their wish to listen to one with a barbarous tongue.[65]

Although Vieira's immediate hope was to serve the Portuguese in any capacity, Maranhão rather than Lisbon was his preferred destination. And with this gaze toward the church in the New World from the church's center in Rome, Vieira returned in his writing to the pastoral concerns of his Inquisition defense. The pope and the cardinals were foreign to him in a way the Indians of Maranhão would never be.

Vieira did not refer to his "barbarous tongue" out of mere self-deprecation. The locution was part of his 40-year effort to invert European perceptions of language and its efficacy in the conversion process. Language was also a defining element of the imperial project. Vieira's distance from the Lusophone world and the Indian languages of the New World represented, for him, a betrayal of the missionary ideal that had shaped his career. Speaking Italian with the pope and cardinals was the apostolic equivalent of carrying on a monologue—the kind of monologue, as Eduardo Lourenço has argued, that crippled the Portuguese imperial imagination and much of the literature and historiography that sprang from it.[66]

Vieira's work in Maranhão, Lisbon, and Rome convinced him that speaking the language of the church leaders would not further the work of universal conversion, but would instead reproduce the empty rhetoric that his sermons denounced. The "barbarous tongues" of the Indians represented an obstacle to conversion that could be overcome through concentrated study.[67] In contrast, Italian—the most civilized language in the world—was barbarous to Vieira, because mastering it drew clerics to the comforts of Rome and away from the missionary enterprise.

---

[65] Ibid., 513.
[66] *O labirinto da saudade*, 37–44.
[67] Vieira, *Exhortação primeira em vespora do Espírito Santo*, 518.

Vieira left Rome for Lisbon in 1675. Between that time and his return to Bahia in 1681, he loosened some of the ties with Portugal that he would eventually sever formally in a famous 1694 letter, in which he took leave of his friends and explained his retreat from public life.[68] When he returned to Brazil, the corruption of the church in Rome and Lisbon increasingly weighed on him, and D. Pedro II was no longer seeking his advice. Back in Bahia after a 40-year absence, Viera focused his attention on the daily struggles of the missionary church, despite his initial intention to reduce his pastoral responsibilities and devote himself to writing. His later letters and sermons (as well as his massive historical and exegetical work *Clavis Prophetarum*) demonstrate, however, that he never abandoned the prophetic vision of the imperial project that he had sought to impart to the Portuguese since he first entered the service of the crown. He continued to look outward from Bahia.

[68] Vieira, *Cartas*, 3: 661–62.

CHAPTER FIVE

Visions of the Portuguese Empire

THE HARDSHIPS of the Maranhão mission and the Inquisition trial transformed Vieira's interpretation of the history of Portugal and Brazil. Between 1661 and 1667, Vieira refined his argument that Brazil occupied a privileged position in the missionary church, and he insisted with unprecedented specificity that Scripture, the missionary enterprise, and the apostleship of the Portuguese nation were interwoven. The *História do futuro* and the *Representations* contain a series of challenges to ecclesiastical authority, grounded in Vieira's theory and methodology of conversion and, above all, in his Christology. Vieira did not see himself as a rebel aiming to restrict the authority of the metropolitan church. But when he reinterpreted the relationship between Portugal and Brazil, and between the church and the Jesuit order, on the basis of his experience in the New World, he called into question the foundations of the missionary enterprise and its place in the imperial project.

The first part of this chapter examines how Vieira's reading of Daniel and Isaiah shaped his interpretation of Portugal's Christian mission and the Jesuits' role in it. The second part analyzes Vieira's defense of his Fifth Empire vision in the *Second Representation* and the ensuing interrogations of the Inquisition tribunal. Vieira's defense in the *História do futuro* and *Second Representation* takes on an increasingly personal tone as he applies biblical and domestic Portuguese prophecies to the empire and the Brazilian Amazon. In the *Livro anteprimeiro* and the more discursive *Representations*, Vieira analyzes the theological, historical, and geographical foundations for his interpretation of the providential role of the Portuguese in the universal conversion. He takes the exegetical component of this enterprise seriously (as the series of discussions of the Fifth Empire in the two texts makes clear), but in summing up his efforts at the end of the *Second Representation*, he assigns prime importance to the historical and geographical knowledge he has acquired through direct experience in the missions.[1]

Just as he did in the *Esperanças*, Vieira in the learned *Representations* argues against the utility of study; he even contradicts the very arguments that explain his Fifth Empire vision. For Vieira, the learned tradition had little value when weighed against the faith of the missionary and his two indispensable allies, the crown and the lay apostle.

Daniel, Isaiah, and the Portuguese Mission

The most important biblical influence on Vieira's vision of the Fifth Empire is the Book of Daniel. Vieira draws on Daniel throughout his prison writings in an attempt to establish formal precedents for the interpretation of human knowledge and the gift of prophecy he presents in his informal meditation on Bandarra in the *Esperanças*. Daniel's prophecies, however, do not figure only in Vieira's general argument for the provisional quality of the exegetical process. He also looks to Daniel in advancing his more specific defense of the interpreter's right to enlist history in the service of exegesis. If prophecy is a gift given to the seer God has chosen, the understanding of prophecy is an additional gift that depends on the times in which the seer lives.

> It is the distinct style of God's Providence, for the greater beauty, admiration and applause of its works, to keep hidden the understanding of the prophecies in which these works are revealed, until the time that has been defined and determined in its decrees. . . . Daniel said: "I heard, but I did not understand." And if the prophet himself did not understand what he wrote, what wonder is it that his interpreters do not understand it, even if they should be as holy and as wise as Daniel? But soon Daniel was answered, with God asking that he be wise: "Go your way, Daniel, for the words are shut up and sealed until the time of the end." . . . And so it is that the very mysteries that were hidden from the greatest wise men and Doctors may become clear to those who know much less, because this knowledge is the prerogative not of learning but of the fortune of the times.[2]

This passage legitimates the continuous process of reinterpreting

---

[1] Vieira, *Representação segunda*, in *Defesa*, ed. Cidade, 1: 253.
[2] Ibid., 234; Dan 12.8–9.

biblical prophecy (of which Bandarra and Portugal's other domestic prophets, as well as disciples such as Vieira himself, are a part). Vieira's words are also an appeal to his fellow Portuguese to accompany the persecuted missionary church in its progress toward the Fifth Empire. The Portuguese are to be the successors to the biblical Israelites; and Vieira, the interpreter of this succession, may rightly be understood to be proposing a "religious theory of Portuguese worldwide expansion."[3] With Daniel and Bandarra providing his point of departure, Vieira posits in the *História do futuro* and the *Representations* a relationship between the Portuguese and the people of Israel that the imperial project will bring to completion.

Several key elements of Daniel's prophecy support Vieira's exegetical project in general and his gloss on Bandarra in particular. The first appears in the text of Daniel well before the dream interpretation that will inspire Vieira's Fifth Empire vision. Daniel blesses God as the one from whom all knowledge comes.[4] This theme, a central one in Daniel, provides a scriptural basis for Vieira's insistence (carried over from the *Esperanças*) that Bandarra's lack of education was an indication that he had been chosen by God to prophesy the mission of the Portuguese. Daniel may or may not have been numbered among the wise men of Babylon to whom the text refers; Vieira would have considered the question unimportant (if he had ever addressed it) compared with Daniel's affirmation that wisdom is something given by God to his seers.[5]

---

[3] Saraiva, "António Vieira, Menasseh Ben Israel, et le Cinquième Empire," 32. Throughout the *História do futuro* and the *Representations*, Vieira sees his text as a source of hope for his people, taking as his model the author of Daniel, who witnessed "the culminating wickedness of the powers of this world . . . 'How long, O God?' (Ps 74.10). One can agree that the Book of Daniel is very like a prophetic answer to this appeal" (Norman Porteous, *Daniel: A Commentary*, 100).

[4] "[H]e gives wisdom to the wise and knowledge to those who have understanding" (Dn 2.21).

[5] The first chapter describes Daniel as one of the youths who "were to be educated for three years" (Dn 1.5). Chapter 2.13 places him among the wise men who are to be executed, while 2.25 presents him as an unknown Jew who sought out Nebuchadnezzar. Davies suggests that the inclusion of Daniel among the wise men in chapter 1 is the result of a gloss by the redactor, and that the contradiction between the two versions "can be removed by extracting 2.13–23 from the narrative, since 24 follows smoothly from 12." Daniel, according to this reasoning, would be an anonymous Jew with no special claim to the gift of prophecy, and the reference to the "wise" in 2.21 concerns "the circles amongst which the Book of Daniel arose" ("Daniel Chapter Two," 393–95).

This affirmation assumes special importance in the context of Vieira's defense of the *Esperanças* before the Inquisition. For Vieira, the story of Daniel and Nebuchadnezzar makes manifest the triumph of the cobbler's wisdom over the Inquisitor's learning. Vieira seeks to make this triumph intelligible to his audience. At the same time, he invokes the lessons of Daniel in arguing for the legitimacy of the exegetical principles he is called on to defend throughout the *Representations*.[6] Vieira argues for an approach to the interpretation of prophecy that at once validates and undermines the interpretive enterprise itself. He considers with wonder (and a hint of irony directed toward his accusers) the realization that to be appointed a seer by God means only that one will speak the prophecies, not that one will understand them. God told Daniel that Daniel would not understand his own words until the appointed time. Less privileged seers, then, are unable to interpret the accidents of history in anything but the most provisional way.

The same passages in Daniel inspire Vieira to make one of the boldest arguments in his prophetic writings: the Portuguese nation will succeed the Jewish one as the temporal locus of the Fifth Empire. Vieira grounds his argument in Daniel's interpretation of Nebuchadnezzar's dream (chapter 2) and Daniel's vision of the four beasts (chapter 7).[7] The four metals in the king's dream are most frequently understood to represent the Babylonian, Persian, Medan, and Greek empires. Vieira collapses the distinction between the Persians and Medes and appends the Roman Empire as the temporal power that will give way to the Fifth Empire of Christ.[8]

---

[6] "Quite apart from the revelation regarding the course and climax of world history which the chapter [Dn 2] is to record and which forms its kernel, it has the secondary but important aim of demonstrating the superiority of the God-given wisdom which is at Daniel's disposal to all the vaunted insight which the sages and diviners of Babylon claim to possess by the exercise of human reason or through their control of magical techniques, and, further, of showing that in the event the world is forced to recognize this superiority. That there is an element of wishful thinking in the expectation that the world will make this acknowledgment cannot be denied" (Porteous, *Daniel: A Commentary*, 37).

[7] Dn 2.31–35, 7.1–27.

[8] John G. Gammie notes that an early interpretation of chapters 2 and 7 identified the four metals and the four beasts with the first four Ptolemies, and that only later was the prophecy taken to refer to the Babylonian, Persian, Greek, and Roman empires. "Such is the nature of apocalyptic literature. Even though born in specific historic [sic] circumstances, it continued to give support and encouragement to later Jewish (and Christian) communities through repeated reinterpreta-

With the exception of the Portuguese Empire (which he places within the Roman one), however, Vieira is interested in the four empires as historical entities only insofar as they refer to the empire that is to come. For this reason (in addition to the rhetorical requirements of his defense of the *Esperanças*), Vieira focuses almost exclusively on those elements of the fourth empire that may be taken as signposts of the Portuguese mission. In the universal message of the Book of Daniel Vieira discerns a particular lesson for the Portuguese as successors to the Israelites.[9] Vieira's interpretation applies to Portugal Daniel's prophecies about the end of time and also exhorts the Portuguese to live up to their destiny in the interim. History and prophecy are inseparable in Vieira's interpretation of Daniel. With the Book of Daniel, Vieira affirms that the transcendent dimension of human history is accessible, albeit mysteriously. It remains for God's chosen seers and

---

tion. By the time of 2 Esdras (c. A.D. 90), the original four kingdoms of Daniel 2 and 7 are reshuffled so that the faithful are told that they must now see in the fourth beast the power of Rome (2 Esd 11:1; 12:11)" ("The Classification, Stages of Growth, and Changing Intentions in the Book of Daniel," 204).

Arnaldo Momigliano, in an analysis that applies to the four beasts as well as the four metals, writes, "The statue is not meant to represent a succession of empires: it rather symbolizes the coexistence of all the past, as it had developed through a succession of kingdoms, at the moment in which all the past is destroyed by the divine stone and replaced by a new order" (*Pagans, Christians, and Jews*, 48). Regarding the interpretation of the dream in chapter 2, Davies argues, "it is unlikely . . . that any historical kingdoms were intended to be signified beyond the Babylonian, and perhaps the Persian, depending on the date at which the interpretation was composed" ("Daniel Chapter Two," 399).

In a similar vein, the theme of the limitations of human knowledge has had a long history of reinterpretation. Analyzing the commentary on chapters 2 and 4 by the sixth-century exegete Cosmas Indicopleustes, Sabine MacCormack writes that for Cosmas, "human reason is not the faculty of discursive or logical thought, but the recipient of divine teaching: animals have no reason, and this is manifest not so much in their inability to think, as in the fact that they are not taught by God . . . there is no way in which one could say that knowledge is generated in man: instead, knowledge is passed on to man from God. The result is a passive human reason, rather than an active one" ("Christ and Empire, Time and Ceremonial in Sixth-Century Byzantium and Beyond," 291).

[9] In his commentary on chapter 7, Lacocque suggests that the prophet's universal message is meant to be particularized by each nation: "Each nation . . . according to the Book of Daniel, has its special angel who represents it. By this, we believe, we should understand that each people has a transcendent dimension, the ultimate meaning of its historical destiny" (*The Book of Daniel*, 128).

interpreters to recognize this transcendent dimension in their own time and communicate it, not only to the non-Christians of the New World but also to the Christians of Europe, whose conversion is not yet complete.

As he does throughout the *História do futuro* and the *Representations*, Vieira holds out the possibility that Europe will be converted from something less than Christianity to the Christianity that the missionary church (particularly the Society) has been carrying to the New World. He draws parallels between his accusers and the Chaldeans, who tell Nebuchadnezzar that God does not communicate with humanity.[10] In contrast, Daniel knows "there is a God in heaven who reveals mysteries."[11]

Vieira begins his explication of his Fifth Empire vision with a thinly disguised attack (in the *História do futuro*) on the presumption of the Inquisitors. He has already underlined the fragility of biblical commands that must be reaffirmed by each succeeding generation.[12] He seeks this kind of reaffirmation at the end of the *Livro anteprimeiro* when he insists on the human failings of every interpreter of prophecy. Arguing that the reader has a responsibility to be critical of this text and those of other writers, Vieira draws an explicit parallel between his own position and that of Augustine, who wrote, in his anti-Donatist tract,

> For we are but men; and it is therefore a temptation incident to men that we should hold views at variance with the truth on any point. But to come through too great love for our own opinion, or through jealousy of our betters, even to the sacrilege of dividing the communion of the Church, and of founding heresy or schism, is a presumption worthy of the devil. But never in any point to entertain an opinion at variance with truth is perfection found only in angels.[13]

[10] "The thing that the king asks is difficult, and none can show it to the king except the gods, whose dwelling is not with flesh" (Dn 2.11).

[11] Dn 2.28. These passages affirm "that God does communicate his transcendence to men, he makes himself immanent for their sake" (Lacocque, *Book of Daniel*, 45).

[12] In addition to the *Esperanças*, see the *Sermão das verdades* (1654), in *Sermões*, 4: 291–317.

[13] Augustine, *On Baptism, Against the Donatists*, Book II, ch. 5: 428; quoted in Vieira, *Livro anteprimeiro*, 12: 373. Augustine's views on the Donatists were not always characterized by the moderation expressed here. Peter Brown argues that Augustine cannot be considered an advocate of religious toleration, although his ideas

Vieira then takes Augustine one step further by attempting to discern the providential effects of failed human communication. He draws his most important example from the experience of the Apostles. Peter's failure to understand Jesus the servant was a necessary product of the kind of liminal period that is characterized by "fruitful darkness" (in this case, the period before the infusion of the tongues of fire at Pentecost).[14] During the transition period that preceded the birth of the missionary church, the Apostles' communication with Jesus was imperfect, and their mistakes stand as a permanent instruction for missionaries in the postprimitive church. But modern missionaries, Vieira insists, must draw another lesson from Scripture and the history of the church: they must recognize that the meaning of prophecy is only incrementally revealed.

The notion of fruitful darkness suggests the imagery of light and shadow with which Vieira argues in the *Livro anteprimeiro* (and again in the *First Representation* and the later sermons) that those who await the return of D. Sebastião have misplaced their hopes. The Portuguese unexpectedly ensured the fulfillment of their hopes by waiting for D. Sebastião rather than for D. João IV: "In their having been mistaken in the one for whom they hoped [*em errarem o esperado*]."[15] Without this mistake, a jealous God would have withheld the redeemer king from his people. Vieira offers a similar treatment of Portuguese hopes in the *First Representation* when he interprets Trova 93 of Bandarra: "Soccedeo a El Rey João em possessão/o Calvario por bandeira,/Leva-lo ha por cimeira."[16] Some editions of the *Trovas* had Bandarra referring in these verses to one named Foão, not João. Vieira rejects the idea that the confusion was a result of the vagaries of Portuguese typography. Instead he argues that the variation adds yet another providential element of suspense to the Portuguese hope of redemption.

---

about coercion were sometimes contradictory ("St. Augustine's Attitude to Religious Coercion"). Robert Joly, by contrast, emphasizes the elements in Augustine's thought that supported toleration ("S. Augustin et l'intolérance religieuse").

[14] The phrase is from Victor Turner, "Betwixt and Between: The Liminal Period in Rites of Passage." It has a corollary in the fruitful silence that Leonardo Boff calls for in the converted Christian: "It is from silence that the fertile word is born" (*Jesus Christ Liberator*, 18–19). Boff's elliptical discussion of the power of "faltering speech" recalls the interpretive framework of the *Livro anteprimeiro* and the later sermons, particularly the 1689 *Sermão do nacimento do menino Deos* (see *Sermões*, 16: 48–69).

[15] Vieira, *Sermões*, 13: 89.

[16] Bandarra, *Trovas*, 93.

What I take to be most certain is that Divine Providence had a great part in this variation in the versions [of the *Trovas*], seeking in this gentle way to preserve, living and in Portugal, the one it had chosen as the instrument of our Restoration; this is something that could in no way occur naturally if there were to be passed on to him [D. João] the hope and expectation that [Divine Providence] permitted to be preserved in the name of D. Sebastião.[17]

This interpretation (like those of the sermons) hinges on the ways divine providence has shielded Portugal from God's jealousy.

The last pages of the *Livro anteprimeiro* narrow the nation's millenarian hopes by focusing successively on the Portuguese discoveries themselves, the missionary church, and the Society of Jesus. Here Vieira finally imposes a kind of loose order on his diffuse discussion of the reversal of expectations. He begins the twelfth and last chapter of the book with a survey of the global missionary landscape, observing that the faith moves progressively from East to West. In making this observation, he underscores the importance of preachers in the imperial project and cautiously assigns a special role to the Jesuits. He is similarly cautious in leading up to his interpretation of the Brazilian colony's role in the conversion of the New World as a whole. Vieira's preliminary application of the Hebrew prophets to Brazil turns on his appropriation of the voice of David in an attempt to address God directly. His subject is the mystery of the reversals suffered by the postprimitive church; his text the words of praise, "Sanctum est templum tuum, mirabile in aequitate."[18]

Only with Portugal's New World discoveries has God brought the world the universal grace for which David praised Him. Vieira extends the psalmist's song into the present, making the often unintelligible history of the postbiblical church a prelude to the renewal of the missionary church in his own time.

During the many years and many centuries that you illuminated some peoples with the light of the Faith, you permitted others, for your own hidden reasons, to remain in darkness (an argument the Japanese put to St. Francis Xavier); yet now that the Faith and Gospel and knowledge and worship of the true God have crossed the seas and reached the most remote nations of the East and West, truly we may say that your Church is

---

[17] Vieira, *Representação primeira*, 1: 87.
[18] Ps 65.4.

admirable in equality, for it treats all equally: *Sanctum est templum tuum, mirabile in aequitate.*[19]

Vieira, like José de Acosta, devoted little attention to why the revelation to the Indians was delayed and placed the sequence of revelation among the many mysteries of divine providence.[20] Vieira differed from Acosta, however, in emphasizing the equality of the New World and Europe in the history of the postprimitive church despite the perceived inferiority of the Indians. (Acosta adopted the commonplace view of America as the "ugly daughter" whose appearance Europeans would improve.[21]) The question for Vieira, as both missionary and interpreter, is, Who will inform the New World of its newly given equality in revelation? Vieira's double-edged answer establishes a pattern that is characteristic of the final section of the *Livro anteprimeiro*. His response first points in the direction of the missionary church, then veers away to affirm the indispensable role of the very people who seem bent on preventing the work of conversion: the explorers and settlers of the empire.

The complexity of this maneuver reflects Vieira's continuing ambivalence about advancing the missionary enterprise in the company of the Portuguese and of clergy other than the Jesuits. His preliminary allusion to the missionary church consists of a series of scriptural refer-

---

[19] Vieira, *Livro anteprimeiro*, 12: 638. The passing reference to Xavier prefigures the extended treatment of the Society later in the chapter.

[20] Acosta emphasizes this point in the Prologue to his manual for missionaries.

> Undoubtedly, it is because of a most high plan (one that is absolutely inscrutable to us) that so many peoples should have propagated themselves for long centuries without knowing the way of salvation. ... We cannot deny that, as a result of the hidden and true judgment of God, there are many men who have been abandoned to their own ignorance, and not only individuals, but families and cities, and often provinces and entire peoples. There were such peoples in past times and there are still such peoples today. ... The reason divine grace and election have kept them excluded for such a long time, losing so many thousands of souls, is an arcane matter that exceeds the grasp of human reason: to seek to penetrate it would be impious (*De procuranda*, 1: 5; cf. 1: 2).

> In *De procuranda* 5: 3, however, Acosta briefly speculates that revelation was withheld because of some deficiency in the Indians; he cites Aquinas's argument that God would have sent preachers to the gentiles if the gentiles "had done what was to be done by them" (*In omnes beati Pauli Apostoli espistolas commentaria ad Romanos*, chap. 10, lectio 3, fol. 43v).

[21] The phrase "ugly daughter" is from the *Parecer de Yucay*, author unknown, quoted in MacCormack, *Religion in the Andes*, 277.

ences that are more poetic than interpretive in their effect. The missionaries God sends to the New World speak with "the strength that he [gives] to the voices of his voice."[22] The shoots (*emissiones*) that God brings forth are the missions of the New World; the mandrakes (*mandragorae*) whose fragrance sweetens the fruits of the vineyards are God's preachers.[23]

Here Vieira abruptly shifts his focus to the evangelical role of the "first fruits" of conquest, the riches the Portuguese have harvested in the New World. The missionaries quickly become followers rather than initiators, and the souls they convert are the "second fruits" of Portuguese expansion. This is as it should be, Vieira argues, in a characteristic attempt to discern the fortuitous results of obstacles to evangelization. He continues this effort in the *Second Representation* with his argument that the conversion process, like the interpreters of the faith and like the church itself, is imperfect in ways that unexpectedly advance the missionaries' work. It is significant that one of Vieira's few references to Francis Xavier in the *Second Representation* challenges the Inquisitors to accept Xavier's view that the missionary enterprise requires a full partnership with temporal powers.

> If we look for the cause of these advances [of the church] among gentiles as well as Christians, we will find that it consists entirely in the very nature and corporality of our beings, in which the apprehensions that are gained through the senses (which are those of the temporal power) have always exercised the greatest force, both in that part of our nature which is given over to hope and in that part which is subject to fear because of the violence and immediacy of [the temporal power's] actions. This violence and this immediacy are not so strongly felt with spiritual injuries and interests, which are more distant in time and more remote from the senses.[24]

---

[22] *Livro anteprimeiro*, 12: 599, 667, 680. The passage paraphrases Ps 67.34, "Ecce dabit voci suae vocem virtutis." The Revised Standard Version ("Lo, he sends forth his voice, his mighty voice") omits the genetive (*voci suae*) on which Vieira's interpretation hinges. Vieira will return to this theme (without specifically identifying the preachers' voices) in the *Second Representation* when he writes of the psalmist's invitation to all the nations of the world to join in the sacrifice as a prelude to their entry into the church. The psalmist, Vieira will conclude, attributes the coming conversion to the "strength of the divine word and voice, the power and efficacy of which nothing in those days could resist; [this voice] repeatedly speaks wondrous effects: *Vox Domini super aquas; Deus maiestatis intonuit*" (*Representação segunda*, 2: 54).

[23] S. of S. 4.13, 7.13.

[24] Vieira, *Representação segunda*, 2: 71. Vieira returns to this argument when he

Vieira accepts as a given the relative remoteness of the missionary's objectives in the context of the imperial enterprise because he believes that this remoteness need not impede the progress of the church. It is the all-powerful king, not the supplicant missionary, who ultimately will determine whether idolatry will be permitted. Vieira understates the conflict between the missionary church and its royal sponsors to demonstrate the efficacy of temporal power in the missionary enterprise. Such efficacy depends on the capacity of kings to inspire fear. The closing pages of the *Livro anteprimeiro* provide a resounding affirmation of the imperial enterprise in its entirety, as befits a work meant to inspire the whole Portuguese nation.[25] These pages portray the missionaries as partners with a succession of royal apostles, beginning with Henry the Navigator.

In his later writings, Vieira will usually identify the work of conversion as the vocation of the missionary church, and more specifically of the Jesuits working in concert with their crown benefactors. In the *Livro anteprimeiro*, by contrast, the Jesuits are not the focal point of the missionary enterprise. Vieira attributes to the Portuguese crown a godlike power deriving from its apostolic role. The enterprise of conversion Vieira will describe (in his works of the 1670s and 1680s) as a collaboration between God and the missionary is here (in his prison writings of the 1660s) assigned to the crown. If the task of conversion is the "greatest work of God's omnipotence," it is also a work of mercy that confers greatness on the founder of the Portuguese Empire and his descendants.[26] With this reasoning, Vieira suggests yet another reversal of expectations that both affirms the apostolic fervor of the Portuguese kings and intertwines the destiny of the crown with the privileged position of the Brazilian colony—especially Maranhão—in the prophecies of Isaiah.

---

suggests that temporal and spiritual benefits both must be used to induce the Jews to enter the church, and that a "finer" form of conversion will be achieved at a later time (ibid., 155–56). For a discussion of the temporal power God granted to the Israelites and how the power given to Christian princes will supersede it, see *Representação primeira*, 1: 196–97.

[25] In contrast, the *Second Representation* examines the efficacy of temporal coercion using criteria that reflect Vieira's position as a defendant addressing the Inquisition tribunal. There, he seeks to establish the proper and improper uses of violence by a temporal power, with which he implicitly identifies his accusers.

[26] Cf. Vieira, *Exhortação primeira em vespora do Espírito Santo*, in *Sermões*, 8: 529, on the missionary's partnership with God.

Isaiah speaks of the great works that the merciful man will perform; and as the greatest work and greatest mercy of all is to free souls from hell (as those of the gentiles are freed when by the light of the Faith they are shown the way of salvation), the prophet spoke words that when considered well cannot be perfectly understood to refer to any other man than our holy Infante Dom Henrique, the first author of the Portuguese discoveries, whose principal purpose in that enterprise (as all our histories attest) was the pure and pious progress of the Faith and the conversion of the gentiles.[27]

It is not the greatness of the Portuguese kings that reveals the empire; rather it is the empire that reveals the greatness of the Portuguese kings, through the work of conversion. D. Afonso Henriques's descendants may not have matched the evangelical zeal of their forebear, but for Vieira the damage these princes have inflicted on the missionary enterprise is more apparent than real. The Portuguese greed that Vieira has regularly condemned from the pulpit now serves to advance the progress of the church.

Vieira seeks in Scripture a vocabulary with which to affirm the apostolic uses of his countrymen's greed. He recites a litany of New World riches, exalting these products as agents of evangelization. The cinnamon, honey, and cedar of the biblical prophecies all have specific Brazilian referents. These goods did not simply invite the Portuguese to the New World but actually compelled them to overcome the hardships of discovery and exploration.[28]

Vieira was a devoted compiler of lists; the rhetorical and artistic function of lists in his writings would itself be worthy of study. In a Vieira sermon, the list becomes a kind of incantation, and it retains something of its hypnotic power even on the printed page in the prophetic texts. Vieira used lists to instruct his audience and to call attention to his

[27] Vieira, *Livro anteprimeiro*, 12: 862.
[28] The riches "forced human greed to prepare itself to overcome all those difficulties and to open and allow us to pass through those doors" (ibid., 752). The image of the door through which the European enters into contact with the non-Christian will appear again in Vieira's 1688 exhortation to the Jesuit novices, where he characterizes language as "the only door by which it is possible to enter into knowledge of others" (*Sermões*, 8: 523). In his analysis of Vieira's interpretation of temporal power, Besselaar argues that for Vieira "a dialectical relationship exists between the subjective intentions of men (such as the ambition for wealth) and the objective ends of Providence (the Christianization of the world)" (*Livro anteprimeiro, Comentário*, 12: 740).

own knowledge of the subject at hand.[29] Lest the protected European readers of the *Livro anteprimeiro* forget that he has just spent nine years in the backlands of the Amazon, Vieira offers a compendium of the spices of Scripture and their counterparts in America. His intimate knowledge of the *drogas das Indias* makes his interpretation at once a poem and an exhortation that resonates in much the same way as the Song of Songs, from which it draws its inspiration.

> The silver, the gold, the rubies, the diamonds, and the emeralds that those lands nourish and hide in their entrails; the unguents, the Brazilwood, the violet, the ebony, the cinnamon, the clove, and the pepper that are born in those lands were such powerful incentives for man's greed that they made it much easier to bear the dangers and travails of the navigation and conquest of one and the other Indies; for it is certain that if God in his providence had not enriched those lands with those many treasures, no amount of religious zeal would have been sufficient to bring the faith to them.[30]

The earthly treasures to which Vieira refers had been invested with evangelical significance throughout the history of the missionary church, beginning with the preaching of Jesus.[31] In the last section of the *Livro anteprimeiro*, however, Vieira assigns unique importance to the physical characteristics of the Amazon and the riverine culture of the Brazilian Indians. Here his exegetical project becomes more explicitly historiographical than at any other point in the *Livro anteprimeiro* or the *História do futuro* proper. Vieira recognizes the novelty of this project and tries to forestall criticism by stating that the specificity with which he applies the prophecies of Isaiah to Brazil is an unfortunate necessity.

---

[29] See, e.g., his incantatory recitation of the months of D. Maria Sofia Isabel's pregnancy, in *Sermões*, 13: 108.

[30] Vieira, *Livro anteprimeiro*, 12: 754.

[31] Vieira will return to this theme in the *Second Representation* when he discusses Jesus' ministry to the Jews. He describes Jesus as "making a concession to human weakness when he exhorted men not to abandon their treasures absolutely but rather to pass those treasures to Heaven, where they might securely possess them." The kings of Portugal, in turn, offer material benefits to neophytes, "hoping that with the help of human and temporal interests the conversion of the heretics might be more copious and that of the gentiles more firm; and experience has shown this to be the case, with divine Providence and grace making use of those means that are most suited to human nature" (*Representação segunda*, 2: 156). For a similar argument, see *História do futuro*, 2: 6; and the 1644 *Sermão de S. Roque*, in which Vieira defends an idea he qualifies in the *Livro anteprimeiro* and *História do futuro* proper: riches gained by impious means may be legitimately used for pious ends (*Sermões*, 12: 22–53).

The claims of lived experience that informed the *Esperanças* once again take precedence over the claims of exegetical caution. His ability to link his knowledge of Scripture to his experience in Brazil, Vieira writes, imposes a special burden to set forth his Fifth Empire vision in detail rather than trim it in the interest of his own safety. The implication is that he would readily desist from this task if anyone else could correctly interpret the prophecies that have been realized in Maranhão in his own generation. But in addressing the king and court as well as his accusers, Vieira relishes the interpretive role he has assumed.

Vieira has already noted, in leading up to his interpretation of Maranhão, that the patristic writers denied the existence of the Antipodes and dismissed as fantasies the navigational feats that the Portuguese eventually accomplished. At the same time, he has noted that those failings of the church fathers were mere accidents of history and human limitations. Yet in these final pages, Vieira makes greater claims for the human capacity to interpret prophecy than he was willing to grant earlier in the text. He argues that the particular manner in which certain of the Hebrew prophecies were fulfilled remained hidden until the time of Acosta, who had wide experience in the New World. Acosta's interpretations, however, were limited (just as his predecessors' interpretations were limited) by his time and place and, above all, by his lack of knowledge of Brazil in general and of Maranhão in particular. Vieira thereby names the province that has eluded all previous interpreters.

With this claim and its accompanying exegesis, Vieira diverges sharply from the interpretive methods of other writers who attempted to incorporate the American Indians into a Christian historical framework. The Andean chroniclers Garcilaso de la Vega, Santacruz Pachacuti Yamqui, and Guaman Poma de Ayala, for example, "drew on European ideas and artifacts to articulate Andean realities."[32] They were interested in the internal dynamics of Andean history, whereas for Vieira, Indian history and religion were relevant only insofar as they helped to illuminate the Bible.[33] Like the Andean chroniclers, Viei-

---

[32] MacCormack, "Pachacuti: Miracles, Punishments, and Last Judgment," 982.

[33] The perplexity manifest in Guaman Poma's narrative is absent from Vieira's writings, even though Vieira emphasizes the chaotic nature of colonial society. For Guaman Poma, the only way to make sense of the tragedy of conquest was to avoid imposing an ordering interpretation on Andean life. "Miracles and punishments listed interchangeably enabled him to articulate his bewilderment at the

ra saw the Indian world of the Amazon as a world of reversals; but for Vieira these reversals only underscored the need for exegetical specificity. Instead of transposing Christian images into Indian ones, as the Andean chroniclers did, Vieira insisted that the tragedies of the conquest could be understood only in traditional Christian terms. Vieira departed from traditional Christian exegesis in his willingness to incorporate Indian realities into his interpretive method, but he did so without ever questioning the importance of the historicity of scripture. The Andean chroniclers "understood Noah's flood as a marker in time, not a date"; Vieira, in contrast, applied enigmatic scriptural passages to Brazil with specificity, just as previous exegetes had done in advancing their theories about the date of the flood.[34]

Thus, instead of rendering traditional exegesis irrelevant to the Amerindian framework, Vieira applied it, with the conviction that the Amazon backlands were the place God had chosen to reveal the mysteries of the Hebrew prophets. Vieira's inclusive exegesis extended to the secular history of the Amazon Indians the same biblical antecedents that Guaman Poma, Garcilaso, and others had extended to the Andean peoples—and that exegetes had traditionally reserved for Europeans.[35]

Vieira's application of biblical prophecy to Maranhão in the *Livro anteprimeiro* focuses on the first two verses of the eighteenth chapter of Isaiah. The differences between the Vulgate and the modern English translations of these verses suggest some of the ambiguities on which Vieira's interpretation turns.

> Ah, land of whirring wings, which is beyond the rivers of Ethiopia; which
> sends ambassadors by the Nile, in vessels of papyrus upon the waters! Go,

---

random injustice of colonial life. In repeating or alluding to the Christian examples of miracle and punishment, Guaman Poma therefore changed the scope and effect of both. For, on the one hand, he regarded as historical and theologically meaningful many episodes from the Bible and from the history of the conquest. But, on the other hand, he explained the moral significance or, rather, the absence of it in these episodes from an exclusively Andean standpoint" (ibid., 987).

[34] Ibid., 980.

[35] The continuing force of this project is reflected in the words of Cardinal Paracattil to the 1970 Synod in New Delhi: "The Catholic Church is neither Latin nor Greek nor Slav, but universal. Unless the Church can show herself Indian in India and Chinese in China and Japanese in Japan, she will never reveal her authentically Catholic character" (quoted in Enrique Dussel, "Theologies of the 'Periphery' and the 'Centre,'" 88).

you swift messengers, to a nation, tall and smooth, to a people feared near and far, a nation mighty and conquering, whose land the rivers divide.[36]

Vieira has argued throughout the *Livro anteprimeiro* that the words of the prophets have traditionally been the most difficult texts for biblical exegetes; he now extends this argument by noting that this passage "was always considered to be one of the most difficult and obscure of all the prophets."[37] Because he is the first interpreter to possess the needed knowledge of the New World to link Isaiah's prophecy to Maranhão,

> it will be necessary that we state it. . . . it is no wonder that our lack of knowledge of Maranhão should have obscured and diverted the honor of this famous oracle of the most illustrious prophet, who so clearly spoke of these people.[38]

The broad outlines of the Brazilian element of Vieira's exegetical project here may be discerned in his interpretation of two words from Isaiah's prophecy: *convulsam* (*arrancada*, or removed) and *dilaceratam* (*despedaçada*, or scattered). For Vieira these words offer ample proof of the text's Amerindian referents, since "only the Holy Spirit could have summoned forth in two words the history and recent fortune of these people."[39] The prophecy refers partly to cannibalism and intertribal warfare, which Vieira has already denounced in his Amazon sermons. In the *Livro anteprimeiro*, he denounces them again, but his condemna-

---

[36] Is 18.1–2. The Revised Standard Version does not suggest several of the specific references to the Indians that Vieira discerns in the Vulgate. The Vulgate on which Vieira based his exegesis reads,

> Vae terrae cymbalo alarum, Quae est trans flumina Aethiopiae, Qui mittit in mare legatos, Et in vasis papyri super aquas. Ite angeli veloces, Ad gentem convulsam et dilaceratam; Ad populum terribilem, post quem non est alius; gentem expectantem expectantem et conculatam, Cuius diripuerunt flumina terram eius.

The King James Version more closely follows the Vulgate.

> Woe to the land shadowing with wings, which is beyond the rivers of Ethiopia: That sendeth ambassadors by the sea, even in vessels of bulrushes upon the waters, saying, Go, ye swift messengers, to a nation scattered and peeled, to a people terrible from their beginning hitherto; a nation meted out and trodden down, whose land the rivers have spoiled!

[37] Vieira, *Livro anteprimeiro*, 12: 953.
[38] Ibid., 1002, 1036.
[39] Ibid., 1079.

tion of the sins of the Indians is overshadowed by an even stronger condemnation of the Portuguese settlers who had recently expelled him from the Amazon. Vieira uses the Indians' so-called barbarism as the basis for his larger effort to locate in Maranhão the scattering and tearing apart of which Isaiah spoke. The ultimate referent of the *gentem dilaceratam* is the Indian nation, consumed not by warriors from other tribes but by the Portuguese themselves.

Vieira explicitly defends the Indians' right to resist the Portuguese, who initiated the cycle of literal and figurative disintegration that has spread throughout the Amazon. Indeed, he sees such resistance as an obligation; the Indians who fought the conquerors acted "with more generous resolution" than those who submitted to the Portuguese.[40] He then identifies a third group of Indians, who neither fought nor submitted but fled into the backlands to inflict on still other tribes the ravages that the Portuguese had committed on them. It is particularly to this third group that the prophet's words refer, Vieira argues, for both the winners and the losers in this second cycle of violence are scattered and torn apart.[41]

Vieira's account is studded with references to the Nheengaiba, the Tupinambá, and the other tribes with whom he had established contact during his term as Superior in Maranhão. In these references he intertwines the history of the conquest with his knowledge of Indian society, particularly Indian navigation on the river. His discussion moves easily back and forth between the contingencies of recent history and the constants of life on the Amazon.

> Having already revealed them by their fortune, the prophet also describes the Indians (and in very particular detail) by the practice and art of their navigation. In this art the Indians of Maranhão were and are especially distinguished.[42]

The manner in which Vieira evokes the importance of water in Amazonian life suggests the polemical nature of his exegesis. Vieira praises these river dwellers for the same skills he once denigrated in the seafaring Dutch, whom the Portuguese had recently expelled from

---

[40] Ibid., 1083.

[41] In emphasizing intertribal warfare, Vieira returns to a central theme of Nóbrega's original criticism of the Brazilian slave system. See Nóbrega, *Cartas*, 323–38.

[42] Vieira, *Livro anteprimeiro*, 12: 1101.

Bahia. Nearly 30 years earlier, as a young missionary, Vieira depicted the Dutch with contempt as he affirmed God's blessing on the Portuguese and dehumanized the invading Protestants.

> In many places [in Holland] the ship makes port at the door of its owner, and in this way the house comes to be the anchor of the ship, and the ship comes to be half the house, as the inhabitants make equal use of both. The Greeks called animals that live in the sea and on land Amphibians . . . these Amphibians are those that as men tried to sieze the City and as fish the Bay, believing that by overcoming our parapet they would win both. But those blind ones did not take note that our parapet was the parapet of St. Anthony.[43]

The amphibiousness of the invaders, Vieira argued, manifested the blasphemy that prevented the Dutch from seeing the banner of St. Anthony. Under this banner the Portuguese returned Brazil to the church's fold. In the *Livro anteprimeiro*, however, it is the Portuguese themselves who are blind, and who betray those who come to them "in vessels of papyrus on the waters."[44] Vieira translates the water imagery of the earlier text into the vocabulary of the Indians of Maranhão, calling them

> the first inventors of the [Amazonian] art of navigation (as a people born and raised more in the water than on land). . . . So much so that the principal nation of that land, taking the name of that very art of navigation and of the vessels in which they navigate there, are called the *Igaruanas*, because their vessels, which are canoes, are called in their language *igará*, and from this name they derived the appelation *Igaruanas*, as if to say "seafarers" or "inventors" or "lords of the ships."[45]

---

[43] Vieira, *Sermão de Santo António* (1638), in *Sermões*, 8: 118.

[44] Besselaar recognizes the importance of Maranhão in Vieira's thought but finds in his interpretation of the masculine *qui* (i.e., *qui mittit*) an extreme example of the excesses of *descobrimentista* exegesis. Noting that the masculine form had proved nettlesome for exegetes (because the preceding verse lacked a masculine antecedent) and that Vieira's interpretation diverges from that of the Flemish Jesuit Cornelius Cornelii a Lapide (1567–1637), Besselaar concludes that in applying the *qui* to the Brazilian Indians, Vieira "attempts a personal interpretation that is not based on a knowledge of the grammar of the original text but rather is completely fanciful and, as always, inventive" (*Livro anteprimeiro, Comentário*, 12: 1117).

[45] Vieira, *Livro anteprimeiro*, 12: 1103. The Iguaranas (as they were later called) inhabited the Serra de Ibiapaba, to which Vieira had conducted a successful expedition (see *Relação da missão da Serra de Ibiapaba*, in *Obras escolhidas*, 5: 72–134). Neither the *Relação* nor the *Cartas* mentions the tribe by name. Leite notes that by 1734 the Iguaranas were extinct, because, as a beleaguered Jesuit stated at the time, their

The seafaring practices that signaled God's curse on the Dutch thus become evidence of God's blessing on the Indians. In this context, Isaiah's first four words—*Vae terrae cymbalo alarum*—assume special significance. The Vulgate and Septuagint, respectively, have translated these words as references to a "land where there are bells with wings" and to a "land where there are ships with wings."[46] Vieira declares that the two translations are in no way contradictory: the Indians of Maranhão represent the only instance in history in which the *sinos* (bells or instruments) of the Latin version may be perfectly reconciled with the *navios* (ships) of the Greek. He therefore concludes that the Indians figured clearly in the language of the prophets, although the existence of these same Indians remained hidden from the church fathers and from their successors until the time of the Portuguese discoveries.

The *cymbalum* of the Vulgate refers not only to the metal cymbal (or bell, in Vieira's Portuguese translation) of the Europeans but also to the generic term with which the Indians denoted instruments, which in turn had a variety of more specific names. The traditional association of the Vulgate's bells with metal instruments was a product not of the text itself, Vieira notes, but of its European interpreters. Vieira's interpretation, like the interpretation by the Spanish exegete Miguel de Palacio (c. 1550–c. 1620) he cites in his text, frees the Indians from this need for European antecedents.

> Why, I ask, should it not instead have been the case that the vessels of which Isaiah spoke were called by or took the name *sinos* not because this name was used among the Hebrews but rather because it was used among those same Indians? . . . And so it is that Isaiah comes to say that the land of which he speaks is a land where the vessels are known as *sinos*; and these very vessels are the *maracatins* of the Maranhão Indians.[47]

---

aldeias "were entrusted to captain-majors, who had their eyes on the Indians only to enrich themselves or at least improve their situation" (*HCJB*, 3: 158–59).

[46] Neither the Revised Standard Version (*whirring*) nor the King James Version (*shadowing*) admits Vieira's emphasis on the bell-like sound produced by *sinos* in his translation of the Vulgate (*cymbalo alarum*) into Portuguese: "Ay da terra, que tem sinos com azas (Woe to the land where there are bells with wings)." Besselaar suggests that Vieira's alternative translation, "Ay da terra, que tem navios com azas (Woe to the land where there are ships with wings)," is based on the reading by the Spanish Dominican Tomás Malvenda (1566–1628) of one of the Latin versions of the Septuagint (*Livro anteprimeiro, Comentário*, 12: 1137).

[47] Vieira, *Livro anteprimeiro*, 12: 1168. Vieira misrepresents Palacio by stating that Palacio's exegesis confers on Isaiah the power to name the Indian *maracás* about

Vieira here rejects the assumptions of traditional exegesis, not to affirm the intrinsic value of Indian social practices but rather to situate the Indians in a biblical framework. The *cymbalos* of the Europeans had their counterparts in the *maracás* hung on the prows of the Indians' battle canoes.[48] The Indians called the prow the *tim*, after their word for a bird's beak; the war canoes were known as *maracatim*. Paddling the canoes, the battle-ready Indians beat on their figuratively winged *maracás* to produce "a barbarously warlike and horrible thundering." In an effort to link the exoticism of the Amazon to something more familiar to his readers, Vieira notes in passing that the Romans, too, referred to the prows of warships and the beaks of birds with the same word, *rostrata*.[49]

Vieira's argument for the autonomy of Indian languages particularizes the elliptical claims he has made earlier in the *Livro anteprimeiro* for the autonomy of the New World itself. He suggests that it is the metropolis that is dependent on the colonies, and compares the empire to a vast body sustained by the fruits that come from its furthest limbs.[50] These fruits were created at the same time as the fruits of Europe, Asia, and Africa, but because they remained hidden, Europeans thought of them as products of a New World. Vieira expresses this perception of the American continent with the same mixture of pride and irony that runs throughout his writings on the New World, which he describes as "new to us, who are the wise ones; but for those savages, its inhabitants, it is old and very ancient."[51]

---

which he prophesied with a word that had currency among the Hebrews. Palacio's conclusion ("perhaps the Indian use of the term *cymbal* to denote a ship took root among the Hebrews in the time of Isaiah") is quite similar to Vieira's. See Michael de Palacio, *Dilucidationum et Declamationum Tropologicarum in Esaiam Prophetam Libri XV tomis tribus divisi* (Salamanca, 1572), 1: 204, quoted in *Livro anteprimeiro, Comentário*, 12: 1168. Palacio's original text is "Sed fortassis Indicus usus nominis cymbali, ut notet navem, antiquitus inolevit apud Hebraeos tempore Isaiae." Vieira's translation reads, "Perhaps ... in the time of Isaiah the ships were called *sinos* among the Hebrews [*Por ventura ... que, no tempo de Isaías, as embarcações se chamarião entre os Hebreos sinos*]." Besselaar notes that this translation is "far from accurate," which is puzzling, given Vieira's eagerness to cite authorities to support his arguments.

[48] The *maracás* were made of coconut or calabash shells filled with seeds (Vieira, *Livro anteprimeiro*, 12: 1156).

[49] Ibid., 1185.

[50] Ibid., 7: 253.

[51] Ibid., 11: 378.

Having identified the *cymbalo alarum* of the Vulgate with the Indians of Maranhão, Vieira extends his interpretation to the *navium alarum* of the Septuagint. He argues that the text refers not to the sails of ships but rather to "the real wings of birds." Like the preceding exegesis, Vieira's interpretation hinges on his knowledge of Indian warfare. The Indians' usual practice, he notes, is to cover their canoes completely, including the *maracás* (as well as their bows and arrows) with the feathers of Amazon birds, especially the bright red feathers of the guará. Therefore the *maracatins*, previously understood to be figuratively winged (because the flying instruments were suspended from the beak of the canoe), may now be seen as literally winged as well; "and for this reason the prophet, who saw and noted all these things because they were so novel, called the canoes *sinos* and '*sinos* with wings': *navium alarum, cymbalo alarum.*"[52]

Having located Maranhão in Scripture, Vieira is ready to interpret the prophecies that refer to the Indians' foremost advocates in the missionary church: the Jesuits. The *Livro anteprimeiro* ends on the celebratory note with which it began, as Vieira continues to assign a preeminent role to the Portuguese crown in the missionary enterprise. At the same time, however, he seeks to remind the crown of the privileged position that God has conferred on the Jesuits as partners in this enterprise.

Though Vieira does not touch directly on the Jesuits' recent setbacks in the Amazon, his history of the church's progress there reflects his determination to revive the Jesuit missions and to strike a blow against the Society's enemies. Isaiah's prophecy about a "nation that is waiting, waiting" (*expectantem expectantem*) refers, like the rest of the verse Vieira interprets, to the Indians of Maranhão. The Indians have been doubly deprived of the means of conversion. First, they were deprived of preachers during the period between the arrival of Pedro Alvares Cabral in Brazil in 1500 and the exploration of the Amazon by Alexandre de Moura in 1615; then they were deprived by the settlers who expelled the Jesuits in 1661.

It is significant that Vieira takes the prophet's opening lament (*Vae terrae*) to refer to this second period of waiting. In a tone more like that of his sermons to the settlers in the 1650s than the exhortatory *História do futuro*, Vieira attacks the Portuguese in Brazil and suggests that it

---

[52] Ibid., 12: 1207.

would have been better for the Indians never to have been granted their first hope than to be summarily betrayed.

> *Vae terrae cymbalo alarum*: because the hope of that land has turned to despair. And do those who have been the cause of these great and eternal injuries hope to save themselves?[53]

Vieira, however, is quick to absolve the crown from any responsibility for these impious acts. He characterizes the Portuguese kings as "knights of Christ" whose principal purpose in building the empire has been the conversion of the non-Christian world.[54]

Vieira concludes his effort to intertwine the fate of the Jesuits with the divinely given mission of the Portuguese by citing the Book of Revelation: "He had a little scroll in his hand. And he set his right foot on the sea, and his left foot on the land."[55] In Vieira's exegesis, the left foot is the church of Rome, whose preachers never leave their homelands; the right foot is the missionary church of the Portuguese and, more specifically, the Portuguese Jesuits. In contrast with his straightforward assertion of personal authority in naming the Amazonian referents of Isaiah's prophecy, Vieira is careful to enlist a previous authority, the sixteenth-century exegete Pierre Boulenger (d. 1598), in making these final claims on behalf of both the Portuguese and the Jesuits.

> We have seen it come to pass in our own times that even kingdoms that are scattered far from us and are unknown, and that have long been enslaved to the most abominable cult of the demons, have been brought to the Christian religion through the works of the fathers of the Society of Jesus. Indeed among the Chinese in the very first year (1564) of the [Jesuit] mission, eight thousand people (among them kings and princes and many chiefs and notables), having left the cult of the demons, received the faith of Jesus Christ. Thereafter many islands and regions of the Indies embraced Christ and Catholic doctrine and entire cities were made holy with the ablution of baptism.[56]

[53] Ibid., 1228.
[54] It is in this connection that Vieira extends his interpretation of the partnership between the crown and the Jesuits to the partnership between the Order of Christ and Francis Xavier, its honorary member. "There is no other among all the orders of Christian knights that can glory in having such an illustrious knight, nor is there any other that, beyond its gifts of glory, can clothe itself with his mantle and his cross; but all this heavenly favor has been merited by the Order that has conquered so many seas, so much of the world, and so many souls for Christ" (ibid., 1404).
[55] Rev 10.2.
[56] Petrus Bulengerus, *In Apocalypsim D. Joannis Apostoli Ecphraseos et Scholiorum*

The concluding passages of the *Livro anteprimeiro* advance a series of far-reaching claims about the Jesuit missionary enterprise that will not be matched until Vieira preaches the visionary *Exhortations* in his old age. Writing while under arrest, and aware of the criticisms that his views have already brought on the Society, Vieira broadens his interpretation of the intersection between the imperial project and Jesuit ministry, as supported by Boulenger. Indeed, Boulenger denies the primacy Vieira has assigned to the crown in the partnership with the Jesuits: Boulenger's exegesis suggests that the nation's prophetic role depends on the deeds of the Jesuits.

José van den Besselaar calls attention to Vieira's marginal notation (in the *Livro anteprimeiro* autograph) to the passage that precedes his quotation from Boulenger. The notation, which reads "Quarta vigilia est tranquillitas magna [in the fourth watch is a great calm]," is a gloss on the gospels of Matthew and Mark.[57] Besselaar notes that this passage in the *Livro anteprimeiro* anticipates Vieira's interpretation of the two gospels in the *Second Representation*. But he ignores a vital difference between the two interpretations, one that represents the larger differences of style and substance between the *Livro anteprimeiro* and the *Representations*. Both interpretations of the calming of the waters prophesy a future age of peace for the church, and in both texts it is the Society of Jesus that provides a signpost of the peace to come. In the

---

Libri VII (Paris, 1639) 10, 2 [fol. 284v–85r], cited in *Livro anteprimeiro*, 12: 1534. Gregorio de Almeida was similarly cautious in his interpretation of Jesuit apostleship, allowing others to speak for the Society's singular role in the imperial enterprise. After praising the apostolic zeal of the Portuguese kings, he turned to the Italian exegete Tomasso Bozio (1548–1620) to underscore the importance of the Jesuits' role in Asia. "With the name Java the prophet signified not only Ionia, from which the Greeks came, but also whatever other regions might be embraced by this word. In the East Indies which have been brought to light for us by the Portuguese there are three great Javas: the Greater and Lesser, which face the Maluccas, and Japan, which faces China. In all these the Christian faith has made great increases through the priests of the Society of Jesus" (Bozio, *De Signis Ecclesiae Dei Libri XXIV* [Rome, 1591], quoted in Almeida, *Restauração*, 1: 36). This reference to Portugal and the Jesuits is not included among Vieira's several citations of Bozio in the *Livro anteprimeiro*.

[57] "And in the fourth watch of the night he came to them, walking on the sea" (Mt 14.25); "And he awoke and rebuked the wind, and said to the sea, 'Peace! Be still!' And the wind ceased, and there was a great calm [*facta est tranquillitas magna*]" (Mk 4.39; cf. Lk 8.24). See Vieira, *Livro anteprimeiro*, 12: 1545; and Besselaar, *Comentário*, ibid., 1534.

Representations, however, Vieira handles the Jesuits' role more gingerly than in the *Livro anteprimeiro*. Not until the last section of his defense does he shed some of his caution and restate his argument that the Jesuits are the carriers chosen by God to reveal the nature and scope of the Portuguese mission.

Vieira has relied heavily on Augustine throughout the *Livro anteprimeiro*, but in the concluding pages his prophetic view of Jesuit ministry diverges from Augustine's interpretation of the history of the postprimitive church. For Augustine, as for Vieira, the temporal and spiritual kingdoms are inextricably intertwined in the church.[58] But when Vieira assigns to the Jesuits a privileged position in the history of the missionary church, he also assigns to human agency a determining role in the missionary enterprise. This view of human agency is at odds with Augustine's interpretation of the contingent progress of the church.

Vieira's argument is rooted in the expulsion from the Amazon and in the Inquisition's attack on him and on the Society as a whole. His voice fades away in chapter 12 (he never completed the book, and the text ends in midsentence), but not before warning that the Portuguese who oppose the Jesuits' work attack the body of Christ. While Vieira in the *Second Representation* assigns primary importance to the Jesuits in the postprimitive church, his approach to the intermixing of the two kingdoms undergoes a fundamental shift when he addresses the Inquisitors directly.

---

[58] Augustine calls the church a "signpost" of the heavenly city; humanity can never know true peace in this world but can experience a provisional sort of peace within the church. In the second half of *City of God* (books 11 through 22), Augustine attempts to make the church's mixed character intelligible to unbelievers by describing "the destined ends of the two cities. One of these is the City of God, the other the city of this world; and God's City lives in this world's city, as far as its human element is concerned; but it lives there as an alien sojourner" (*City of God*, bk. 18, ch. 1). Jean-Claude Guy aptly summarizes the progress of the city of God as an alien sojourner: "The city of God will undoubtedly be unable to render present beforehand to the unbeliever that bliss that she knows cannot be tasted here below except in hope, in a sort of eschatological prelibation. She can, however, show now how the vision of God that [the unbeliever] awaits might furnish him with a reading of present history and contingencies that leaves nothing unexplained" (*Unité et structure logique de la Cité de Dieu de Saint Augustin*, 128).

Fiet unum ovile: The Progress of the Church in the *Second Representation*

Vieira's Inquisition defense does not provide the kind of extended analysis of Brazil's place in the prophecies that is found in the *Livro anteprimeiro*. Throughout the text (particularly in the concluding sections of the *Second Representation*), Vieira avoids antagonizing his accusers with either the broad prophetic claims of the *História do futuro* or the more specific references (found mainly in his letters and sermons) to rivalries among the religious orders in the colony and the superior mettle of the Jesuits. He does, however, speak with considerable specificity, even when his words have no obvious target; and his discussion of the Fifth Empire is a case in point. The universal conversion that will complete the progress of the church is the underlying link between the disparate themes of the second part of the defense.

The *Second Representation* is loosely organized around a series of 30 *questões*. Beginning with Question 14, Vieira digresses from his discussion (familiar to readers of the *Esperanças* and the *First Representation*) of prophecy and how to discern it. He now turns to the uncertain progress of the missionary church throughout its history, specifically in the Portuguese Empire. He puts a new gloss on the exhortatory message of the *História do futuro* by affirming the prophetic role of the Jesuit order in terms that strongly recall his application of biblical prophecies to Brazil in the earlier text. The rest of the *Second Representation* is an evocation—by turns lyrical and angry—of the process by which an institution that is necessarily incomplete will be completed through the intervention of a merciful God. Throughout the conclusion of the defense, Vieira places central importance on the service of the Jesuits (particularly those in the Amazon) to the faltering Portuguese missionary enterprise.

The universal conversion will transform not only the non-Christian world but also Christian Europe.

> The Church and the Kingdom of Christ shall come to a perfect, complete, and consummated state that will be distinct [from their present one], though without essential novelty. . . . The difference and perfection consist in the fact that the whole world will convert and will be universally Christian; that all Christians will be, for the most part, observant; that all princes and nations will live in peace, doing away with all arms and wars; and that

during this happy time, grace being abundant, the number of the saved will abound among all the gentiles. And this will at last be what with all propriety will be called the Kingdom and Empire of Christ.[59]

When the non-Christians are converted, Vieira continues, the world that is now Christian in name only will become truly Christian for the first time. The completed church will be continuous with the present one, in that the present church is a living figure of the future one. It will be distinct from the present church, however, because humanity will be united in faith. Even this celebratory passage, however, concedes that the church's progress has been uncertain. Vieira's reference to the newly converted Christians who will be "for the most part" observant reflects his doubts about the efficacy of even a divinely ordained conversion. Not everyone will be reached, but the missionary church, particularly its preachers, must do everything within its power to prepare Christians and non-Christians alike to hear the message of conversion.

Vieira begins to carry this premise to its logical conclusion by asking, in Question 14, "May the universal conversion of the World be proven by the extinction of all forms of paganism?" His answer contains one of the text's few references thus far to Brazil. These passages and the references to Brazil that they introduce constitute a key element of the increasingly personal narrative style of the second half of the defense.

In this section, Vieira suggests a revision of the traditional tripartite division of the non-Christian world that distinguished among Jews, Muslims, and other non-Christians. The revision is part of his longstanding effort to demonize the Muslims and to incorporate the Jews and other non-Christians into Christian history. Vieira never pursues this distinction with any rigor, but his proposal and its accompanying interpretive passages emphasize that his concern with the Jews and the non-Christian inhabitants of the empire (particularly the Brazilian Indians) excludes the Islamic world.[60]

---

[59] Vieira, *Representação segunda*, 1: 222.

[60] For Vieira, the Muslims posed a threat both political and spiritual to Christian unity, to which the *Second Representation* responds. The text directs some glancing blows at the Muslims' imperial designs; more direct attacks are found in Vieira's letters and later sermons. The letters of the late 1660s and early 1670s, for example, reflect his continued preoccupation with the war against the Turks. He calls repeatedly for Christian unity against the Muslims, who thrive on divisions in Chris-

Vieira is quick to note that the Muslims are not the only ones who have banished the true church. Drawing on recent events in Europe, he points out that the church has been expelled from the heart of Christendom itself. With each exclusion, however, comes a compensating inclusion, and in this ebb and flow lies the significance of the Portuguese Empire. Banished from England and other parts of Europe, the church has moved on to Brazil, the rest of the Americas, and Asia, in a continuing process of growth.[61]

With the notable exception of the Muslims, Vieira characterizes the non-Christian world as being led astray by leaders who blind their flocks. As he did in the *História do futuro*, he turns to the Song of Solomon to discern the places to be converted and the means of their conversion. The southern regions to which the prophecy refers denote "our discoveries, and other [lands] that are still to be discovered and that are properly called *Terra australis.*"[62] Equally important for his apostolic purposes is the role he assigns to Ignatius. As noted earlier, Vieira's exegesis of the tenth chapter of Revelation identified the right foot of Christ with the Jesuits. Vieira now adds a final, more particular gloss, arguing that the great star that fell from heaven was Luther and the mighty angel who came to do battle was Ignatius,

> who with an open book in his hand and with one foot in the sea and the
> other on land shone like the sun and roared like a lion. The Council of Tar-
> ragona understands this angel to be St. Ignatius Loyola, sent to the World
> at the same time as Luther as the enemy of [Luther's] heresy. And this con-
> clusion not only was adopted by all the historians of Ignatius's life but al-

---

tendom: "The Turk, according to the latest warnings, appears to be waiting to see the Christians warring among themselves before taking up his own arms" (see *Cartas*, 2: 455, and passim). Vieira's antipathy toward the Turks was still strong as late as 1689. See the *Discurso apologético* on the death of the prince D. João, in *Sermões*, 13: 139–276. For Bandarra's formulation of the same distinction between the Muslims and other non-Christians, see *Trovas*, 46–47.

[61] *Representação segunda*, 2: 20. MacCormack, commenting on the "providentialist claims" of early New World chroniclers, notes that these writers "found in the events they chronicled examples of both miracles and punishments. God had miraculously aided the conquerors, it was held, so as to replace from among the Indians the souls that the Catholic church had lost to the [Protestant] reformers" ("Pachacuti," 975). Vieira embraced the miraculous element of the conquest as an act of divine restitution in the face of the Protestant challenge; but he never followed his predecessors in attributing calamities, such as the decimation of the Indian population by plague, to divine punishment for the sins of paganism.

[62] Vieira, *Representação segunda*, 2: 22.

so was confirmed and approved in his canonization by the Supreme Pontiffs.[63]

Besides containing the text's only reference to Ignatius, this passage exemplifies one of Vieira's most important rhetorical strategies. When it comes to interpreting church history, the authority conferred by canonization once again relegates the authority of even the celebrated Jesuit hagiographers (to whom Vieira also has referred in the *História do futuro*) to an ancillary role. Deprived as he was, in prison, of the texts he needed to support his arguments, Vieira in this passage is nonetheless able to recall the concrete actions of the church's highest authorities to support the orthodoxy of his application of Revelation to Ignatius. Equally important, he enlists the documents of canonization in his cause without citing them, and thereby moves beyond the text of the breviary he was granted in his prison cell.

By invoking the canonization of Ignatius, Vieira questions the Inquisitors' wisdom in challenging the orthodoxy of one of Ignatius's disciples. He also recasts, in a slightly different light (namely, with a new emphasis on the Society's founder and on European heresy rather than on American paganism), his interpretation from the *História do futuro* of the Jesuits' role in building the missionary church.[64] Embedded in Vieira's reference to Ignatius is a warning to the Portuguese, similar to the earlier one: those who impede the work of the Jesuits are denying the will of God and his spiritual and temporal vicars on earth (the popes and the Portuguese kings, respectively). All this is achieved in a short passage that mentions neither the Inquisition nor the Society of Jesus by name.

Vieira will return to the imagery of Revelation in his closing reference to the missionary church as a ship battered by the waves. Out of deference to the Inquisitors, this passage generalizes the interpretation of the approaching time of peace from the *Livro anteprimeiro*. Here, Vieira confines himself to an implicit reformulation of the exhortation to his fellow Jesuits (especially those who are scattered throughout the empire), which was explicit in the earlier text. Throughout this passage, Vieira's rhetorical strategy allows him to angle a blow at his accusers while ostensibly speaking generally about the fate of the ship that is the missionary church.

[63] Ibid., 2: 23; Rev 10.1–3; cf. Vieira, *Livro anteprimeiro*, 12: 1528. Ignatius was canonized with Francis Xavier in 1626.
[64] See Vieira, *Livro anteprimeiro*, chaps. 10, 12.

Even when [Jesus] has his feet on the land, he has his eyes on the ship, because in the very heavenly safety in which he dwells, the dangers and travails of the ship are his greatest care. We men and the Disciples of Christ themselves (and those of the Apostolic College) believe that the Church Militant must remain in this state until the day of glory dawns, and that it is the duty of its name forever to do fierce battle with the fury of the waves and the contrariness of the winds.[65]

Against the certainties of the Inquisitors, Vieira once again places the evidence of history, and above all the revelation of the church's uncertain progress that the Apostles and their successors in Rome have provided.

Vieira's earlier hesitation concerning the number of the saved now reappears as the premise of Question 15: "Shall this universal conversion of the World, as it is understood to include all kinds of Infidels, also be understood to include all individual men?" Because Vieira poses the question reluctantly, he gives it, not surprisingly, the briefest treatment of any of the 30 questions in the text. He argues that all nations, but not all individuals, will be gathered into the completed church.[66] Yet even here, he holds out the hope that divine providence may yet bring each individual into the fold. In any event, he concludes, those who stray from the flock will be so few as to be relatively insignificant.[67] The vagueness of his analysis stands in sharp contrast to the specificity of his call to the Portuguese 20 years later to heed the prophecy of Isaiah and not be left behind.[68] The inclusive exegesis that earlier was applied to the Indians here extends to the Portuguese, in-

[65] Vieira, *Representação segunda*, 2: 229. As Besselaar notes, Vieira in the *Livro anteprimeiro* confuses the texts in Mark concerning the calming of the waters (*Comentário*, 12: 1540; cf. Mk 4.39, 6.48, and Lk 8.24). The image of the ship battered by the waves is a common motif in religious art of the period; see, e.g., the frontispiece of the first volume of Simão de Vasconcelos, *Crônica da Companhia de Jesus* (Lisbon, 1663).

[66] Vieira, *Representação segunda*, 2: 36–39. Vieira makes similar arguments in the *Sermão da quinta dominga da quaresma* (1655), in *Sermões*, 11: 432–69, esp. 464; and in the *Discurso apologético* (1689), in *Sermões*, 13, 139–276, esp. 270–76.

[67] Vieira will briefly reconsider this problem in Question 24, in which he introduces a series of mathematical calculations and again argues that the millennium will come when "all or almost all men are saved" (*Representação segunda*, 2: 197–205).

[68] "Thus shall it be in the midst of the earth among the nations, as when an olive tree is beaten, as at the gleaning when the vintage is done" (Is 24.13; cf. Vieira, *Discurso apologético*, 274–76).

cluding the Inquisitors and other clergy with whom Vieira has done battle for much of his life.

Like the historical contingencies that slow the progress of the missionary church and that the exegete must painstakingly interpret, Vieira's principal points in the *Second Representation* (particularly his analysis of Brazil and the universal conversion) must be culled from a collection of discursive passages that lack the relative logical coherence he achieved in the *Livro anteprimeiro* (itself an unfinished and imperfectly organized work). The deficiencies of the defense can be attributed partly to Vieira's lack of access to a bible and exegetical literature (which he laments at intervals throughout the text). But these deficiencies have a more intimate point of origin; in the end, Vieira argues that his inability to systematize his argument reflects both the permanent state of the missionary church and the persecution he personally has suffered. The text, incomplete like the *Livro anteprimeiro*, contains "only the thread of the argument; some texts have been cited in it, but they have not been checked, nor have they been treated in the way that the material demands; in sum, [the text] is similar in all things to the present state of its Author."[69]

Not until the last section does Vieira bring into clear focus the underlying thread to which this passage alludes. These are among the most effective passages of the *Second Representation*. Vieira links Brazil to his Fifth Empire vision with the same specificity that characterized the *Livro anteprimeiro* (though still without a comparably systematic analytical structure and scriptural exegesis). As he did in the earlier text, he places greater value on the experience of missionaries in the New World than on the writings of cloistered scholars, and laments that his application of his own experience to the interpretation of Scripture should have brought about his present difficulties. He recognizes that his argument in the *Representations* may strike the reader as "extraordinary and strange," but insists that, aside from identifying the Portuguese princes as the agents of universal conversion, his interpretation is entirely based on Scripture.[70]

When Vieira speaks of the persecution he has suffered in both the colony and the metropolis, his style is less characteristic of the *Repre-*

[69] Vieira, *Representação segunda*, 2: 290.
[70] Again Vieira hedges, in deference to the Inquisitors. Throughout the *Sermões* and the *História do futuro*, he has sought to establish the scriptural basis for his interpretation of the apostolic mission of the Portuguese crown.

sentations than of the letters he wrote from prison during the same time. Vieira offers a despairing view of the church's progress in Brazil, contrasting with the generally hopeful view in the rest of the defense. He bitterly laments, moreover, his internal exile in Portugal following the expulsion from Maranhão. Vieira does little to disguise either his pride or his fatigue as he nears the end of the trial, during the spring and summer of 1666. Casting a backward glance at his 40-year missionary career, he affirms successively his Jesuit vocation, his personal missionary vow, and his fulfillment of this vow in the Brazilian missions. It is this missionary experience that informs the defense (particularly the *Second Representation*), which Vieira characterizes as the work of a religious

> who by the profession of his habit, and by a special private vow ... had dedicated himself to the ministry of saving and converting souls; and who, after having disputed throughout Europe with the heretics, atheists, and Jews (always, by the grace of God, with manifest victories for the faith), had spent ten years in America bringing to the faith many thousands of gentiles; and who has currently been exiled in this Kingdom for defending the same cause. The only thing human in that matter [the *Esperanças*] (all else being sacred and divine) was in his [the prisoner's] having said that the principal instrument of [the faith] for temporal conquest and domination is (or shall be) a Portuguese Prince. But if in this application my love and pious devotion to the *Patria* deceived me (along with many others), the error was for noble reasons.[71]

The Inquisition has inflicted on Vieira a second exile, more bitter than the first. The Portuguese settlers were impious; but in Vieira's view, most of them acted out of ignorance. The Inquisitors, in contrast, are learned men who have impeded the work of conversion and denied Vieira the right to draw on his missionary experience in interpreting Scripture. Once again he defends this practice, but this time he extends the argument: the exegete requires not only a thorough knowledge of the New World but also

> the geographic, historical, and chronological knowledge of all the lands, peoples, and kingdoms [of the Bible], whether near or remote, and of the nations with whom they were at war or at peace (the particular situations of each one), and of the seas and the rivers and the very winds that are the

[71] Vieira, *Representação segunda*, 2: 290. Cf. Question 25 (p. 180), in which Vieira indirectly compares himself to Paul, who wondered whether he had not been too selfless in his work as a missionary (2 Cor 11.2).

vocabulary—the phrases and metaphors—in which the Prophets very frequently expressed themselves.[72]

Vieira does not have in hand the texts with which to perform such a reading of Scripture, nor has he visited the Holy Land. His vocabulary is that of the missions.[73]

Vieira has focused up to this point on the faltering progress of the postprimitive church, particularly the Portuguese church. He now reformulates his analysis of church history so as to apply it more specifically to the missionary enterprise as he experienced it in Brazil. His evaluation of the efficacy of preachers in the New World differs strikingly from his grim assessment in the *Livro anteprimeiro* and in the lapse just cited.

The reason for this more sanguine assessment lies with Vieira's audience. In the *História do futuro*, Vieira summoned the crown and the Portuguese elite to the work of conversion and urged them to control the excesses of the settlers in Brazil. In the defense, he addresses a tribunal whose excesses he considers greater than those of the settlers. (Indeed, as the experience of D. João IV showed, the Inquisitors were even less responsive to royal authority than were the crown's disorderly subjects in the Amazon.) The *Livro anteprimeiro* assigned the heroic roles in the imperial project exclusively to the Portuguese princes, with the navigators and even the Jesuits appearing mainly as useful surrogates. The *Second Representation*, in contrast, unstintingly praises the heroism of these empire builders, even as it recalls the obstacles the Portuguese navigators and settlers placed in the church's path.

Vieira's praise for Vasco da Gama and Pedro Alvares Cabral as discoverers of "two new worlds" replicates the heroic discourse of the chroniclers of the empire, and serves as a kind of codicil to the discussion in the *Livro anteprimeiro* of the crown's apostolic zeal.[74] The paean to the navigators also reflects Vieira's lifelong ambivalence about how to incorporate them (and the traders and settlers who followed them)

[72] Vieira, *Representação segunda*, 2: 291.

[73] See Vieira's criticism of those who read but cannot understand the truths of Scripture because they lack pastoral experience (*Representação primeira*, 1: 148–49).

[74] Vieira inexplicably cites 1501 as the date Alvares Cabral discovered Brazil (*Representação segunda*, 2: 245). Among the chroniclers Vieira cites are João de Barros (who figured prominently in the *Livro anteprimeiro*) and Jerónimo Osório (Hieronymus Osorius), author of *De Rebus Emmanuelis Regis Lusitaniae Invictissimi virtute et auspiciis [. . .] Libri XII* (Cologne, 1574).

into the missionary enterprise. On one level, Vieira wants to argue that the physical obstacles the missionaries faced—not the opposition of their fellow Europeans—were the primary impediments to the work of conversion. In summing up the missionary church's erratic progress since the first discoveries, Vieira writes that the Portuguese supported the work of conversion as well as could be expected. This claim, however, rests on the official support the church received. Significantly, Vieira here abandons his focus on the heroic navigators and names the actors in the same order as in the *Livro anteprimeiro*: first the Portuguese kings and then their servants in the missions (particularly the Jesuits).[75] When Vieira turns to examine the concrete work of conversion, however, he recognizes the obstacles the church has faced in specific mission fields.

At this point, Vieira's knowledge of Brazil informs his larger discussion of the missionary enterprise as an international undertaking that by its very nature cannot be successfully completed.[76] In the 150 years since the Europeans' knowledge of the world was transformed, he notes, only the smallest part of the newly discovered lands has actually been explored. In areas such as Brazil, where significant exploration has already been undertaken, vast regions remain where no contact has been made with non-Christian peoples. Such contact as has been made, moreover, has often impeded rather than advanced the church.

Vieira now extends his analysis of specific obstacles to evangelization by considering the Jesuit Cristóbal de Acuña's account of his travels with the notorious bandeirante Pedro Teixeira. This discussion serves a threefold purpose: it provides a source besides Vieira's own experience to suggest the vastness of the missionary project in Brazil; it once again underlines the heroism of the Jesuits by calling attention to

[75] Vieira, *Representação segunda*, 2: 245. The passage contains the text's only reference to Anchieta and another of its few references to Xavier.

[76] Vieira here makes explicit the comparison between the contemporary missionary church and the primitive church that was implicit in the interrogations. The New World churches were blessed with "those same gifts of his grace that the primitive church planted in the World, calling to those latecoming fields of his harvest not only tillers chosen from the Spanish and Portuguese nations but also from the Flemish, English, Germans, Poles, Italians, and French" (ibid., 345–46). Vieira's list of the foreigners who served the Iberian missions prefigures his emphasis in the later sermons on incorporating missionaries of all nationalities into the Portuguese church. Cf. *Sermão de acçam de graças*, in *Sermões*, 13: 65–137; and *Discurso apologético*, 139–276).

the sins of a persistent enemy of the Society in the colony; and it draws conclusions concerning the future of the missionary church throughout the world by holding out Brazil as an example of the obstacles that the Portuguese settlers routinely have placed in the path of ministry.

Vieira juxtaposes the 1640 Teixeira expedition with the expedition headed by António Raposo Tavares the previous year. He reiterates his claim that only a fraction of the American backlands has been penetrated by the Portuguese and that any statement about the continent must be based on limited knowledge. The logic of this argument parallels the logic of the one concerning biblical interpretation. Just as it is impossible to determine what the Apostles believed about Jesus' identity except with reference to a particular passage in Scripture, so, too, it is impossible to claim any knowledge of the church's task in Brazil except with reference to the few hints that may be gleaned from expeditions such as those of Teixeira and Raposo Tavares. Vieira affirms that the bandeirantes and settlers who pose the greatest threat to Jesuit ministries in the New World are also the people who make those ministries possible. Christian ministry in Brazil becomes a contradictory enterprise in this account, but an enterprise to which Christians must perforce accommodate themselves until the universal conversion. The Amazon backlands are the reality to which Vieira refers in his prophecies about universal conversion; at the same time, they are the primary indicators of the provisional progress of the missionary church.

> We can only state with certainty that in the course of traveling down a single branch of the great Amazon River, which runs from Quito to the sea, Father Christoval de Acunha saw or heard reports about 150 nations, all with different languages, as he affirms in a report on that expedition that he published in Madrid and presented to the King. And on the entrada that the field captain António Raposo Tavares made into the Brazilian backlands on another branch of the same river for 11 months during 1639, he traveled at least 3,000 leagues, and all this country was inhabited by an infinite number of [Indian] nations that no men of Europe besides those travelers had ever seen; and those same men left behind many examples of their cruelty and greed but not a single example of their faith.[77]

[77] Vieira, *Representação segunda*, 2: 248; cf. Cristóbal de Acuña, S.J., *Nuevo descubrimento del gran río de las Amazonas*. Philip IV immediately suppressed the book to prevent its detailed account of the Amazon region and its inhabitants from circulating among the newly independent Portuguese. A second edition did not appear until 1891. Acuña and the Teixeira expedition have been expertly analyzed by

This passage suggests the multiple layers in Vieira's defense narrative, layers only provisionally accessible to the Inquisitors and unexamined by later readers. Vieira's generation witnessed some of the most daring feats of exploration ever accomplished in the Brazilian backlands. The expeditions of Teixeira and Raposo Tavares were the best documented of those journeys. Acuña had ample opportunity to observe the injuries the Indians suffered at the hands of Teixeira, the Captain-Major of Pará, and his account of the crimes he witnessed circulated widely among the Jesuits.[78] Raposo Tavares's exploits were equally well known. Raposo Tavares launched his career as a bandeirante in 1629 on the largest slaving expedition the colony had ever seen. To investigate the crimes against the Indians committed on this expedition, Philip IV appointed a special junta, including the jurist Juan de Solórzano Pereira and the future bishop of Puebla (and sworn enemy of the Jesuits) Juan de Palafox.[79]

David Sweet and George Edmundson. See Sweet, "A Rich Realm," chap. 4, esp. 191; and Edmundson, "The Voyage of Pedro Teixeira."

[78] A 1640 attack on the Society's critics in Brazil by the Jesuit Provincial Francisco Carneiro contains a reference to Teixeira's expedition that resembles in style and substance several central passages of Vieira's defense. Describing the impiety of the Portuguese settlers, Carneiro states that the missionary enterprise appears irreparably at odds with the imperial one. Carneiro notes that while in the Amazon, Acuña and his companions

> found and spoke with Tupinambá Indians who were fleeing the aldeias of Bahia in great numbers to escape persecution and mistreatment by the Portuguese; the Indians fled for more than three or four hundred leagues ... and truly it is something for which to cry tears of blood that we should see that the very Catholic Portuguese nation, which was so pious and firm in the faith that it was chosen by Christ on the field of Ourique to spread that faith throughout the world (a task for which many great Portuguese have opened wide rivers that have never before been navigated and discovered regions that have never before been seen or known, risking their lives in some lands and shedding their blood in others to advance the faith) ... should sacrifice the glory and stain the honor of such glorious deeds in exchange for a most miserable profit (*Resposta a uns capítulos, ou libelo infamatório, que Manuel Jerónimo procurador do Conselho na cidade do Rio de Janeiro com alguns apaniguados seus fêz contra os Padres da Companhia de Jesus da Província do Brasil, e os publicou em juízo e fora dêle, em Junho de 1640*, in Leite, *HCJB*, 6: 587–88).

[79] Among these crimes, "[Raposo Tavares] destroyed innumerable reductions [Indian settlements controlled by Jesuits], imprisoning the Indians, expelling the Jesuits of the lower Paraná, and razing the Spanish settlements at Vila Rica ... and Ciudad Real" (Buarque de Holanda, *História geral da civilização brasileira*, 1: 287).

Raposo Tavares and his companions were to be tried in Lisbon, but they were not soon brought to justice. After the expedition described by Vieira, Raposo Tavares conducted another expedition that remains the most famous *bandeira* in Brazilian history. Then he made his way from São Paulo to Belém (where he met Vieira in 1656) only to find that his previous misdeeds had been remembered in Portugal.[80]

The immediacy of the events in the Amazon to which Vieira refers in these closing pages has the effect of tying together several important strands of the text. Vieira restates his argument about the long duration of the missionary church, but now writes specifically about Brazil and Asia, providing a more detailed report on the current state of the missions throughout the world than in any of his other writings. In this text it becomes difficult to distinguish between the field report of a missionary, addressed to the church hierarchy (and to the Portuguese nation as a whole), and the defense of a prisoner, addressed specifically to the Inquisitors. As he did in the *História do futuro*, Vieira seeks to make his method of interpretation integral to the progress of the missionary church; to challenge the method, he implies, is to impede the church's already slow progress in the two new worlds he describes.[81]

Vieira is by turns confident in the successes of the church and dismayed by its setbacks. No one passage in the text and no single series of historical contingencies adequately characterizes Vieira's portrayal in the *Representations* of the church on pilgrimage. Vieira's references to Brazil and his evocation of the task that lies ahead indicate that as he concludes the defense and prepares for the interrogations, his assessment of the situation in the missions of the New World is by no means uniformly bleak.[82]

[80] "Raposo naturally expected to receive some reward from the home government for this outstanding feat, which is unsurpassed in the history of the exploration of the American continent. When his claims were referred to the Overseas Council, Salvador [de Sá] recommended that the explorer's services in other fields of activity should be duly rewarded, but not those connected with *bandeiras* in the interior, 'for these are not meritorious or deserving of recognition.'" These last words were penned by one of the colony's outstanding supporters of the Jesuits (see Boxer, *Salvador de Sá*, 129, 298).

[81] For his present purposes, Vieira concentrates on the "two new worlds" of America and Asia, but he is also careful to note the importance of "the first discoveries by the Infante D. Henrique on the Coast of Africa" (*Representação segunda*, 2: 245).

[82] Cidade takes the opposite view of these passages, but analyzes them as if they were written from the standpoint of a Brazilian missionary, ignoring the fact that

The discussion of the sins of Teixeira and Raposo Tavares constitutes not so much a signal of despair as an affirmation of the necessary obstacles to conversion the church will face on its temporal journey. Indeed, it is at this point that Vieira insists for the last time in this text on the necessary convergence of spiritual and temporal interests in the imperial project. In the Portuguese case, he argues, the zeal of the crown has thus far compensated for the excesses of the navigators and settlers, and "the preaching to the [non-Christian] nations, and the conversion of those nations, were in all their particulars the most insistent, supported, and sustained efforts that the forces of humanity and nature permitted."[83] Although individual Portuguese kings have often fallen far short in their support of the missionary church, this failure is part of the very nature of the missionary enterprise. Vieira emphasizes the slow progress of the church; completion of the missionary enterprise must await a moment of divine intervention that remains in the distant future.

According to Vieira's estimate, after 160 years of evangelization the number of converted Christians in America and Asia has reached perhaps 6 million. He concludes that at the present rate, universal conversion by human means will take 2,850 years, not counting the preaching that will be needed in lands still unknown, which may equal or exceed the known world in size and in the number of non-Christians it contains. To those who suggest that conversion will proceed more easily as the church penetrates farther into the New World, Vieira responds that the opposite is true; and again he emphasizes the apostolic uses of the temporal interests that have forged the partnership

---

Vieira wrote the defense after he had returned and had been placed in the Inquisition's custody. Cidade's characterization thus lends the texts a univocal quality that disregards the continued development, in prison, of Vieira's theory of mission.

Traveling through the interminable solitary expanses of Amazonia, often accompanied only by the father who, according to the rule of the Order, was designated as his companion, Vieira must have felt with each step the enormous disproportion between the small number of sowers of the Gospel and the vast fields that remained to be planted. He is afflicted [in writing the defense] by the grimness of the missionary enterprise, by the little progress that had been made in the East and West Indies over the course of 150 years of European expansion, and by what could be hoped for in the future, above all (he notes ironically) in the lands where there is neither cinammon nor diamonds" (*Obras escolhidas*, 6: xli).

[83] Vieira, *Representação segunda*, 2: 245.

between the crown and the missionary church. The material support that the missionaries receive from the temporal power, as they move away from the coastal strongholds of the Christian princes, is essential for the success of the missions. Vieira adds that the church's limited progress in coastal areas of America and Asia has been accomplished by missionaries who have been

> defended and assisted by fear or respect for the arms of their princes and permitted to enter and be introduced [into the nations] by the desire of the gentiles for trade and often by gifts, which win over and tame the souls of the *barbaros* more effectively than is possible using reason alone; and without these two means which are of such great importance and efficacy, and which would not have been available had it been necessary to penetrate these same nations by land (as these people are always enemies in the beginning and are the more barbarous and wild the deeper into the backlands they live) it is apparent for all to see (though none will understand it as completely as those who have experienced it) what a slow enterprise it will be to convert not every one of these many nations, but any single one of them.[84]

In making this argument directly to the Inquisitors, Vieira insists on a distinction in church history between temporal and spiritual power that the Inquisition has blurred. He has argued for the orthodoxy of his views throughout the defense; here he shows that his recognition of the distinctions between the two kingdoms is a fortuitous result of his missionary experience, enabling him to point out the obstacles to the progress of the missionary church that his accusers are holding in place.[85] Within the new worlds discovered by the Portuguese lie a

---

[84] Ibid., 251.

[85] Cidade notes that Vieira's emphasis on the apostolic role of the Portuguese kings provides a theological underpinning for a role the Inquisition recognizes de facto. Throughout his missionary writings, Vieira is more concerned with the efficacy of temporal power in the missionary enterprise than with the Inquisition's subordination of temporal to spiritual power. Cidade's analysis of the interrogations is one of the few places in the critical literature where the missionary orientation of Vieira's theology is brought into full focus.

> The Inquisitor defends the doctrine that is most commonly accepted by the Christians of our own time. Let us note, however, that this inquisitorial spirituality is more apparent than real. [Inquisitor] Alexandre da Silva was not unaware that although the kingdom of Christ was not of this world, it was a doctrine of the Church that the princes of this world must submit to that kingdom in conferring upon the church the powers on which [Silva's] position as an Inquisitor rested. When the church gave the prisoner to the secular authorities, it was cer-

multiplicity of non-Christian societies whose conversion will become increasingly difficult as the missionaries work their way toward the farthest reaches of the empire. Vieira's language recalls in style and substance one of the most politically charged treatises of his career, his response to the allegations of the mutinous settlers of Maranhão, which he wrote just before his arrest.[86] His reference to the reader's inability to understand his words has a leveling effect: the Inquisitors' discernment is no greater than that of any other reader, for the dangers of the missionary enterprise are unimaginable to all Portuguese who lack direct experience of the New World.

Vieira's lengthy treatment of the trials of the missionary church is one of the few sections of the defense in which he allows himself to lapse into the first person.[87] The first such lapse occurs when, having recited a litany of New World dangers ranging from hostile Indians to poisonous snakes, he again emphasizes the things that cannot be learned from study. He has analyzed successively the theological, historical, and geographical foundations for his interpretation of the universal conversion. He now wishes to assign to his first argument (the theological one) a role secondary in importance to the two experientially based arguments that follow. Lacking a core of shared experience, Vieira appeals directly to his readers' reason.

> If I were to study only within the walls of my cell and were to remain fixed to my desk, and if I were then to read through (with greater aptitude than I possess) the interpreters of St. Thomas and Duns Scotus, it might be that on the first of the three propositions for which I have argued [the argument from theology] I might draw the same conclusion as others and would fol-

---

tain it did so because that authority obeyed its judgment with the same passivity—and efficiency—as if it were an ecclesiastical authority. Vieira's position was more consistent. He argued on behalf of both kingdoms, and for reasons of far greater religious import than those that determined the subjection of the temporal power to the spiritual. His objective was the Christianization of the world rather than the defense of dogma and morality in the areas that were already Christian. He was concerned more with the apostolate than with policy (Vieira, *Representação segunda*, 2: 316, n. 1).

[86] Vieira, *Resposta aos capítulos*, in *Obras escolhidas*, 5: 174–315.

[87] Vieira's style in these passages is by turns conversational and homiletic, justifying a characterization that Cidade applies, albeit too sweepingly, to the text as a whole: "the polemicist, even in the silent isolation of his cell, is before an audience that he seeks to move with the most powerful oratorical resources" (*Representação segunda*, 2: ix).

low the opinion that they follow. But combining the Theology of that first supposition with the historical truth of the second and with the certain geography of the third, and above all with the lived knowledge of both propositions, and of the arguments and impediments that may only be read in experience itself [*que só se podem ler na mesma experiencia*] and may not in any way be discovered in books; this is the reason why, in the well-known argument of this text, I hold that the conversion of the World and universal preaching of the Gospel shall be the special work of Divine Omnipotence and Providence.[88]

Conjectures about when this special work will be accomplished must be made with caution. Vieira states that the fear with which people greet his own speculation is a natural result of the demands placed on individual Christians by the missionary enterprise he has been discussing. The completion of the church requires that Christians remain "doubtful or fearful ... and in that uncertainty and suspension with which Divine Providence wished them to be." Vieira argues, however, that this uncertainty must not compromise either the "moral certainty" with which they wait or their resolve to work within the missionary church in its present persecuted state.[89]

With this mixed message of caution and certainty, Vieira, in effect, comes full circle, asking, in the final question of the *Second Representation*, "From what land or nation will the Emperor be whom God will take as the instrument of this enterprise [universal conversion]?"[90] He maintains the text's personal tone when he returns to the prophecies (both scriptural and domestic) with which he set forth his interpretive claims in the *Esperanças*, the *História do futuro*, and the opening sections of the *First Representation*.

Vieira casts his interpretation of the fulfillment of the prophecies by the Portuguese in increasingly specific terms. As he did in his earlier validation of geography over theology, he discerns an apostolic purpose in the physical location of Portugal in general and of Lisbon in particular. The seat of the empire possesses "a certain median quality and even a proximity" to all parts of the world, and these physical characteristics have been shaped so as to enhance the natural missionary disposition of the Portuguese. Nature and spirituality converge in Portugal. In these passages, Vieira's most cherished hopes for Portugal

[88] Vieira, *Representação segunda*, 2: 253.
[89] Ibid., 254.
[90] Ibid., 261.

amid his internal exile come to the surface. Invoking D. Afonso Henriques's defeat of the Muslims, Vieira writes that the Portuguese are raised from the womb to do battle with Islam, and that "he is not Portuguese who does not hold that the conquest of Jerusalem is our own."[91]

Turning to the apostolic zeal of the more recent Portuguese kings, however, Vieira provides a new gloss on the theme of Portuguese piety. Instead of focusing, as he did in the *Esperanças*, on the hidden graces of D. João IV, Vieira takes those of D. Manuel I as his example. He posits an informal periodization of modern Portuguese history, making D. Manuel the central reference point. This discussion of D. Manuel formalizes the transfer of Portuguese hopes from D. João IV to the Portuguese crown itself that has been proceeding in the rest of the text. Vieira's closing elegy to the crown makes clear that his previous arguments for the resurrection of D. João IV present no obstacle to his continuous reinterpretation of the apostolic role of the successors of D. Afonso Henriques.

Vieira applies to D. Manuel the conceit of innate "dispositions" he used earlier to describe the physical and spiritual character of Portugal and the Portuguese. But Vieira also employs an argument he has not used in his prophetic writings since the *Esperanças'* barbed references to the hidden greatness of D. João IV. In an effort to provide further evidence for his interpretation of Portuguese dispositions, Vieira cites two apparently ill-advised policies—the admission of the Jews to Portugal and the exploration of Asia—as examples of the unexpected ways prophecy is fulfilled in successive Portuguese kings.[92]

The two cases facilitate Vieira's final discussion of the apostolic uses of events that pose an apparent threat to the Portuguese nation. In the first example, Vieira recasts arguments that go back to his earliest days as an adviser to D. João IV. After admitting the Jews, the crown initiated a process of forced conversion and assimilation. At the same time, it sponsored a series of overseas explorations that many believed a country as small as Portugal could not sustain.[93] Vieira's account turns

---

[91] Ibid., 272, 275.

[92] It was in fact D. João II (1481–1495)—not D. Manuel, as Vieira states here—who admitted into Portugal as many as 120,000 Jews who had been expelled from Spain in 1492. See Kayserling, *História dos judeus em Portugal*, 98.

[93] Referring to Vasco da Gama's voyage, Vieira notes the common opinion that it seemed to be "a thing that was truly beyond the bounds of prudence and good

what appears to be a concession to the Inquisition about the problem of purity of blood into a lesson for his accusers about the workings of divine providence. He offers these two policies of the crown ("which were and are reproved by many") as part of his ninth and final proof that the Fifth Empire will be that of the king of Portugal. Vieira thereby provides a material basis for the innate dispositions he has already traced back to D. Afonso Henriques and forward to D. João IV. In the admission of the Jews and in the building of the empire,

> it appears that a large part was played by Divine Providence, which chose [D. Manuel] as the conqueror of so many and such new peoples; and through these peoples God worked with ends that were higher and more hidden than human arguments could contemplate or follow . . . it was most fit that the two extremes of that same Union [the universal conversion] (which are the Jews and the gentiles) should be united in the same Kingdom and under the same Prince, and that this Prince and this Kingdom should be Portugal. And thus we may say that the dispositions of that same union and conversion have been materially begun since the reign of el Rey D. Manoel. During this reign the discoveries began, along with the preaching of the gospel throughout the World. And it was this very king who began at the same time to bring to his Kingdom and unite in his Empire the Jewish People (the Jews of Europe) and the gentiles (the peoples of Africa, Asia, and America).[94]

---

judgment to wish to join so vast a body to so small a head and to bring life to such divided and remote limbs with so distant a heart" (*Representação segunda*, 2: 276). Concerning D. Manuel's supposed admission of the Jews, Vieira writes, "though his purpose and intention were to convert these people to the faith, as he immediately sought to do, nonetheless . . . the purity of blood [*limpeza do sangue*] of the Kingdom was corrupted, as was the purity of faith (an additional result of this contagion), which brought infamy to the entire Portuguese Nation, as those who speak this language are generally considered in the World to be Jews" (ibid., 2: 275–76). It is not surprising that Vieira disregarded the well-known circumstances of the Jews' forced conversion—a conversion that was ordered by D. Manuel—in his effort to affirm the importance of the apostolic partnership. He had been preoccupied since the 1640s with how to incorporate the New Christians—and Portuguese exiles in Amsterdam and elsewhere who had returned to Judaism—into Portuguese religious and economic life. See Vieira's practical proposals of the 1640s on behalf of the New Christians, in *Obras escolhidas*, 4, especially *Proposta feita a El-Rei Dom João IV, em que se lhe representava o miserável estado do Reino e a necessidade que tinha de admitir os judeus mercadores que andavam por diversas partes da Europa* (1–26). For a valuable discussion of Vieira's ideas about the New Christians, see Graham, *The Jesuit António Vieira and His Plans for the Economic Rehabilitation of Seventeenth-Century Portugal*.

[94] Vieira, *Representação segunda*, 2: 276–77.

Vieira's argument about the simultaneity of the crown's efforts to convert the Jews and the peoples of the New World—compromised though it is by the incorrect attribution to D. Manuel of the decision to admit the Jews to Portugal—focuses the last passages of the defense on the prophecy of Daniel that is at the heart of Vieira's millenarian project. The Portuguese Empire has given the world a first glimpse of the fifth and final empire, which would eliminate all distinctions between the empires that had come before. The Jewish people were inseparably linked to the Portuguese in this prophetic enterprise: instead of placing them in opposition, as the Inquisition did, Vieira placed them together (along with the non-Christians of the New World) in the larger story of Portugal's place in the postprimitive church. By converting the Jews and other non-Christians at the same time, D. Manuel provided a foretaste of the universal conversion that will be accomplished by his successor on the Portuguese throne (the temporal vicar of the empire) in partnership with the pope (the spiritual vicar). It is the interpreter's task to recognize, in the accidents of the missionary enterprise and in the strengths and limitations of its leaders, the seeds of the completion of the church.

CHAPTER SIX

The Ignatian Mission Renewed

V IEIRA MADE his last journey to Brazil in 1681. He would assume one more administrative post for the Society, serving as Visitor in Bahia from 1688 to 1691. Vieira returned at what appeared to be an auspicious moment for the Jesuits. The laws issued by D. Pedro II in 1680 placed the Society in a strong position in the Amazon for the first time since its expulsion from the region in 1661.[1] With the Jesuits' exclusive jurisdiction over the Indians restored, the victory Vieira had dreamed of since the 1660s—one that precluded any compromise with the Portuguese settlers on the Indian question—seemed finally within reach. The Society was granted little time to savor its success, however. Writing from Lisbon in 1680 to the Jesuit Superior in Maranhão, in one of the few letters from this period that addresses the Indian question, Vieira anticipated the difficulties the Jesuits would face in enforcing the new laws.

The letter occupies a crucial place in the periodization of Vieira's texts. Along with the 1678 report to D. Pedro, it begins a new body of writings about Brazil and the missionary enterprise there. Vieira, the former Superior, presents to his successor, Padre Pier Luigi Consalvi, a series of guidelines for enforcing the laws and administrating the missions, along with a disingenuous account of his own role in writing the new laws. A correspondent in Pará had informed him that Ignácio Coelho da Silva, the new governor of the state of Maranhão and Pará, was angry because of rumors that Vieira had criticized him while arguing for the Jesuit cause in Lisbon.[2] In the letter, Vieira denies these ru-

---

[1] For the texts of the laws, which were published on April 1, 1680, see Reis, ed., *Livro grosso do Maranhão*, 51–59.

[2] Consalvi served as Superior from 1674 to 1683. His name has been alternately

mors, stating that in the discussions about the new laws he had asked that the Jesuits not be entrusted with exclusive responsibility for the distribution of Indian labor (the *repartição*).[3] He also cites his refusal, almost 30 years earlier, to accept the same responsibility from D. João IV. The purpose of his refusal in 1680, however, was very different from what it was in 1653, and the difference underscores the change in Vieira's thinking about colonial society.

After settlers anticipating his arrival rioted in São Luiz in 1653, Vieira chose not to invoke the privileges that D. João IV had granted the Jesuits. As noted earlier, his sermons, letters, and state papers from this period make clear his wish to accommodate both the settlers and the colonial administration. In 1680, however, Vieira wanted the Jesuits to exercise the powers they had won, albeit without demanding control over the *repartição*. The reinstatement of the Society's sweeping powers in the manner he had proposed was a direct result of Vieira's influence at court.[4]

---

spelled Consalvi by Leite (*HCJB*, 4: 217) and Gonsalvi by Betendorf (*Chronica*, 300) and Azevedo (in Vieira, *Cartas*, 3: 428).

[3] The Jesuits in the aldeias shared his view. The issue was a volatile one within the Society; Vieira's contemporaries feared that the order's very survival in the Amazon might depend on eliminating its role in administering the *repartição*. This was demonstrated by the question posed by one unnamed missionary, writing to Rome in 1681: "Should the Prince order that the Indians be distributed by the Padres (which would cause a thousand squabbles and disputes), what is to be preferred [by the Jesuits]: to accept this [administrative] role or to abandon the care and conversion of the Indians?" (Leite, *HCJB*, 4: 129).

[4] As Leite observes, "Vieira came to be the arbiter, the man to whom people turned and listened, the inspiration for the new law" (ibid., 62). The privileged position granted to the Jesuits by D. Pedro II, whom Alden has described as "perhaps the most able of the Bragança monarchs," was continuously challenged. The fragility of the Jesuits' power was especially evident in the gradual weakening of the provisions of the 1686 *Regimento das Missões*, which in turn reflected "the spirit of the age of D. Pedro II. . . . the heroic age of Nóbrega, Anchieta, Figueira, and Vieira was passed: militancy had given way to accommodation. . . . [the] Black Robes' very success led to their undoing, to their definitive expulsion from all Portuguese lands in 1759" ("Black Robes versus White Settlers," 33–38).

Alden's bleak view of the Jesuits' long-term prospects in the Amazon extends, like Azevedo's, to the period of Pombal. Alden's interpretation differs from Azevedo's, however, in acknowledging that the missionaries' "primary goal" was to convert the Brazilian Indians; in contrast, Azevedo, particularly in *Os jesuítas no Grão Pará*, attaches little importance to religion and, with rare exceptions, portrays the Society as merely one competing interest group among many in the colony.

The Laws of 1680 and the Jesuit Missions in the North

With few exceptions, Vieira's purpose during these last years in Brazil was to distance the Jesuits and their Indian converts from the rest of colonial society. He took no pleasure in this separation from the Portuguese; in the 1680 letter, describing the Jesuit monopoly established by D. Pedro's advisers, Vieira's tone is cautious.

> The Society has great reason to thank God, for despite the usual murmurings against us, and the complaints of those who envy us, when it came to deciding on the Indians—the instruction and administration of those who are already Christian, the conversion of the gentiles, and the liberty and protection of both—all [the crown advisers] by acclamation said that [this work must be done] either by angels or by the Society. ... First and foremost ... we must ensure that no hint of covetousness is seen in the Society. ... Your Excellencies must know that [our enemies] will make of any speck a log, and that there is not a secular or regular religious in this entire State who is not our watchman, and a lynx in this matter. When we absolutely prohibit the Governor to occupy the Indians in these [illegal] works, and when we do the same to the Bishop, note that both will be able to write against us, and that it will be to our advantage to give them little with which to make their case.[5]

In theory, the Society participated in economic life—in Europe and in the New World—solely to facilitate its pastoral work. In the 1650s, Vieira had accepted the necessity of borrowing money from settlers, and of sustaining the Jesuits' traditional economic links to Portuguese society.[6] For this reason, he had adopted a tone of surprise and indignation when charges of financial misconduct were directed against the Jesuits and other religious in the colony. By the 1680s, however, Vieira had concluded that only a withdrawal from economic life would preserve the Society's prestige. Such a withdrawal would allow the Jesuits to enforce the letter of the law, unimpeded by accusations of corruption leveled by hostile settlers and clerics. The jealous prying of the

---

[5] Vieira, *Cartas*, 3: 431.

[6] "No Father among those responsible for the Aldeias may give or take for himself more than the sum of one cruzado, nor will he contract by any means a debt in excess of ten cruzados for himself or for the Aldeia" ("Visita do Padre António Vieira," in Leite, *HCJB*, 4: 111). The text of the *Visita* is a primer on all aspects of the missionary vocation.

clergy (particularly the newly powerful secular clergy) into Jesuit affairs Vieira took as a natural condition of colonial life. He never became preoccupied with specific examples of corruption; nor did he make any distinction between clergy and settlers. His letter portrays the two groups as united in hostility to the Jesuits and the work of conversion.[7]

Affirming the Society's missionary focus in Maranhão, Vieira urges Consalvi to suspend all work on Jesuit buildings in the capital, even the mission's patron church, Nossa Senhora da Luz, in an effort to direct all the Society's resources toward the conversion of the Indians.

> For this is not the time or occasion for us to use the few men and little money we have for anything but the task with which we have been entrusted. . . . All our effort and application should be to take charge quickly of the aldeias . . . for our greatest obligation is not the service [of the settlers] and their slaves; rather it is the service of the free Indians, Christian and gentile, leaving the rest for when there are more missionaries, which I hope will be very soon.[8]

The councils in which Vieira participated in 1680 created the Companhia de Comercio do Estado do Maranhão to supply slaves and basic goods to the colony. The settlers initially set out to protest the company's monopoly, but their leaders soon shifted to a "campaign of libel" against the Jesuits, focusing on the Society's control over the Indian labor force. In 1684 the settlers rebelled against the colonial administration and expelled the Jesuits from Maranhão for the second time.[9] This time, however, the Society was joined in its complaint to

---

[7] Vieira, *Cartas*, 3: 436–37. The only cleric to whom the letter refers directly is the corrupt D. Gregório dos Anjos, who arrived in Maranhão in 1679 to serve as its first bishop. He soon came into conflict with the Jesuits because of his illegal appropriation of Indian labor and subsequent disregard for the Society's jurisdiction over the aldeias. D. Pedro's letters to Gov. Menezes express the king's anger at the abuses committed by the bishop, as well as by the governor himself (see Reis, *Livro grosso*, 33–36; Azevedo, *Os jesuítas*, 136).

[8] Vieira, *Cartas*, 3: 432–33.

[9] For a detailed study of the leader of this revolt, see Maria Liberman, *O levante do Maranhão: "Judeu Cabeça do Motim," Manoel Beckmann*. Beckmann and Vieira's old enemy Jorge de Sampaio received the death sentence, though the Jesuits interceded with the crown on their behalf. Liberman emphasizes Beckmann's self-perception as a defender of the king and the settlers against the colonial administration and the Jesuits.

> The temporal administration mixed with the spiritual one did not suit the economic interests of the settlers. . . . What the rebels coveted was the freedom to work and develop in the region in which they had chosen to live. The authori-

Lisbon by a local elite, concerned that the poorer settlers who were protesting posed a threat to order. Although the Maranhão settlers succeeded in abolishing the Company's trading privileges, the Jesuits were vindicated—at least temporarily—with the publication of the 1686 *Regimento das Missões*.[10]

After his return to Brazil, Vieira's references to the need to convert the Portuguese (and the Indians they had enslaved) grew vague and increasingly rare. With the report to D. Pedro and the recommendations to Padre Consalvi, Vieira sought to turn the Jesuits' attention away from the Portuguese, and from their Indian slaves as well. He had seen that the settlers could turn on the Jesuits at any moment, and he refined his missionary strategy accordingly. Abandoning the building program was simply one element of that strategy; but its symbolism was never more evident than after the Jesuits' second expulsion. The *obras* the Society left behind were, in Vieira's terms, works of conversion that did not depend on the settlers' goodwill. These works would continue even if the Jesuits should be forced to flee.

In defining Vieira's last years in Bahia, and particularly his service as Visitor, the events of 1684 suggest two lessons. First, Vieira was at least partly successful in translating his pastoral ideals into action in the Amazon missions. The expulsion served, for Vieira and for the Society, as one more fruitful reversal. Second, Vieira had earlier won, in the 1680 laws, a concrete victory that would outlive the expulsion. This victory came in the form of a little-noticed provision in which D. Pedro granted funds for Jesuit education in Maranhão.[11] Although the success

---

tarian and independent actions of the Jesuits, the exploitive structure of the monopoly [the Companhia de Comércio], the Indian laws, the despotic attitudes of the governors, were all factors that in their totality represented not only an obstacle to the hopes of the people, but also an impediment to work and to the development of commerce, and a menace to the very survival of the population (93).

Varnhagen describes Beckmann as a noble precursor of Brazilian independence. Divine justice, Varnhagen writes, was on the conspirators' side: "History in any case cannot but sympathize with those generous souls who were treated so cruelly. Manuel Bequimão went to the scaffold a true hero" (*História geral do Brasil*, 3: 252; see also Leite, *HCJB*, 4: 69–85; and Azevedo, *Os jesuítas*, 143–47).

[10] For a detailed account of the Jesuit missions in the aftermath of the Beckmann revolt and the *Regimento*, see Kiemen, *Indian Policy*, 139–80; cf. Leite, *HCJB*, 4: 87–94; and Azevedo, *Os jesuítas*, 187–226.

[11] The debate over Jesuit education in the seventeenth-century Amazon is a

of this measure proved to be limited by conditions in the colony (as well as divisions within the Society), D. Pedro's official support for Jesuit education culminated a 30-year effort on Vieira's part to establish a course of study adapted to the needs of the Amazon missions. Never was Vieira's remaining influence with D. Pedro more evident than in the provision's language mandating that the Jesuits to be trained in Maranhão should study Indian languages and remain in the Amazon.

> And because it is necessary to have a greater number of Missionaries for those Missions and camps in the backlands, and because it is certain that men who are trained in that climate will be better suited for this ministry, the Religious in the novitiate that has been founded in the city of São Luis do Maranhão will pursue the course of study that is necessary for the missions, and there will always be [in the novitiate] twenty men beyond the number that has been there until now; and these men will be exclusively destined for and assigned to the Missions of that State.[12]

The *provisão*, published the same year Vieira wrote to Padre Consalvi, followed the educational strategy Vieira had advocated since the 1650s. Vieira envisioned the São Luiz novitiate as "a kind of seminary for all the missions" that would nurture the novices' missionary vocation in the Amazon itself.[13]

Underlying Vieira's hope were both the mistrust of higher learning and the emphasis on language study that would reappear, with a more combative edge, in the *First Exhortation*. While the novices were studying theology in São Luiz, Vieira wanted them to master the languages of the Amazon Indians. D. Pedro had now mandated this commitment to language study, and Vieira assured Padre Consalvi—who, unlike Betendorf, had endorsed Vieira's efforts to establish the novitiate—that this commitment also had the support of Tirso González, the Jesuit General in Rome. In addition, Vieira persuaded D. Pedro to instruct the crown authorities in Maranhão to outfit Jesuit *entradas* at crown expense, specifying that the missionaries must be "men who are expert at languages." Finally, Vieira emphasized in his letter to Consalvi (as he would in the *Exhortations*) that language must never serve as a barrier

---

complex story that remains to be written. Leite, the only writer to address this subject, provides a useful introduction; but his analysis reflects his preoccupation with the European end of the debate and neglects Vieira's writings of the 1680s (*HCJB*, 4: 233–37).

[12] Reis, *Livro grosso*, 54.
[13] Vieira, *Cartas*, 3: 435.

to saving Indian souls.

> I have no doubt that your Reverence must seek to extend as much as possible the name and knowledge of Christ, and to succor the souls of so many dying innocents who can be won for Heaven even without the resource of language [*sem cabedal de língua*].[14]

Vieira, who had battled the settlers for years over money, offered his suggestions with the concern that the capital (*cabedal*) of the Jesuits always have a sacred point of reference. Learning Indian languages was to be above all a symbol of the Jesuits' commitment to the missionary enterprise and to the call for Jesuit separateness that became the defining element of Vieira's missionary strategy in the Amazon. Vieira's letter to Padre Consalvi is the most striking example before his return to Brazil of the language and logic with which he justified this separateness. The lesson of the 1650s was that the Jesuits must focus exclusively on the conversion of the Indians. Vieira had formally postponed the conversion of the Portuguese to the uncertain future; he hoped that this conversion would come soon, but he was uncharacteristically cautious about predicting with any degree of specificity the time at which it would occur.

The *Exhortations*

Vieira spent the first few years following his return to Bahia in writing and reflection at a Jesuit retreat outside the city.[15] Then he entered the public sphere once more to preach a series of sermons reflecting his continued preoccupation with the Brazilian missions and Brazilian society as a whole.[16] In these sermons, Vieira addressed the Jesuit order and the Portuguese nation in an effort to recast the pastoral and political projects he had pursued throughout his life.

---

[14] Ibid., 434–35.

[15] Barros, *Vida do padre António Vieira*, 271–72; Azevedo, *HAV*, 2: 225.

[16] The most important of these sermons were the *Exhortaçam I em vespora do Espírito Santo* (1688), *Sermões*, 8: 514–34; *Exhortaçam II em vespora da visitaçam* (n.d.; preached during Vieira's term as Visitor), ibid., 534–48; *Palavra de Deos desempenhada: sermam de acçam de graças pelo nacimento do principe D. João* (1688), ibid., 13: 65–137; and *Palavra do pregador empenhada, e defendida: empenhada publicamente no sermam de acçam de graças pelo nacimento do principe D. João, primogenito de SS. Magestades que Deos guarde; defendida depois de sua morte em hum discurso apologético, offerecido secretamente à Rainha N. S. para alívio das saudades do mesmo principe* (1689), ibid., 139–276.

Vieira's two *Exhortações* were preached to the novices at the Jesuit college in Bahia. He addressed the novices both as a missionary who himself had set out from the Bahia college almost 60 years earlier and as a voice of authority and conscience to remind them of the meaning of the Jesuit vocation. The *Exhortations* may best be understood as an intimate statement of Vieira's theory and methodology of mission and as an attempt to implement some of the suggestions he had made 8 years earlier in his letter to Padre Consalvi. Like that letter, the *Exhortations* emphasize the singular role of the Jesuits in the postprimitive church. Vieira continued to refine his interpretation of the Jesuits in the history of the church as he postponed his hopes for the conversion of the Portuguese in Brazil.

At the age of 80, Vieira accepted the post of Jesuit Visitor in Brazil, with the provision that he not be obliged to make inspection tours of the missions in the backlands.[17] He preached the *First Exhortation* on Pentecost 1688, at the beginning of his three-year term. Besides calling this sermon and an undated companion sermon *Exhortations*, Vieira underlined the singularity of the texts by presenting them with a special dedication to the "Brothers, Novices, and Students of the Society of Jesus, zealous, as they all must be [*como todos devem ser*], to devote and sacrifice their lives for the conversion and salvation of the gentiles in the Missions of our Conquests."[18]

[17] Barros, *Vida do padre António Vieira*, 284; Azevedo, *HAV*, 2: 270.

[18] Vieira, *Sermões*, 8: 514. The two sermons at the Bahia college are Vieira's only published exhortations. For a discussion of the effective use of this form of "in-house" preaching by Ignatius's companion, Jerónimo Nadal, see O'Malley, *First Jesuits*, 13–14, 63–69. The *Exhortations* have received little attention in the literature on Vieira. Azevedo presents them in a purely instrumental light, as strategy papers designed solely to attract more novices to the Bahia college. "It was necessary that more followers come to the Society, and that they take on the task [of learning languages] and prepare for this task with the appropriate course of study. This is the purpose [of the *Exhortations*] ... fanning the emotions of the negligent scholars, the Visitor sought to increase the ranks of the apostles" (*HAV*, 2: 276). It could be argued alternatively that Vieira, far from seeking to fatten the college's enrollment, intended to discourage even the novices who had already committed themselves, unless they were prepared to embrace the missionary vocation as he envisioned it. Cantel does not examine the development of Vieira's thought during the 1680s, nor does he see Vieira as centrally involved in missionary work during those years. His generalizations about the *Exhortations* and their historical context could apply to any period in the history of the Brazilian missions: "The clergy too carries its share of responsibility for the evils that afflict Portugal. ... Missionary vocations are becoming increasingly rare. Vieira reproaches many religious for preferring the

The inconspicuous interjection *como todos devem ser* contains the plea that lies at the center of these sermons. For Vieira, the missionary vocation of the Jesuits—particularly the young Jesuits—is not readily apparent. His dedication to the novices thus carries a burden of both affirmation and doubt. The novices are committed to the missionary enterprise by their very presence at the college, but this commitment (which Vieira compares to the saving mission of Jesus, who spoke to John from Mary's womb) must be reaffirmed throughout their time at the college. He portrays the college as a womb for the nurturing of missionaries; from the college the Society sends its ministers into the world to do the work of conversion.[19]

For the *First Exhortation* Vieira took his text from Acts: "And there appeared to them tongues as of fire, distributed and resting on each one of them."[20] In this image, Vieira finds three distinct thematic strands, which he will weave together in his exploration of the mystery of Pentecost.[21] The first is one of his oldest preoccupations: the primacy of language in the work of conversion. The second is the special Jesuit vocation for mastering languages, especially the *línguas barbaras* of the Brazilian Indians. The third strand is another theme to which he has been drawn since his first years with the Jesuits: the need to connect intellect with passion and scholarship with action.

Vieira seeks first not to celebrate the unity infused by the tongues of fire but to recognize the chaos out of which the tongues appeared. Therein lies the miracle of Pentecost: in igniting the tongues of fire, God granted a felicitous sequel to the confusion that descended on the world with the destruction of the Tower of Babel. The proliferation of languages with which God punished human pride inflicted a wound; that wound healed only with the infusion at Pentecost of the gifts of the spirit, which restored to the world the languages it had lost.

The tongues of fire were a sign of the Apostles' mission to construct a second tower—the church—out of the wreckage of Babel. Vieira's

---

comforts of Lisbon to the rigors of the climate of America or Asia" (*Prophétisme et messianisme*, 167).

[19] "For behold, when the voice of your greeting came to my ears, the babe in my womb leaped for joy" (Lk 1.44).

[20] "Apparuerunt dispertitae linguae tanquam ignis, seditque supra singulos eorum" (Acts 2.3).

[21] Vieira's most famous Pentecost sermon is the 1654 *Sermão do Espírito Santo*, preached in Maranhão (*Sermões*, 3: 392–429).

exegesis of the text from Acts contains the kernel of his later pastoral thought: he seeks (particularly in the context of the Brazilian missions) to transform multiplicity into unity and to find seeds of renewal in the chaos of the colony. Put differently, Vieira suggests a new tropology for the Babel story. The infusion of the gifts of the spirit need not be seen as a final remedy for the destruction of the tower. Instead, these gifts constitute a historic reversal, in which the precedent of Genesis contains a lesson for the Portuguese world equally important as the lesson of Pentecost. For Vieira, the seeds of renewal for the missionary enterprise lie in the ruins of Babel as well as in the gifts of the spirit. What was disastrous for the Israelites is a blessing for the Portuguese world in general and for the Jesuits in particular.[22]

The church, Vieira argues, came into a world that had been cursed with a multiplicity of languages. In blessing the first apostles, God took instruments of destruction—the languages with which He had divided the nations—and transformed them into instruments of conversion.

> Just as by confusing the languages of the builders of the tower God impeded the work that they intended [to create], so by infusing the tongues in the Apostles and Preachers of the Faith he founded, established and propagated His own work, which was the church.[23]

These same instruments of conversion must now be acquired through the hard work for which the Jesuits have been chosen. To make this point, Vieira presents to the novices a picture of the first apostles that is as revealing for what it omits as for what it includes. Seeking to draw parallels that establish the apostles as the predecessors of the modern Jesuits, Vieira ignores passages from Luke and Acts that express the fear and doubt he will explore at length in other contexts.[24] The revi-

[22] Like Vieira and the Brazilian Jesuits, missionaries in Spanish America recognized the need to provide religious instruction in the languages of the Indians. Variations on Vieira's interpretation of Babel in the context of the New World were common. See Pagden, *Fall of Natural Man*, 181.

[23] Vieira, *Sermões*, 8: 516. For an exegesis that takes a different approach to the passage from Acts, see the *Sermão da sexagésima*, wherein Vieira emphasizes that each apostle was called on to use the gift of language in a way that suited his particular mission. Of the tongues of fire, Vieira asks, "And why each one on each one, and not all on all? Because all languages do not serve for all [the apostles], but rather each one serves its own." Every apostle, however, is called to use the gift of language in the work of conversion (*Sermões*, 1: 56–59).

[24] See, e.g., the *Sermão do Espírito Santo* (*Sermões*, 3: 424), in which Vieira preaches on Acts 1.11: "Men of Galilee, why do you stand looking into heaven?"

talization of the Brazilian missions will require the certainty of the post-Pentecost, spirit-infused apostle, not the tentativeness of the apostle-in-waiting. Vieira thus will move seamlessly from Exodus to Ezekiel to Paul—not the Paul of the road to Damascus, however, but the Paul of the Epistles, the perfect missionary.

The perfect missionary must know the language of the people to whom he has been sent. Yet the missionary's use of language in the work of conversion is so difficult a task that even in the time of Moses, God recognized that his servants would require help. Vieira now turns to the Exodus story as the first biblical precedent for the missionary's transformation of impairments into sources of strength. This process of turning even the most disastrous reversals into what Peter Berger has called "signals of transcendence" is a central element of Vieira's later pastoral thought.[25] When Moses protested that he could not speak to the Israelites, "for I am slow of speech and of tongue," God rebuked him for presuming to be independent. Moses would speak to the Israelites through his brother Aaron; the political leader and the priest would work together to convert the Israelites. This interdependence is the norm Vieira wants to establish not only among the novices but among all the Jesuits in Brazil.[26] Just as Moses alone could not bear God's word to Israel, no missionary can carry the Gospel's message by himself.

God deprived Moses of the gift of speech to provide an example to future apostles. In the modern missionary enterprise, Vieira argues, all Jesuits must work together to achieve the mastery of languages that no missionary can achieve alone. Vieira repeats throughout the *Exhortações* his belief that only hard work and a deep-rooted acceptance of human limitations can overcome the obstacles the Jesuits must face. He likens the missionary strategy of the Society, which sends each priest into the field in the company of a brother, to the mutual dependence common among the Chinese. Father Nicolas Trigault, noticing that some Chinese men were carried about on the shoulders of others,

[25] Peter Berger, *The Sacred Canopy*, 185.
[26] Ex 4.10. It is an image to which Vieira will return in both the *Discurso apologético* and *Clavis prophetarum*, where he writes of the division of secular and priestly power in Moses and Aaron "so that we might understand that they must be united in brotherly love" (*Obras escolhidas*, 9: 252). For a similar application of the story of Moses and Aaron to the Jesuit missions in the New World, see Acosta, *De procuranda*, bk. 4, ch. 9.

observed that those who were carried on the shoulders were lame, and that those who carried them were blind. So that the lame man, because he had eyes, lent his eyes to the blind man; and the blind man, because he had feet, lent his feet to the lame man; and in this way necessity contrived to make of two incomplete men one whole man [*inventou a necessidade fazer de dous homens defectuosos hum homem inteiro*]. We [Jesuits] should do the same, obligated by the same necessity. The Priest will supply what the Brother lacks, and the Brother what the Priest lacks: the Priest without language administering the Sacraments, and the Brother with language instructing and teaching those who shall receive them.[27]

The lesson of Moses' mission is that the apostle must find strength in his very weaknesses, and he provokes God's wrath when he fails to do so. In citing the text from Exodus and linking it to the mission of the Jesuits, Vieira might also have looked to another passage in the same chapter: "Go back to Egypt, for all the men who were seeking your life are dead." The Jesuits, as noted earlier, were making their first sustained efforts in the Maranhão mission field since the expulsions of 1661 and 1684, and these renewed efforts had not won unanimous support within the Society. Recalling how Moses abandoned pastoral life and returned to Egypt, Vieira criticizes the pastoral failings of his fellow Jesuits and calls on them to bring the gospel to the Brazilian Indians even in the midst of the Society's most implacable enemies (the Portuguese settlers), just as Moses returned to the Jews, though God had hardened Pharaoh's heart.[28]

Vieira continues to pursue the linked themes of language and the missionary's lack of autonomy by looking to the words of Ezekiel and Paul. Ezekiel, like Moses, told God that he could not carry out his mission to the Israelites, and, again like Moses, he was rebuked.[29] If Ezekiel, who spoke the same language, feared his mission nonetheless, it was not surprising that the Jesuits of Brazil were fearful: they had to learn not only the *língua geral* but also the various other languages of the Brazilian Indians. Vieira insists on the Jesuits' responsibility to master these languages while, finally, undercutting that insistence by proposing a vision of the missionary calling that goes far beyond cateche-

[27] Vieira, *Sermões*, 8: 525.
[28] Ex 4.19.
[29] "Son of man, go, get you to the house of Israel, and speak with my words to them. For you are not sent to a people of foreign speech and a hard language, whose words you cannot understand" (Ez 3.4–5).

sis. The Jesuits' dedication to the mastery of languages becomes a crucial symbol of commitment to this vision of the calling, but not an end
in itself. This is why Vieira progresses from Moses to Ezekiel and finally to Paul: Paul's mastery of languages—a God-given mastery, to be
sure—was not finally what made him the perfect embodiment of the
missionary vocation. Vieira emphasizes instead (in a passage linking
the mission of Jeremiah to that of Paul) the *ad omnia* in God's instruction to Jeremiah.

> This *ad omnia* is and must be the enterprise and the insignia of every true
> Missionary . . . all for all, and for all everything. Not only to catechize the
> gentiles, baptize the catechumens, and instruct the Christians, but also to
> nourish them when they are hungry, to clothe them when they are naked,
> to heal them when they are sick, to ransom them when they are held cap-
> tive, to bury them when they die: as Teachers, as Fathers, as Pastors, as Tu-
> tors, as Doctors, as nurses, as servants, as their slaves in all things, to live
> with them always and to die with them, and for them, and also at their
> hands. . . . All this is signified by that *ad omnia*.[30]

This is the consummate expression in the *Sermões* of the missionary
vocation. The importance of Vieira's final qualification concerning the
missionary who is unable to communicate with words cannot be overstated. With Paul as his exemplary missionary, Vieira resolves the
problem that the *Exhortation* poses. Language might appear to occupy
a prime position in the missionary enterprise, but as the Exodus story
shows, language is only one means of conversion, and mastery of languages need not—indeed cannot—reside solely in one agent of conversion. It is in this context that Vieira cites the rebuke of Ezekiel, in
which language is a gift of God, serving as a universal means of understanding under conditions of God's choosing. Finally, Vieira sets
before the novices the example of Paul, which teaches that the missionary enterprise recognizes no barriers (linguistic or otherwise) between peoples, and that language mastery does not determine success.

Vieira sees no contradiction in preaching a sermon about the importance of language in the work of conversion and then undercutting
this idea by a further example. He cites not only Paul, who worked

---

[30] Vieira, *Sermões*, 8: 526. The text is, "Do not say, 'I am only a youth'; for to all
[*ad omnia*] to whom I send you you shall go, and whatever I command you you
shall speak" (Jer 1.7).

miracles with the gift of language, but also Xavier, who worked miracles without that gift. Vieira need not have gone as far afield as Xavier. He himself had marveled at how much he and his companions had achieved on Cabo Verde (while detained en route to Brazil in 1653) in the space of one month, with no knowledge of African languages.[31] His concern, then, is with language mastery not as an end in itself but as an affirmation of the commitment to self-sacrifice on which the success of the missions depends.

Drawing on this connection, Vieira moves from the general to the particular. He weaves the first strand of the *Exhortation*—the primacy of language—into an argument that theological study must be firmly linked to the work of conversion. It should be remembered that Vieira is speaking to the novices in his role as a Visitor for the Society and he intends to implement the suggestions he has already made to Padre Consalvi. His attempt to strengthen his listeners' missionary vocation leads him back to the first principles of the Jesuit vocation itself; that is, to Ignatius. In Ignatius he finds the link to the tongues of fire that most Christians believed were lost with the primitive church. The founder of the Society of Jesus was "a giant of fire [*ignis*], therefore called Ignatius."[32]

The *First Exhortation* can be read as an orderly conclusion, after more than 25 years, to the disparate arguments Vieira presented in the *Sermão da sexagésima*. In that sermon, Vieira suggested that the gifts of the spirit were lost not with the primitive church but with the Jesuits who succeeded Ignatius and the Society's third General, Francisco de Borja.[33] Now he invokes once more the heroic period of the Jesuit missions and places the responsibility for reigniting the tongues of fire squarely on the shoulders of the present generation.

Ignatius sought to renew the Christian faith in Europe and to bring that faith to the New Worlds of America, Asia, and Africa, which had

---

[31] Vieira, *Cartas*, 1: 294–98. In his report on his second term as Visitor, Vieira was careful to include instructions on how the missionaries should proceed in the absence of interpreters. Referring to the Indians, he writes that the missionaries "shall show them Images and Crosses, and make them assist in the ceremonies and in the Christian community, so that if necessary, the Padres may baptize them with gestures, for as there is no way for them to receive the faith through their ears, at least *sub condicione* no one shall die without baptism" ("Visita do padre António Vieira," in Leite, *HCJB*, 4: 116).

[32] Vieira, *Sermões*, 8: 518.

[33] Ibid., 1: 77.

been opened to the church in his own lifetime. In founding the Society, he had called on men who were willing to sacrifice themselves in the most humble ministries, first in Europe and later in the mission fields. Vieira is thankful, he tells the novices, that the Jesuits have not been granted the gifts of the primitive church. God made Moses slow of speech as a lesson for future apostles—particularly the Jesuits of Vieira's own day. By not infusing the missionaries in the New World with the gifts of the spirit, God was commanding them to serve the church in a new way. Vieira, ever attentive to the links between Jesuit history and Scripture, notes that like the text from Acts, the Society's *Constitutions* permit no exemptions to this command. Novices and elders alike share the responsibility to make manifest in the New World the apostolic fire that began with Ignatius.

Vieira's interpretation of the Pentecost lesson hinges on an apostolic reversal, which he characteristically transforms into a sign of God's mercy. In turning Luke's text into a specific instruction for all Jesuits, Vieira calls on the novices to transform the tongues of fire into a fire of tongues that will convert the non-Christians throughout the New World. The deepest meaning of Pentecost is to be found in the inextinguishable fire of the Holy Spirit, not in the transient tongues themselves.

> "There appeared to them tongues as of fire, distributed and resting on each one of them." So that it was not the tongues that rested on them, but rather the fire. And why? Because the tongues were transient, passing on with the primitive church; while the fire of those same tongues did not pass on but remained and stayed fixed: *Sedit*. And what fire of tongues is this? It is the zeal and the burning fervor that the heirs to the Apostolic spirit have for knowing, studying, and learning strange languages in order to preach the Gospel, propagate the Faith, and make great the Church.[34]

Just as God chose the Apostles to build a second tower—the primitive church—to reunify the world after the destruction of Babel, so Ignatius and his successors have been chosen to build a third tower—the modern missionary church—where all the languages of the New World will be found. Far from lamenting the withholding of the gifts of the primitive church, Vieira continues, the Jesuits should rejoice in the greater glory that will be theirs as a result of hard work alone.

[34] Ibid., 8: 518.

The first tower was that of Nimrod, in which the tongues were confused; the second tower was that of the Holy Spirit, in which they were infused; the third tower is that of St. Ignatius, in which they are neither confused nor infused. They are not confused, because they are learned in a distinct and orderly manner. Neither are they infused, because they are not given by grace, like the gift of tongues. They are instead acquired and purchased at the price of much study and great labor; and it is for this reason that they bring many great rewards.[35]

While Vieira believes that the Society as a whole is destined to receive these rewards for leading the postprimitive church in the work of conversion, he sees the Society in Brazil as an institution in decline, which needs to reaffirm its traditional missionary vocation if it is to survive in a colony where it has never been welcome.

An admonitory tone runs through the *Exhortation*: Vieira sounds at times as if he is determined to demonstrate that the missionaries of the future will be unable to match the heroism of his own generation and those that preceded it. He speaks of a time "that we old men remember, when the native Portuguese language was no more common among us than the Brazilian. That was my work, but it is not what I see today." Looking back to the heroic period of the missions of southern Brazil, he speaks of José de Anchieta not only as an author but as an inventor: Anchieta produced a unique grammar for the *língua geral*. It spawned a body of Jesuit literature in Brazil that "appears to be more suited to making theologians out of Christians than to making Christians out of gentiles." Through language study, then, the founders of the missions performed the hard work of conversion; they showed that no European catechism was too complex for the Brazilian Indians, whom so many in the church said were unteachable. Language, as Anchieta employed it, was an instrument with which to work miracles; and his *Gramática* itself was a miracle, not for the number of Indians it converted but for the vision of the Jesuit vocation that it embodied.[36]

Vieira warns that the legacy of the first Jesuits in Brazil is in danger of disappearing with his own generation. This crisis, however, gives the novices an opportunity to reverse the danger, within the Society itself, by committing themselves to the work of conversion. The means Vieira proposes for accomplishing this reversal reveal again the trans-

[35] Ibid.
[36] Ibid., 520; José de Anchieta, *Arte de grammática da língua mais usada na costa do Brasil* (Leipzig, 1876).

formation of his missionary strategy. In spite of his bitter battles with the settlers in Brazil, Vieira insists that the external circumstances for the Society have never been more favorable. He can make this declaration because he no longer considers partnership with the Portuguese to be a necessary condition for the success of the Brazilian missions. Instead, he looks to the Jesuits' internal strengths, and also assigns a lesser, though nonetheless crucial, role to the Society's traditional partnership with the Portuguese crown.

As he does throughout his later sermons, Vieira affirms the piety of the royal family, even as he distances himself from the society it rules. This praise for the crown (and for the privileges it has bestowed on the Jesuits) is especially noteworthy here in the *Exhortation*, considering Vieira's problematic relationship with D. Pedro II. Singling out D. Pedro from his predecessors, Vieira instructs the novices that

> God has given us a King (may God keep him) who is so noble an heir of his glorious progenitors, and whose soul is so pious and truly Apostolic, that from the multitude of his cares the greatest of all is the propagation of the Faith, entrusting everything in this State [Bahia], and much more in Maranhão, to the zeal and instruction of the Society. God has given us at the same time for universal Father and [Jesuit] General the most illustrious Spanish Missionary of this century [Padre Tirso González], whose spirit (like that of Paul) is not attached to Rome and makes itself present to us in his letters, in all of which the fire of St. Ignatius ignites us more than it exhorts us to the Missions. And what shall I say to the Bahia College, or what will it say to me, when in this great Community the *língua geral* is now so uncommon [*pouco geral*] that there are few in whom it can be found? Shall I say that by chance or by a great misfortune the tongues have been muted or diminished, because the fire has gone out or grown cold?[37]

Vieira's characterization of D. Pedro employs the same language he used to describe the ideal missionary. His juxtaposition of the king's apostolic orientation with that of Tirso González creates the impression of a seamless connection between the project of the Portuguese nation and that of the Jesuit order. In the course of the *Exhortation*, Vieira has pointed to apostolic predecessors in the Society, and he has underlined the support the Brazilian missions have received from both the Jesuit hierarchy and the Portuguese crown. It remains for the present generation to commit itself to the missionary vocation. Language study

---

[37] Vieira, *Sermões*, 8: 521.

once again is the most telling measure of this commitment. The reordering of the Society's educational priorities that will permit the novices to act on this commitment constitutes the third strand of the *Exhortation*. Vieira restates here the agenda he pursued in Maranhão during the 1650s and reiterated in Lisbon: he emphasizes the need to direct all Jesuit education toward the practical necessities of the missions, and the futility of learning that does not lead to action.[38]

The Jesuits, Vieira admits, face an apparent dilemma. On the one hand, the Society has tried to reemphasize the importance of language study as an entry requirement for the colleges. On the other hand, few students are interested in studying Indian languages. The number of Indians has declined dramatically since the early contact period, and young men entering the novitiate have increasingly sought the Society's traditional instruction in rhetoric, philosophy, and theology. For Vieira, nevertheless, the Ignatian pastoral ideal demands that the Society rededicate itself to the study of Indian languages. While he recognizes why the Jesuits have not mastered those languages, he is finally unsympathetic to any response short of a radical reorganization of missionary education in the colony.

> On the present occasion, when to the obligations of this [Jesuit] Province are added the conquest of the new world of Maranhão and of the great Amazon River, there is no doubt that [Jesuit ignorance of] the *língua geral*, which is the only door by which it is possible to enter into knowledge of others, is the cause of the privation and difficulty [*aperto*] in which we find ourselves.[39]

Vieira returns here to his well-known argument that Maranhão itself is a new world, occupying a unique position in the Portuguese Empire and the Fifth Empire. And in speaking of the *aperto* (literally, narrow strait) the Jesuits are in, he enlists the size of the Amazon to suggest the necessary grandeur of the Jesuit project. In both the *Livro anteprimeiro* and the *História do futuro* proper, Vieira frequently contrasted the boundlessness of the missionary enterprise with the limited

---

[38] Cidade summarizes Vieira's view of the ideal missionary education as follows: "It is not necessary to know Greek or Hebrew. It is sufficient to know the languages of the gentiles. . . . The word of the preacher of the Gospel is still the instrument of the man of action. To speak for [Vieira] is almost always to act" (*Padre António Vieira*, 1: 11, 15).

[39] Vieira, *Sermões*, 8: 523.

imaginations of those responsibile for carrying it out.[40] In the *Exhortation*, his *aperto* may be read as a literal reference to the missionary enterprise: without a fundamental reorientation, the Society's constricted vision will be no match for the immensities of the Amazon. Similarly, when Vieira speaks of "the only door by which it is possible to enter into knowledge of others," he is speaking not only of the door leading to the multiplicity of languages with which the Indians of the Amazon must be converted, but the door to the physical world itself. The Indians inhabit a world of "others," a world that lies beyond the walls of the college and of Portuguese society. The door to that world is being shut as the Jesuits retreat into scholarship.

Recognizing the need for the kind of language study that Vieira prescribed, the Jesuit hierarchy had recently changed the curriculum and granted a special dispensation to those novices willing to go to the Maranhão missions before formally completing their studies. Vieira preaches against knowledge that is unconnected to action and, more specifically, against theological learning that leaves behind the work of conversion.

> The strongest appetite of the rational nature is the desire for knowledge. This was what killed Eve and many others. It is what exhausts the Society, which spews out of its mouth blood that would be better spent on the commentaries and petitions of which the Archives of Rome are full. And what petitions are these? They are the continuous requests and letters written not with ink but with the very blood that all the Provinces of Europe have shed, petitioning on their knees for the supreme Government of the Society to establish overseas missions, which are the most exposed and dangerous missions.[41]

In this passage, and throughout his writings on the missionary church, Vieira attempts to invert European expectations of the New World. This inversion is particularly evident in his references to the importance of language in the conversion process. Even when he was one of Rome's celebrated orators and a potential preacher to the papal court, Vieira spoke of the mastery of foreign tongues as a skill valuable

[40] See, e.g., Vieira's lament that the Portuguese people are needlessly "narrow of heart [*estreitos de coração*]" (*História do futuro*, ed. Buescu, bk. 2, ch. 6). His purpose, there as in the present exhortation, is to enlist the pastoral energies of the Portuguese public and the novices, respectively.

[41] Vieira, *Sermões*, 8: 527.

only insofar as it furthered the work of conversion. He mocked himself for his immersion in the subtleties of Italian. He wanted to preach to the Indians of the Amazon, not to the pope and the College of Cardinals.

In his new position as Visitor, Vieira again delegitimates the learning that Rome prized. The only archives the church needs, he tells the novices, are those that refer to America and other mission fields. During his term as Visitor, the very word "archive" becomes for Vieira something of an epithet when it refers to anything other than the Bible or the affairs of the missionary church.[42] The facts registered in the archives of Lisbon and Rome are superseded by those found in the mission records and in Scripture, which may be interpreted in the Amazon more readily than in Rome. Here the problem of access to texts, which occupied Vieira in the *Representations*, appears once more. It suggests the conflicting impulses in Vieira's view of intellectual life. Access and censorship were problems most apparent during Vieira's years in prison, but in Brazil, too, he constantly seeks access to books that are difficult to obtain. At the same time, he dismisses the learned inquiries of other writers and insists that the only book he needs is the Bible.

Vieira's view of how the Jesuits should proceed as a corporation, however, expresses no such tensions. For all but the few faithful who have a gift for theology, to seek knowledge of Christ is to be not a theologian but a missionary. Brazil—the beloved "milch cow" of D. João IV—is now at the center of the church. Lisbon and Rome are auxiliary to the project of conversion. Vieira uses the terminology of the academy to subvert the academic enterprise. With undisguised contempt, he calls on the theologians to leave behind their commentaries and follow the example of Christ and his imitators in the missions.

> "To give knowledge of salvation to his people": The knowledge [*sciencia*] of salvation alone, and this taught not to the great ones of the world, but to the people [*plebe*]. . . . And in view of this truly great example, is there anyone who would wish to be graduated in some other science?[43]

[42] See, e.g., a revealing letter to the queen's Jesuit confessor, Padre Leopoldo Fuess, in which Vieira notes that he was temporarily disconcerted by the death of the heir to the throne but that "in the midst of my perplexity I turned again to the Holy Scriptures, the archive in which Divine Providence has deposited her secrets" (*Cartas*, 3: 583).

[43] Vieira, *Sermões*, 8: 528; Lk 1.77.

This unequivocal condemnation of the academy, and of theological study in particular, is not found in all of Vieira's later writings. It is characteristic, however, of the writings in which he analyzes the crisis in the mission field.

Vieira proposes a sharply focused definition of the Jesuit vocation and the place of scholarship in that vocation. Some Jesuits, he anticipates, will liken the scholars who devote themselves to the mission field to the servant in the gospel of Matthew who buried his talents. Vieira mocks those who would make this analogy. Invoking, by comparison, the field of athletic competition, he tells the aspiring Jesuits, "many compete in the stadium and in the end find themselves tired, not crowned [*cançados, e não coroados*]." There is no sin in not being a great athlete. The sin lies in becoming "idolaters of learning."[44] Not every Jesuit is meant to be a scholar, but every Jesuit is meant to bear a personal responsibility for the Indian souls that will be lost during his years of study.

Vieira's disdain is palpable when he speaks of the *honrinhas* that so many in the Society covet. Such honors trivialize the Jesuit vocation and ultimately represent a refusal to serve God. The argument that only a chosen few in the Society will make theological contributions valuable enough to justify their absence from the backlands comes not only from Vieira's impatience with the Jesuit impasse in the colony but also from his insistence that the missionary submit to God's will by renouncing the pursuit of knowledge that does not serve the work of conversion.

> And what greater honor (seeing that we are so attached to these *honrinhas*), what greater honor than for me to enter with God into my part in the greatest work of His omnipotence? Who converted these gentiles? God, and I. God with His grace, and I with my teaching. God entered into this work with His part, and I with mine. "With the mighty deeds of the Lord God I will come." Here there is nothing for us to do but cross our arms, place our fingers over our mouths, and confess either our ignorance or our little faith.[45]

---

[44] Vieira, *Sermões*, 8: 529.

[45] Ibid.; Ps 71.16. The passage about the athletes illustrates how difficult it is to argue, as critics such as João Francisco Lisboa have done, that Vieira was an elitist (*Jornal de Timon e vida do padre António Vieira*). The qualities that might be considered elitist in Vieira were finally inseparable from his missionary strategy, as Cidade emphasizes in his description of the *First Exhortation* (*Padre António Vieira*, 14–15).

The statement is so personal that Vieira can no longer be speaking in his official role as Visitor, but instead as one for whom conversion is a greater mystery after a lifetime in the missions than it was when he was young. The missionary enterprise in Brazil began for Vieira with a loudly proclaimed partnership with the Portuguese; it is ending with a partnership with God that renders the preacher mute. In the presence of conversion—"the greatest work of His omnipotence"—the response of faith is silence.

The *Exhortation* concludes with an appeal to the conscience of each novice. Vieira's retreat from the world of the Portuguese is nowhere more evident than in this summation and in the *Second Exhortation*, which restates it. For the true missionary—the *verdadeiro missionário* whom Vieira so often addresses—the Society of Jesus, like Augustine's church, becomes no more than an imperfect signpost. In contrast to Augustine's emphasis on community, however, Vieira here proposes a solitary vision of apostleship. Moving from the general to the particular, Vieira asks each novice to examine his own soul to discern his proper vocation, as Vieira himself did long ago.

> Leaving behind lofty arguments [about the Jesuit vocation], let each one argue to himself and with himself. When I was in the world, did I not leave the world of the world to save my soul? And now that I am a religious, shall I not leave the world of Religion to save many souls?[46]

The pervasive corruption among both settlers and clergy in Brazil forces the missionary in the colony to become a servant of the Indians, turning away not just from the world of the Portuguese, but from the world of religion itself. The institutional church—even the missionary church in the New World—cannot provide an adequate foundation for the missionary enterprise. The *Exhortation* thus demonstrates the progressive narrowing of Vieira's pool of potential collaborators, until finally there is only the individual missionary team, consisting of the priest and the brother who accompanies him. It is impossible to do the work of conversion as a pastor among pastors.

The missionary's need to withdraw from the world of religion is the theme of the *Second Exhortation*. For his text, Vieira turns once again to Luke: "And the angel departed from her. In those days Mary arose and

[46] Vieira, *Sermões*, 8: 530.

went with haste into the hill country, to a city of Judah."[47] The sermon, which was preached on the eve of the novices' renewal of vows, reaffirms Vieira's Pentecost lesson on the Ignatian vocation by discerning in the text a question: Who got the better road, the angel who returned to heaven or Jesus, who had just been conceived and whose suffering lay ahead of him? For Vieira, this question differs from those that generate the prideful commentaries he dismissed in the *First Exhortation*, for the novices' understanding of the missionary enterprise hangs on the answer. Vieira has addressed this question in various guises all his life, and the answer he now provides offers a measure of the distance he has come since he first began to preach on the missionary calling. The fire of tongues can now be ignited only by the Jesuits.

In 1642, when Vieira preached the *Sermão de Santo António* in Lisbon, the theme of conversion had a political context. Vieira wanted to awaken an entire society to its duties in the face of the Spanish threat to Portuguese independence, and he asked all three estates to transform themselves for the common good. The *Sermão de Santo António* emphasized the transforming power of fire. The conservation of Portugal depended on a conversion to be accomplished by fire, air, and water, with fire symbolizing the church, "the highest element of all, closest to Heaven and most removed from the Earth; the element that all the others sustain, though it is exempt itself from sustaining any others."[48] Forty-six years later, the fire that Vieira analyzes rests exclusively with the Jesuits. Looking at his work as a pastor and trying to describe it to the novices, moreover, Vieira abandons the rhetoric with which he tried to bind together post-Restoration Portugal and pins his hopes on the missionaries sitting in front of him. The Jesuits will walk Jesus' road. To the question of who got the better road, there can be only the answer offered by Ignatius, who, "with the heroism and sublimity of his spirit," said he would remain on earth serving God, even if in doing so he risked his own salvation. This is the example that Paul

---

[47] "Discessit ab illa Angelus: Exurgens autem Maria abiit in montana cum festinatione in Civitatem Juda" (Lk 1.38–39).

[48] *Sermões*, 11: 138. The sermon was preached on the eve of the convocation of the Cortes. Vieira commanded the nobles, the clergy, and the *povo* to understand literally its text, "You are the salt of the earth" (Mt 5.13). Even at this early point in his career, Vieira insisted on physical conversion as a sign of the conversion of the heart. "We have already been fishermen; it remains for us now to become salt."

followed when he remained in the world instead of joining Christ in heaven, and it is the example every Jesuit must follow.[49]

Vieira is more hopeful about the missionary enterprise in the *Second Exhortation* than in the first. He also introduces a mystical, Joannine element. He looks to John when he preaches that in bringing the gospel to the non-Christian world, the Jesuits are blessed not as men or even as angels, "but blessed with the glory of the Son of God when he was seen on earth: 'We have beheld his glory, glory as of the only Son from the Father.'"[50] In this vision lies a link between Luke and John that holds a key to Vieira's theory of mission. For Vieira, sanctification—the hard work of conversion that is carried out on earth and brings grace—is a greater mission than glorification, a gift given in heaven. Sanctification lies at the heart of the missionary vocation that Vieira tells the novices to ponder before entering the Society.

> Within the very greatness and omnipotence of God it is a greater work to sanctify than to glorify, because to glorify is to give glory, while to sanctify is to give grace, which is better than glory. . . . This, dear Brothers, is our vocation and your vocation, something many do not recognize when they ask to be admitted to it.[51]

When John speaks of glorification he is speaking of Jesus' death. Vieira follows the Joannine interpretation, but in his effort to understand Jesus as missionary he looks to Luke. His address to the novices focuses on the work of conversion that comes before glorification.

In Lukan theology, the success of all missions, even that of Jesus, depends on the help and nurturing of others. Jesus was carried by Mary into the hills of Judea, and he spoke to John through the womb of John's mother, Elizabeth. Vieira, drawing on the imagery of the *First Exhortation*, compares the mission that Jesus began in Mary's womb to the unique two-year novitiate within the Society. He sees the novitiate as a time not only for nurturing the missionary who will leave the world that is familiar to him, but also for binding him to the larger institution that serves as the mother without whom he will literally be

---

[49] See Phil 1.21–24. Vieira even looks to Ignatius as if Ignatius were the model for Paul, concluding with mock regret that he is "almost pained that St. Paul made a similar resolution [to that of Ignatius]. But with such a companion one can well give up the singularity" (*Sermões*, 8: 535).

[50] Jn 1.14.

[51] Vieira, *Sermões*, 8: 539.

rendered mute.

> I cannot fail to note here our custom in the backlands when the Missionary does not know the language of those he is to convert. In this case, one and not infrequently two interpreters go along: one interpreter through whom the Missionary speaks and another through whom the gentiles listen. The Virgin and St. Elizabeth were such interpreters at the time of the Incarnation. Christ, who was not yet able to speak, spoke through the voice of the Virgin ("the voice of your greeting"); and the Baptist, who was not yet able to hear, heard through the ears of Elizabeth ("in my ears"). In this same manner the mute man may speak to the deaf one, and the Missionary may convert, and the gentile may be converted: not by themselves, but by means of their mothers when each one is in his mother's womb.[52]

This image of the missionary concludes one of Vieira's last explorations of Jesuit apostleship. The very act of speaking the language of conversion establishes the missionary's dependency. This dependency is something that the novices (like their predecessors in the Society) are called upon not to resist but to "recognize and make manifest."[53]

The Fifth Empire and the Portuguese Succession

Vieira's term as Visitor coincided with the birth and death of D. João, the firstborn son of D. Pedro II and the king's second wife, D. Maria Sofia Isabel. The birth, and the prince's death less than three weeks later, produced a new crop of millenarian expectations that inspired Vieira's last two public sermons: the *Sermam de acçam de graças* (*Thanksgiving Sermon*) and its companion piece, the *Discurso apologético* (*Apologetic Address*).[54]

These sermons are unrivaled in Vieira's writings in terms of the specificity with which they link contemporary political contingencies to his longstanding preoccupation with the Fifth Empire. Together they constitute a restatement of the implications of prophecy for public

---

[52] Ibid., 543–44.

[53] The phrase is from William Sloane Coffin's interpretation of the Easter lesson, in *Sermons from Riverside*.

[54] These sermons, along with the 1684 obsequies for D. Pedro's first wife (D. Maria Francisca Isabel) comprise volume 13 of the *Sermões*. The *Sermam de acçam de graças* was preached in the cathedral of Bahia in December 1688. The *Discurso apologético* was written in 1689 and never preached; it was formally intended only for the eyes of the mourning queen, but Vieira also clearly intended it to circulate in Bahia and Lisbon.

life that Vieira addressed throughout his career. Vieira's insistence on the illusoriness of human hopes and the lack of autonomy of the agent of history, and his command that partnership be the organizing principle of mission, are all developed in a new direction in these sermons on D. João.

This study has argued that Vieira's interpretation of church history was designed to accommodate the faltering progress of the church in both Portugal and the New World. This interpretive method is crucial to the *Sermam de acçam de graças*. The sermon shows that Vieira, even in the act of giving thanks for the birth of the prince, anticipated the tragedy that the *Discurso apologético* would explain. Put differently, Vieira in the *Sermam de acçam de graças* laid the foundation for a reversal that he would need only to interpret, just as he had interpreted for the novices the contradictions inherent in the missionary church, which must work without the gifts of the spirit.

The coincidence of his term as Visitor with the birth and death of D. João was weighted, for Vieira, with unmistakable symbolism. He interpreted this symbolism in detail, especially in the *Discurso Apologético*. Vieira had lived long enough to interweave the destinies of the prince and the missionary so closely as to make them virtually indistinguishable. In these sermons, the prince and the missionary are agents of both history and providence. Neither agent is autonomous, and each fulfills his destiny by recognizing and finally sacralizing his lack of autonomy.

In the sermons on D. João, Vieira ascribes to human agency in history the same polymorphic quality he has attributed to language in Scripture. The inversions and reversals that punctuate history are signals for human beings; they tell us that we court disaster when momentary enthusiasms cause us to forget the precariousness of our hopes. The death of the newborn prince served for Vieira as a powerful personal reminder of this precariousness and of the danger of placing our hopes in any single individual.

Critics have suggested that Vieira was forced in the *Discurso apologético* to perform a desperate act of reconstruction to rescue the crumbling edifice of the *Sermam de acçam de graças*. This view misreads both sermons by failing to connect them to the body of Vieira's writings.[55]

---

[55] We have no record of the derision with which some readers must have greeted Vieira's attempt. Cidade suggests the possible reception by sympathetic

Vieira's apologia was addressed not directly to his readers but to God and the queen, who served as an instrument of divine providence. If, indeed, he sought to respond to the derision he encountered in some quarters, the text of his response cannot be read as a straightforward act of self-defense.

The rhetorical structure of the *Discurso apologético* itself is as complex as the dynastic reversal that Vieira seeks to interpret. The passage early in the sermon in which he appears to acknowledge that the prince's death poses a problem of interpretation turns out to be a preemptive strike against his would-be attackers.

> No one will call this task [explaining the thanksgiving sermon] difficult, because everyone, and with reason [*e com razão*], will take it to be impossible.[56]

The *com razão* that suggests a concession on Vieira's part is in reality an act of personal and exegetical defiance. Vieira acknowledges that those who take his exegetical task to be impossible would appear to be correct to do so. At the same time, he condemns those skeptics for their arrogance. They use their reason to conclude that the prince's death has undone Vieira's predictions; yet it was precisely his reliance on the evidence of history, Vieira argues, that brought him to his present exegetical predicament and may have helped to bring the prince's life to an early end. Vieira's mistake in the *Sermam de acçam de graças* was to reformulate the Juramento d'Ourique: he replaced a present hope ("he will look upon, and will see") with an accomplished fact ("he looked upon, and saw").[57] The consequences of this presumed omniscience are painstakingly described in the *Discurso apologético*. Nowhere in this description does Vieira cede any ground to those who have derided his earlier words or, more important, those who would allow the prince's

---

skeptics when he argues that Vieira was forced to struggle "to keep on its feet the daring architecture of the chimerical political sermon" (*Padre António Vieira*, 153). Cantel, like Cidade, posits a building metaphor in discussing Vieira's exegetical work in the sermon: "He remains a prisoner of his system. All the agility of his spirit will not enable him to escape, for this is a question of faith. His agility permits him only to keep the structure standing in an ever more precarious equilibrium each time events seem to be at the point of bringing it down" (*Prophétisme et messianisme*, 130–31). Neither writer grants that it was because of these reversals—not in spite of them—that Vieira's certainty grew stronger.

[56] Vieira, *Sermões*, 13: 147.

[57] "Respiciet, et videbit"; "Respexit, et vidit."

death to inspire doubts about the national mission that has been sealed in the Juramento.[58]

Even as he rejoiced at the birth of the prince, Vieira found reason to be cautious about the fulfillment of Portugal's hopes. In no sense may the *Sermam de acçam de graças* be interpreted as a mere restatement of Vieira's youthful obsessions.[59] The *Sermam de acçam de graças* and *Discurso apologético* are the most important late examples (along with the letters) of the complex interplay between hope and *desengano* (disillusionment) in Vieira's thought. As a nation that has been given a unique blessing by God, the Portuguese have greater reason than any other nation to fear both divine providence and human envy. Vieira posits a God who lovingly withholds from His chosen nation the blessings it expects, then bestows those same blessings in unexpected ways. In this way Vieira provides a new gloss on a theme that he treated in detail in the *História do futuro* and gives his listeners a foretaste of the arguments he will deploy in his defense of the sermon.

The only thing certain about our hopes, Vieira preaches in the *Sermam de acçam de graças*, is that in fastening on the wrong object (D. Sebastião) they have assured their own realization. Had the Portuguese hoped for D. João IV from the beginning, their hopes would have been destroyed by the envy of their rivals.

> The Portuguese have always hoped for a King who would restore them. And in what way was their hope justified? In their having been mistaken in the one for whom they hoped [*Em errarem o esperado*]. If they had hoped correctly for Dom João IV, both he and we would have been lost, for if God's jealousy and fear of that hope had not taken him [Dom João IV] from the world, they would surely have taken him from Portugal. And what did divine Providence do to reveal his destiny to him, and through him to us? It made the Portuguese give themselves over to their hope in Dom Sebastião.

---

[58] Vieira returns throughout the *Discurso apologético* to the Juramento, to which he refers in the thanksgiving sermon as "our text, from which I shall not depart, not even in a single comma" (*Sermões*, 13: 111). He warns frequently in his other writings of the potentially fatal effects of the wavering faith of the Portuguese; cf. the "Brief Warning to Unbelievers" in the *Livro anteprimeiro*, 4: 222–96.

[59] Cf. Cantel, who writes that with the birth of the prince Vieira "rediscovers all the exuberance of his youth," and that "Emerging from his long retreat [in Bahia], Vieira rediscovers the enthusiasm of his youth and makes of this sermon a public exposition of his messianic doctrine" (*Prophétisme et messianisme*, 127, 184). Cantel ignores or misinterprets the writings in which Vieira underlines the illusoriness of human hope.

For what purpose? So that their hope for the dead King (a hope in which there was nothing to be feared) would preserve without danger the succession of the living King.[60]

This interpretation of the efficacy of reversals in history—reversals that make human society aware, however fleetingly, of the precariousness of its hopes—runs throughout the *Sermam de acçam de graças*. Vieira thus introduces in a public context the theology he developed in the private *First Exhortation*, which was preached within months of the *Sermam de acçam de graças*. When he speaks of the foundering of hopes— even the best-founded hopes—in the face of envy, he echoes his experience in Maranhão 30 years earlier, for he has not forgotten the enmity he encountered from rival religious orders when the Jesuits exercised D. João IV's mandate. For Vieira, the most visible symbols of hope (particularly the church) are the least likely instruments of divine providence. In the missions, he called for a long-term recommitment by the Jesuits to the work of conversion; in the temporal sphere, he looks to the fulfillment of the Juramento in D. João IV and his successors.

The underlying link between the Jesuit mission and the vagaries of Portuguese succession is made concrete in the miraculous role Vieira ascribes to Francis Xavier in the conception of the newborn prince. D. Maria Sofia made weekly visits during her pregnancy to the Jesuit church of São Roque in Lisbon to ask for Xavier's protection, and she attributed the conception of her child to his intercession. Vieira seeks to discern logical reasons for the queen's faith. He finds them in the time of conception of the newborn prince, and he methodically takes his listeners through the months of the year to demonstrate that his conclusion is sound.

From the dates of the labor and the birth we may naturally infer those of the conception. And when was our Prince born? On the thirtieth of August.

---

[60] Vieira, *Sermões*, 13: 89. The most important warnings in the *Sermões* of the danger of placing hope in the agents of divine providence are found in the *Sermão da primeira oitava de Paschoa*, 1647 (8: 197–226), on the Israelites' veneration of Moses; the *Sermão da primeira oitava de Paschoa*, 1656 (4: 396–433), in which Vieira discerns providential effects in the failure of a large gold-seeking expedition; the *Sermão do mandato*, 1643 (3: 355–91), on the example of David's love for his wife; and the *Sermão das exéquias do sereníssimo principe de Portugal D. Theodosio*, 1654 (16: 253–78), which declares that D. Theodosio was denied the throne because his talents had awakened God's jealousy.

So we may justifiably infer that he was conceived either on the eve of St. Francis Xavier's feast day, or else on the day itself, these being the first and second of December. Let us now count. December, January, February, March, April, May, June, July, August: exactly nine months. Let us all then say (giving thanks to St. Francis Xavier), "Your prayer is heard," and (congratulating the King), "Your wife Elizabeth [Isabel] will bear you a son."[61]

The sermon's emphasis on Xavier's intercession for the queen accomplishes two purposes. Vieira establishes, first, the central and unexpected role of this foreign-born missionary in the Portuguese Empire, both during and after Xavier's lifetime; and second, the position of both Xavier and the infant prince as singled out by God in the Juramento, the one to serve as a Portuguese missionary, the other as vicar of the temporal kingdom.[62]

The most important of the sermon's claims concerning Xavier centers on the unforeseen circumstances that led to his initial journey to India under the patronage of D. João III. Xavier had intended to remain in Rome to assist Ignatius after Nicolas Bobadilla departed, but he undertook the mission when Bobadilla fell ill. To that account Vieira adds the miracle by which God grafted a Portuguese birthright onto Xavier, who was born in Navarre. Vieira's language here recalls his discussion of Moses and the missionary vocation in the *Exhortations*. Portugal could not carry on the work of conversion by itself: it had to rely on foreign-born missionaries.[63] At the same time, Vieira argues, a non-Portuguese missionary clearly could not be God's chosen instrument for converting the New World. Xavier's so-called naturalization by D. João therefore represented more than a renewal of God's promise to the Portuguese.[64] Vieira discerns in the king's patronage so singular a manifestation of divine providence that he unhesitatingly

---

[61] Vieira, *Sermões*, 13: 108. The text is Lk 1.13.

[62] Xavier became an increasingly important reference point in Vieira's theory of mission after his return from Maranhão in 1661 (particularly in the *História do futuro* and the *Exhortations*).

[63] On the shortage of missionaries throughout the Iberian world, see Boxer, *Church Militant and Iberian Expansion*, 112–21.

[64] Xavier was not formally naturalized by D. João, but it is clear that he considered himself Portuguese in his capacity as a missionary (his family had long opposed Castilian power in Navarre, and he never thought of himself as Spanish). In a letter he wrote while en route to Japan from Goa in 1549, for example, he noted, "We are three Portuguese traveling." The other two Jesuits, Cosme de Torres and Juan Fernández, were, like Xavier, of Spanish origin. See Xavier, *Epistolae*, 111.

compares Xavier's assumption of two nationalities to the Incarnation. Turning to the Letter of James ("receive with meekness the implanted work, which is able to save your souls"), Vieira links the Incarnation directly to Xavier and the Juramento.

> Having united in one man two natures (one heavenly and divine, the other earthly and human), the Word could preach, suffer, die, and save the world. Likewise with Xavier. As Xavier was a Navarran, God implanted him in a Portuguese, uniting in the same man two natures. Through one of these natures he was a native of Navarre. Through the other he became a native of Portugal that he might preach, labor, and live for the conversion of the new world, and thereby save those souls whose salvation God had specially entrusted to the Portuguese: "I chose them as my messengers to faraway lands."[65]

In noting the Portuguese birthright of Xavier (and other foreign-born Jesuits who won his favor), Vieira calls attention to the relationship between the missionary work of the Society and the advancement of the temporal interests of the Portuguese crown.[66]

Vieira's affirmation of the shared mission of Xavier and the Portuguese nation completes his thanksgiving vision of the dependency of the missionary, the empire, and finally, Jesus. D. João and Xavier together converted Asia, something that neither one could accomplish alone; and Christ, in the Juramento, established the Portuguese king as the vicar of the temporal kingdom in the same way he established Peter as the vicar of the spiritual one. In Jesus' words to Peter ("on this rock I will build my church"), Vieira finds the model for shared rule that the kings of Portugal will inherit.

> I shall establish an Empire, Christ said, in you, *in te*, but for me, *mihi*: and what is the meaning of "in you," and "for me?" The meaning is that it will be an Empire of Christ and the King of Portugal together. Because it is founded for me, *mihi*, it is mine; because it is founded in you, *in te*, it is yours. And if this Empire is mine, and yours, it belongs to the two of us.

---

[65] Vieira, *Sermões*, 13: 102; Jas 1.21. The closing reference is to the Juramento: "Elegi eos in messores meos in terris longinquis."

[66] He commended an Italian Jesuit in a 1685 letter to the Duke of Cadaval by explaining that Padre Candoni, who had served with distinction in the China missions, "is Sicilian by birth, but by love and zeal he is as passionately Portuguese as if he had been born in Lisbon; what is more, he is working not only for the preservation and increase of Christendom but also for the rights and privileges of the crown and for the authority and greatness of the monarchy" (Vieira, *Cartas*, 3: 518).

Who are these two? They are Christ, who spoke it, and the King of Portugal, to whom he spoke.[67]

The partnership of the *Exhortations* ("God, and I") is given a new temporal locus—the king of Portugal—in the service of the same apostolic ends. The progeny of the sixteenth generation to which the Juramento refers is the newborn prince. Still, the Portuguese must pray for their prince just as D. Maria Sofia continued to pray to Xavier after she had conceived. The *Sermam de acçam de graças* sounds a final prophetic warning about the precariousness of even those hopes founded in Xavier and the Juramento.

Vieira's defense of the *Sermam de acçam de graças* begins in a tone full of confounding echoes of his angry 1642 *Sermão pelo bom sucesso das armas de Portugal*.[68] The resemblance, however, is only superficial. Instead of angrily questioning God's purposes, as he did in the earlier sermon, Vieira in the *Discurso apologético* finds signs of God's mercy even in his opening lament. Arguing against the widely shared perception that it would have been better for the newborn prince never to have been given to Portugal than to have been given and taken away after eighteen days, Vieira returns to the conceit of looking and seeing on which the *Sermam de acçam de graças* was based. God took the prince from his people to protect him not only from the hurtful eyes of Portugal's enemies but also from the reverent gaze of the Portuguese themselves.

> When God hurries to take from this world those who are well looked upon by Him, it is not because His eyes cast His *olhado* on them, but rather because His eyes see and foresee the *olhado* from which He wants to deliver them. And this was the reason (one that we neither expected nor imagined) why divine providence gave and took away within so few days the desired one of our eyes and the promised one of its own. These are the second effects of the gaze and sight of God, which do not undo but rather perfect the first effects. He wished that our Infante should be born into this life, in order that he might live into the other, not dead exactly, but transported.[69]

[67] Vieira, *Sermões*, 13: 117; Mt 16.18.
[68] Vieira, *Sermões*, 3: 467–96.
[69] Portuguese conveys Vieira's understanding of *ver* and *olhar*, the two verbs on which the passage hinges.

De sorte que quando Deos se apressa a tirar deste mundo os que delle são bem vistos, nam he porque os seus olhos lhe dem olhado, mas porque vem, e prevem o olhado de que os quer livrar. E esta foy a razão de nós nam esperada, nem imaginada, porque a providencia divina nos deu, e levou dentro em tão

These "second effects" are the central conceit of the *Discurso apologé-tico* and a foundation block of the religious and social thought of Viei-ra's last years in Bahia. His professed guilt consists in his having forgot-ten the very precariousness he has attributed to God's promises. In an affirmation of the efficacy of his preaching that goes even further than his customary broad claims, Vieira now argues that his *Sermam de acçam de graças* took the prince's life. Words are actions.[70] The way he arrives at his conclusion concerning the prince's death reveals much about how Vieira understood the act of prophecy and the responsibilities of its practitioners.

Vieira in the *Sermam de acçam de graças* took a divine promise (*respiciet, et videbit*) and located it in history (*respexit, et vidit*). To the public celebration of the prince's birth, Vieira added a prophecy that denied the tenuous hold on life given by God's first look (*olhar*). The sermon thus served as a kind of provocation. In offering thanks for what had been given, Vieira assumed too readily that what had been given would not be taken away. The result was God's second look, one of the second effects with which human hopes are brought low. The workings of divine providence are completed when these hopes are raised up again, as Vieira shows his readers they must be. Vieira dis-cerns a tension between faithful affirmation and prideful expectancy, and it is in navigating between these two that the preacher who claims a gift of prophecy puts the object of his prophecy at risk.

> It was I who put our Prince in this second danger, one in which I was also the cause of death, for when we were celebrating his birth as a child I added to him the title and destiny of Emperor; and in this way I announced the news and provided more reason for the *olhado* that took his life.[71]

Vieira's expression of culpability demonstrates the fragility he hinted at in the *Sermam de acçam de graças* and prepares the ground for a new understanding of divine providence. The *Sermam de acçam de graças* provoked God to protect the newborn prince from the admiring gaze

---

poucos dias o desejado de nossos olhos, e o prometido dos seus. Estes são os se-gundos effeitos do olhar, e ver de Deos, que não desfazem, mas aperfeiçoão os primeiros. Quiz que o nosso Infante nacesse a esta vida, para que fosse viver à outra, não morto propriamente, mas trasladado (*Sermões*, 13: 146).

[70] For another example of this argument, see the *Sermão do nacimento do menino Deos*, in *Sermões*, 16: 48–69.

[71] Ibid., 13: 143.

of the Portuguese. Vieira moves on, in the *Discurso apologético*, to a more cautious effort to discern and understand the second effects that shape Portuguese history.

Vieira's analysis in these passages of how the temporal kingdom will be governed is one of his last explorations of the nature of apostolic and political dependency. He draws here on the historical particularity of the succession tragedy to underline the lesson that no single brother can serve as an autonomous agent of history. Anticipating his audience's wary reception of the argument that D. João will govern through an unborn brother (a brother who in turn will govern through his father until he comes of age), Vieira declares,

> For me, though it be a marvel, it is not a novelty; for this is God's way with the Kingdoms that He has made and of which He is the King. And the only two Kingdoms of this kind that the world has seen are the Kingdom of Judah, and afterward that of Portugal.[72]

The concrete personal and political disappointments of his last years in Bahia are thus woven seamlessly into Vieira's interpretive project. Far from forcing him to leap to save a crumbling edifice, the *Sermam de acçam de graças* anticipates the dynastic crisis that the *Discurso apologético* interprets. The *Discurso apologético* allows Vieira and his readers to incorporate the recent succession tragedy into a new understanding of the tension between the illusoriness of human hopes and the irrevocable promises of the Juramento and the Bible.

Vieira has written and spoken many times of the need to understand the mysteries of Scripture in their literal sense.[73] It is therefore not surprising that in the two sermons on D. João, which allude frequently to the Juramento, he is concerned with the physical activity of looking and seeing. The hope contained in Hannah's prayer, *Si respiciens videris*, carried with it a promise that her child would be given to the service of God.[74] It also carried the conviction that God's sight is beneficent. Vieira shares this conviction, but with a difference that only becomes fully apparent after D. João's death.

[72] Ibid., 165.
[73] Vieira's most detailed justification of this exegetical tradition is found in the *Livro anteprimeiro*, ch. 12; see also *História do futuro*, ed. Buescu, bk. 1, ch. 5.
[74] "If thou wilt indeed look on the affliction of thy maidservant" (1 Sam 1.11). The Revised Standard Version does not suggest a potential disjunction between looking and seeing.

Before the succession tragedy, Vieira had never considered the literal sense of the text from Samuel, but the prince's death suggests a
new exegesis. The eyes of God that attended the birth of Samuel are
fixed not only on God's servants but also on the society in which those
servants live. In a lapse that suggests the fundamental tensions in the
theology of his later years, Vieira for a moment had turned his view
away from society and had seen only the destiny of the prince.

> I founded [the interpretation of D. João's destiny] in the words and prom-
> ises of God. How could I fear that the eyes of the very God who gave him
> life would cast the *olhado* upon him, since only the one who gave him his
> existence could take it away? The power of this conclusion caused me at
> first to think that God's eyes, too, can cast the *olhado*. But after the clouds of
> pain and sadness had dispersed a little, they helped me to perceive a
> greater light; and in this matter (which is all a mystery) I discovered an-
> other circumstance that I had not imagined and that indeed could not eas-
> ily be imagined. And what mystery was this? That it was not the *olhado* of
> God that took the life of our Prince, but rather it was God who took the
> Prince's life so that the world might not give him the *olhado*.[75]

Vieira recalls his sermon as both an act of prophecy and an act of creation. The words with which he begins his explanation—"I founded
it"—refer not only to the hope but also to the realization of that hope.
At the same time, a passage that briefly had the look of an apology becomes a vehicle for Vieira both to reaffirm his exegetical method and to
remind his audience that his prophetic powers produced results that
were fatal only in appearance. Wary, perhaps, of exhausting the pa-
tience of his readers, Vieira offers a somewhat elliptical treatment here
of the gaze of God. But this brief passage provides an effective link to
his larger argument concerning the specificity of the scriptural references to the shared rule of the Portuguese heirs.

Vieira has already wondered, Joblike, "Alive, and dead! Given, and
then denied! And in the space of eighteen days!"[76] Ascribing the removal of the prince to God's wish to protect the prince from even the
most loving gaze, the sermon posits an implicit withdrawal from sight
that has its corollary in the explicit withdrawal from birth (emphasized
here by the neologism *desnacer*) on which, according to Vieira's interpretation, D. João's vicarship is founded. That withdrawal from sight

---

[75] Vieira, *Sermões*, 13: 144.
[76] Ibid., 140.

becomes the chosen instrument for the realization of Portugal's destiny; it extends the reversal of human expectations in history one step beyond the prince's birth and brief life. Vieira may be understood literally when he repeats his sense of wonder over the interpretation at which he arrived earlier (one "that I had not imagined") and says that D. João and his brother

> together formed one Emperor of a kind that had never been seen or imagined, composed of two, one living, the other dead. I said "never seen or imagined" because outside Portugal such a thing has not been seen, nor has it been imagined; but in Portugal it has been.[77]

Vieira thus discerns, in the withholding of the prince, the privileged vision that divine providence has granted the Portuguese in the present mysterious circumstances.

The very nature of the vision that has been withheld and then granted affords further proof of the singularity of Portuguese destiny. The historical circumstance of shared rule allows Vieira to insist again on the specifity of the scriptural references to the succession tragedy. He shows that D. João's succession could have been realized only through the kind of division of Portuguese hopes that he gleans from Matthew's genealogy of Jesus. Of all the pairs of brothers included there, the evangelist mentions the second brother by name only in the case of Zerah and Perez. The principal reason for this inclusion, Vieira argues, is the order of the brothers' birth: Zerah emerged first from the womb but gave way to Perez. D. João and his unborn brother exceed even the singularity of Jesus' forebears.

> Never before has there been such a turn of events or such a [divine] favor, if we reflect well. . . . For truly, to be born and quickly to die, as happened to our Prince, is to be born and unborn [*nacer, e desnacer*]: and if from two Brothers (the first unborn so that the second might be born) the Evangelist made one first-born heir, much more wondrous a matter is (or rather, will be) that of our two Princes, the one who has already passed from this life and the one who is to come.[78]

Vieira in this passage provides his own "second effect" by suggesting that the granting of vision has a further corollary in the vision that has been withheld from all other nations throughout history. At the same

---

[77] Ibid., 169.
[78] Ibid.; Mt 1.3.

time, the image of joining two men in one recalls the second effects that Vieira identified in Moses and Aaron in the *Exhortations*. The precedent of Moses and Aaron is scarcely mentioned in the *Discurso apologético*, but the importance of the Exodus story is demonstrated by Vieira's choice of words. In the *First Exhortation*, Moses' dependence on his brother was seen as an example to future generations, "that we might understand that out of one Moses who could not speak, and a brother who could, we can create a perfect Missionary."[79] The biblical and extrabiblical references Vieira derives from this model of the perfect missionary all number among the second effects that transform the brothers' lack of autonomy into an example to Christians and, for the Portuguese, a specific instruction concerning the vicarship with which their kings have been entrusted.

Vieira's understanding of Portugal's singular mission and singular devotion suggests further links between the pastoral and political concerns of the *Exhortations* and the *Discurso apologético*. In both *Exhortations*, Vieira linked his demand that the Jesuit affirm his calling from the beginning of his novitiate to Jesus' call to John from Mary's womb.[80] In the *Discurso apologético*, Vieira transforms the nation itself into an agent of history from the time it was in the womb. In doing so he offers one of the sharpest contrasts in his writings between the blasphemy of Christendom's enemies and the devotion of the Portuguese. The contrast suggests how far Vieira extends the logic behind his earlier treatment of Xavier's divinely given naturalization. He dehumanizes the Turks literally to incarnate the Portuguese nation. The Portuguese hatred of the Turks is the hatred "not of men for men," but of Christians for blasphemers, whose destruction they have been charged, from the womb, to carry out.

> The Kingdom of Portugal was conceived before it existed in the person of Dom Henrique, and while still in the embryo it was already animated by the spirit of the conquest of Jerusalem. . . . The same Kingdom was born on the Fields of Ourique in the fighting arms of Dom Affonso I.[81]

Vieira extends this interpretation still further when he returns, near the end of the sermon, to the queen's prayers to Xavier. He praises the devotion of D. Maria Sofia Isabel, for whom the sermon was written; at

[79] Vieira, *Sermões*, 8: 524.
[80] Lk 1.44.
[81] Vieira, *Sermões*, 13: 220.

the same time, he affirms the role of Xavier and the Jesuits in the conception of the prince and the fulfillment of Portugal's historical mission. Adding to the complexity of these final pages is the interweaving of the Portuguese and Jesuit missions; here Vieira undercuts the historical role of the father of the prince whose destiny he is prophesying.

In singling out D. Maria Sofia Isabel as an instrument of divine providence, Vieira repeats a process that was familiar to his readers. In the *Exhortations* he began with a wide circle, which he gradually tightened, analyzing the mission of the primitive and modern churches, then focusing on the Portuguese church and the Jesuit order, and proceeding finally to a discussion of the Jesuits in Brazil. Vieira's web of associations is less carefully ordered in the *Discurso apologético*, but his purpose is the same. He moves from his opening discussion of Portugal's mission and Xavier's role in Portuguese history to an exegesis of scriptural references to the birth of the brothers, and concludes with an interpretation of texts that foretell the providential role of the queen.

For Vieira's purposes, the most important of those prophetic texts are the extrabiblical writings that have attained canonical status among the Portuguese. Specifically, Vieira interprets the foreign birth of Frei Zacharias, the thirteenth-century seer in whose words D. Maria Sofia Isabel is most clearly prefigured, as constituting a Xavierlike reversal of Portuguese expectations.[82]

Vieira's appropriation of Frei Zacharias is surprising, because although Vieira uses uncritically a variety of sources, he generally cites only the most widely diffused and accepted Portuguese prophecies (notably the Juramento and the prophecies of S. Frei Gil and Bandarra) to support his arguments. Vieira seizes on the reversal offered by Frei Zacharias both on principle and for practical reasons. If Vieira's role as interpreter is to make the strange less new and threatening, it suits his purposes to find that he must naturalize the prophet and domesticate the prophecy. He therefore introduces the Frei Zacharias text as "another domestic Portuguese prophecy [following Frei Gil], though its mother and father are of foreign origin (if indeed this may be said)."[83] The last phrase serves to emphasize the accidents of birth to which Vi-

---

[82] Fr. Zacharias, to whom Vieira refers as Fr. Zacharias of Guimarães, was better known as Fr. Zacharias of Alenquer. See Cardoso, *Agiologio lusitano dos sanctos*, 2: 508, 3: 61.

[83] Vieira, *Sermões*, 13: 256.

eira customarily pays minute attention. He appropriates Frei Zacharias as a Portuguese, though he assigns a less prominent role to divine providence in the case of Frei Zacharias than he does in the case of Xavier.

The significance of Frei Zacharias hinges on his prophecy that "in the last days of greater Spain there will reign a King two times piously given [*duas vezes piamente dado*]: and he will reign through a woman whose name will begin with *I* and end with *L*; and this King will come from the East."[84] Vieira's interpretation of this passage contains two striking elements. First, he forges a link between Frei Zacharias's prophecy and his own veiled suggestion elsewhere in the *Discurso apologético* that not only the promised king but also the queen will be "two times piously given." Vieira's antipathy for the late D. Maria Francisca Isabel was well known; here it takes on a more complex shading. In his 1684 obsequies for the queen, Vieira pointed to the renewal of the dynastic line that he hoped would follow her death.[85] The obsequies antagonized D. Pedro II, who had never shared his father's esteem for Vieira. Five years later Vieira is unrepentant, and even more unmindful of D. Pedro's reaction to his words.

> God took away one Queen, in order to give us another. He took away Her Serene Highness of Savoy to be able to give us Her August Highness of Austria; He took away the sterile queen to be able to give us the fecund one; He took away the one who after so many years of hope and *desengano* obliged us to look outside the *Patria* to become subjects and vassals of a foreign Prince. He did all this in order to bring us from even farther away

[84] Ibid.

[85] Vieira, *Sermam de acçam de graças empenhada: sermão nas exéquias da rainha N.S.D. Maria Francisca Isabel de Saboya* (*Sermões*, 13: 1–64, esp. 59–60). Azevedo and Cidade differ sharply over the tone of this sermon. Azevedo finds in it an unmistakably malicious intent (*HAV*, 2: 239–42). Cidade sees it as a complex "extension of [Vieira's earlier] praise" that goes beyond celebrating the queen in the traditional style to embrace the king and the fertile bride Vieira hopes he will find (*Padre António Vieira*, 148). These two views are not as incompatible as Cidade suggests. D. Pedro's evident displeasure with the sermon, and his subsequent low regard for Vieira during Vieira's old age in Bahia, suggest that Azevedo has accurately identified the malice in the text. Vieira clearly relished the opportunity to repay, if only by omission, the late queen's low esteem for him. At the same time, the obsequies show that Vieira was already applying himself to the interpretive project that would come to fruition in the *Sermam de acçam de graças* and the *Discurso apologético*. The obsequies gave Vieira an opportunity to suggest that the queen's death would be followed by triumphs, which he could reveal to D. Pedro.

one who within the first year restored to us the Lordship of native-born Kings.[86]

With these words Vieira links Frei Gil's prophecy that salvation will come from afar to Frei Zacharias's prediction that salvation will be accomplished through a woman.[87] The redeemer from afar presents the Portuguese with a twofold reversal of expectations: redemption will come unexpectedly, and it will come from an unexpected king.

Vieira has been refining this argument for almost 50 years, but the replacement of the so-called sterile queen with the fertile D. Maria Sofia leads him to take a new approach to the prophetic texts. The late queen came from afar and possessed a name that lent itself to the fulfillment of Frei Zacharias's prophecy. Symmetry requires, however, that not the queen from Savoy but another, still more distant Isabel be the instrument of divine providence. The masculine and feminine endings may thus be applied interchangeably to the participle in the prophecy.

A final indication of the singular destiny that Vieira reserves for the second queen is the image in the *Sermam de acçam de graças* of D. Maria Sofia Isabel as an instrument of restitution. God removed the newborn prince to protect him from the gaze of the Portuguese, but God's own gaze came to rest on the prince's mother. The prophecy requires not only that the king be twice given but that the restitution be accomplished by this particular twice-given queen.[88]

[86] Vieira, *Sermões*, 13: 68. D. Maria Francisca Isabel was not sterile; she gave birth to a daughter, D. Isabel Luísa Josefa, but no sons.

[87] The section of the prophecy of particular interest here is "Salvation will come from far off, and by one who has not been expected you will unexpectedly be redeemed [*Salus à longinquo veniet, et insperate ab insperato redimeris*]" (Ibid., 254). Among Vieira's many interpretations of the prophecy is his 1642 *Sermão dos bons annos*, announcing the destiny of D. João IV, which was the first sermon Vieira preached in the royal chapel (*Sermões*, 11: 399–431). Frei Gil's prophecy is also examined in the *Livro anteprimeiro*, 12: 666.

[88] Vieira's identification of the queen who will rule in the name of a king from the west with the queen who will be twice given is one of two pieces of evidence he introduces to support this part of his analysis of the Portuguese succession. The second piece of evidence is his appropriation of John Chrysostom in interpreting the role of D. Maria Sofia Isabel in propagating the royal line. "By no means," Chrysostom wrote of Samuel's mother, Hannah, "shall one err who calls this woman at the same time both mother and father of this child, for even though the man might have contributed the seed, nonetheless her prayer both supplied the efficacious force and brought it about that Samuel would be born with more auspicious

The *Discurso apologético* extravagantly praises D. Pedro's heroism and identifies the king as the appointed guardian of the Fifth Empire, which his son will inherit.[89] Vieira had identified D. Pedro 30 years earlier as the rightful heir to his brother, D. Afonso.[90] In his old age, Vieira places his hope in the queen as well as in D. Pedro and the Jesuits. By affirming the queen's role, he radically expands the idea of apostolic partnership that underlies the *Exhortations* and the sermons on D. João.[91]

Vieira expands this partnership still further when, in attributing the birth of the prince to the prayers of the queen, he extends his interpretation of gifts given twice to include the repeated intercession of Xavier. The prince was conceived as a result of the queen's veneration of the image and biretta that had been brought from Goa (thus the dual interpretation of the prophecy that the king will come from the East). The second son, too, will come from the East.

> Because if, when given the first time, it came from Goa in the reliquary and biretta of St. Francis Xavier (as we have already noted), in the same way when given the second time it will come from that same East through the intercession of the same Saint, whose proven power and favor were sought in the prayers and novenas of Her Majesty. At the time when the nine

beginnings" (John Chrysostom, *De Anna, Sermo 2.1,* in *PG* 55.641A; Vieira, *Sermões,* 13: 260).

[89] See especially part 4, in which Vieira notes the symmetry in the names and destinies of the agents to whom the spiritual and temporal vicarships would be entrusted. Peter (Pedro) was appointed the first vicar through whom the Father would subject the world to Jesus; the second vicar will rule through D. Pedro II, in whom "this beautiful architecture shall bring forth in equal proportion and grace not only the correspondence of the office but also the consonance of the name in one and another Empire" (ibid., 199). Cidade notes that this passage is among the most lyrical of the many passages in the *Sermões* praising the Portuguese kings (*Padre António Vieira,* 154).

[90] The beginnings of the transformation in Vieira's thought that led to the *Discurso apologético* may be discerned in the words with which he voiced his support for D. Pedro in the *Sermão da Epiphania* (*Sermões,* 4: 547). There, Vieira still saw the missionary enterprise as a burden to be shared by Portuguese society as a whole under the leadership of a powerful missionary king. D. Afonso was clearly unfit for this enterprise. That sermon provides a vivid analysis of the responsibilities of the monarchy. Vieira linked a thinly veiled reference to the invalid king and his heroic brother to an explicit summons to pursue conversion over empire.

[91] Similarly, in *Clavis Prophetarum,* he extends the notion of the partnership between brothers in the temporal and spiritual kingdoms (Moses and Aaron) to the partnership between king and queen, with the queen representing the spiritual kingdom. Vieira draws here on Is 49.23: "Kings shall be your foster fathers, and their queens your nursing mothers" (see *Obras escolhidas,* 9: 252).

months of the first pregnancy began, the Image of St. Francis Xavier was brought from São Roque [the Jesuit church] to the Palace, and speaking with the Image our Lady the Queen told it in words most Portuguese [*com palavras muito Portuguezas*]: "My Saint, give me a son if God should wish it." God wished it, and wished that it be not only His gift, but also that of the Saint.[92]

Vieira here ties together the diverse strands of the *Discurso apologético* by focusing on the shared destiny of Xavier, the queen, and the Portuguese nation. The foreign-born queen becomes the instrument chosen by God to express, "with words most Portuguese," the singular devotion of her adopted homeland. Similarly, divine providence turned a Navarran into a Portuguese who would convert the East. Together, the queen and the missionary would twice bless the nation with the sons who would receive from Christ the vicarship of the Fifth Empire.

The *Discurso apologético* might have concluded here, but Vieira leaves his listeners with a warning, lest his words invite complacency. Although the Fifth Empire has been irrevocably promised to the nation, the Portuguese cannot be assured that they will share in the promise as individuals. Vieira praised the queen in the *Sermam de acçam de graças* for her devotion to Xavier even after she knew that she had conceived; she knew that God, "though he cannot fail in his word, nevertheless wishes that we ask him for the very thing he has promised us."[93] Vieira goes on to cite Isaiah's prophecy for the day of judgment: "For thus it shall be in the midst of the earth among the nations, as when an olive tree is beaten, as at the gleaning when the vintage is done."[94] The remnant of which the prophet speaks will be the Portu-

---

[92] Vieira, *Sermões*, 13: 261. For Vieira's initial discussion of Xavier's intercession for the queen, see ibid., 181–87.

[93] Ibid., 136.

[94] Is 24.13. The passage (the text for the feast day of Xavier that coincided with the announcement in Bahia of the birth of the prince) recalls a prophecy from S. Frei Gil, which Vieira omitted from his earlier discussion of the Dominican but cited in a revealing 1678 letter to Duarte Ribeiro de Macedo.

> Domus Dei recuperabitur
> Pax ubique erit.
> Aetas aurea reviviscet:
> Felices qui viderint.

[The house of God will be regained/Peace will reign everywhere./The golden age will live again:/Fortunate those who shall see it.] Vieira, *Cartas*, 3: 251.

guese, but only those Portuguese whose actions deliver them from punishment.

The conversion of the Portuguese nation thus emerges as the ultimate consequence of the devotion of its queen and of her intercessor, Xavier. This conversion was Vieira's constant preoccupation during his sermons of the 1650s, and though it appears less frequently in his writings after his final return to Brazil, he never abandoned it. In the final passage of the *Discurso apologético*, Vieira once again seeks to prompt the Portuguese to act.

> If this paper should pass into the hands of the Portuguese, I would wish to tell them that placed between the danger and the hope in which this prophecy puts us today, each person should see and consider carefully whether it is better for him to mend his mad ways and live with the few, or to continue in these ways and perish with the many.[95]

Between the danger and the hope lie the second effects through which history unfolds. No longer affecting to speak only to the queen, Vieira sees a final instructive example of these second effects in the circuitous manner in which his text will reach its readers. The preacher who could once command a crowd in Lisbon must now speak to his audience indirectly, through the eyes that might come upon this avowedly secret sermon. Vieira's interpretation of Portugal's mission is an inclusive one inasmuch as it assigns to all Portuguese a role in establishing the Fifth Empire. The fulfillment of that role has been sealed by the Juramento. The Portuguese, blessed with another saving reversal of expectations, will be set on the road to conversion by those faithful who providentially receive and act on Vieira's warning.

The Uses of Silence

The fire of tongues with which the Jesuits were to convert the non-Christian world was at the heart of the missionary project as Vieira interpreted it during his last years in Bahia. Yet even as he preached his *Exhortations* to the novices, Vieira recognized that not all missionaries would be prepared (at least in the short run) to construct the third tower with which the Jesuits were to complete the postprimitive church. Some

[95] Vieira, *Sermões*, 13: 274.

were too young and inexperienced to draw their apostolic strength from the spoken word. Others—including Vieira himself—were too old and infirm to preach as they once had. In addressing these problems, Vieira employed the same rhetorical strategy he had followed in the *Exhortations*: he transformed a potential obstacle to the progress of the missionary church into a blessing that would move the church forward.

In his later sermons, Vieira affirmed that the church could prosper in the New World only if the missionaries' mastery of indigenous languages was complemented by other forms of apostleship. Whereas the *Exhortations* focused on language study as a sign of commitment to the missionary church, Vieira composed two other sermons for the Bahia college—the *Sermão do nacimento do menino Deos* and the *Sermão de Santo Estevão*—in which he sought to identify for the novices an instrument of conversion more immediately attainable than convincing speech.[96] He found such an instrument in the muteness of the newborn Jesus and the martyred St. Stephen. Imitating the newborn in the manger and the apostle under the hail of stones was to be as integral a part of the Jesuit vocation as studying Indian languages and cultivating the art of preaching.

The *Sermão do nacimento* and the *Sermão de Santo Estevão* consider the apostolic uses of silence and sacrifice, with particular reference to the non-Christians of the New World, around whom Vieira constructed the image of the fire of tongues. These sermons gently remind the Jesuits that the fire of tongues can be ignited only by missionaries who preach with compassion. Vieira shows in these texts that the silence in which he wrapped himself in his old age was not only a concession to his isolation in Bahia and to the defeats he had suffered there, but also a constituent element of his pastoral strategy.[97]

[96] Vieira, *Sermão do nacimento do menino Deos*; *Sermão de Santo Estevão, na primeira oitava do Natal*, in *Sermões*, 16: 48–69 and 70–90. The two sermons are undated companion pieces, published posthumously by João de Barros. They were written most likely during Vieira's term as Visitor. A note accompanying the texts states that they were composed "to be preached in the college by a young Religious during the examination that the Society wished to make of his talent for the ministry of preaching. As this was the purpose . . . the Great Vieyra accommodated himself to the temperament, condition and age of the young Orator" (*Prologo, e noticia prévia ao leitor*).

[97] Azevedo titles his chapter on Vieira's last years in Bahia "The Vanquished" (*HAV*, 2: 219–304). Like "The Politician," his chapter on Vieira in Europe in the 1640s, the title is a misnomer, but it accurately indicates the argument of both vol-

The *Sermão do nacimento* is a particularly revealing text for its emphasis on Jesuit missionaries who, in their muteness and suffering, have become the privileged successors to Jesus. As in the *Sermão da Epiphania*, the work of the unschooled shepherds is more instructive for the Jesuit missionaries than the work of the learned Magi. The shepherds knew instinctively what the Magi learned from the star and the evangelists later recorded: that Jesus as a newborn child, without the gift of speech, began the work of teaching and speaking that the Jesuits would continue.

> He teaches and speaks now as Man, as he acted and spoke as God ... and just as God before becoming Man taught without the confusion of words (because he spoke inwardly to the heart), so in being born a Child he teaches without the confusion of words, because he speaks outwardly to the eye: *Et videamus hoc Verbum.*[98]

Vieira takes as his text the words of the shepherds: "Let us go over to Bethlehem and see this thing that has happened."[99] Much of the force of his message, however, is concentrated in the words with which Luke summed up his gospel: "I have dealt with all that Jesus began to do and teach."[100] It is the vast scope of Jesus' mission that feeds Vieira's hope for the future of the church. The work of the missionary, like that of Jesus, is to persuade and to move. Jesus began this work even before his birth, when he cried out to John from Mary's womb; his ministry continued, but did not complete, his mission. The *imitatio Christi* that Vieira demands in his old age consists as much in imitating Jesus in the manger as in imitating Jesus preaching to the crowds.

With the exception of the *First Exhortation*, the *Sermão do nacimento* is

---

umes of the biography and of Azevedo's other work on the Jesuits in Brazil. For Azevedo, the pastoral work of the Jesuit missionaries represented one element (and often not the most important one) of the Society's larger endeavor to maintain and expand its central role in the Luso-Brazilian imperial enterprise. Azevedo evaluates Vieira and the Jesuits in terms of their success in that endeavor; he concludes that Vieira failed in his projects, and that his last years in Brazil were bitter ones. Boxer also calls "The Vanquished" a misnomer, for somewhat different reasons; but he provides an effective response to Azevedo, emphasizing that Vieira was "a bonny fighter" until the end (*A Great Luso-Brazilian Figure*, 29–30).

[98] Vieira, *Sermões*, 16: 54.

[99] Lk 2.15. Neither the Revised Standard Version nor the King James Version conveys the sense of the *verbum* of the Vulgate on which Vieira bases his interpretation of the word made visible.

[100] Acts 1.1.

the most specific critique of the Society's shortcomings to be found in Vieira's later sermons. He identifies the works of the Jesuits as "the works of Christ himself continued," and argues that it is not the settlers but the missionaries who must answer for their own failure to act on their faith.[101] Vieira asks his Jesuit listeners how to address the problem of pride within the Society. His answer provides the link between the fire of tongues and the babe wrapped in swaddling clothes: "What shall we do? Let us go over to Bethlehem, and let us go no further." On this connection Vieira constructs the missionary strategy of his last years in Bahia.[102]

The last six words of Vieira's gloss on Luke ("and let us go no further") state the task that Vieira sets before the postprimitive church. He anchors these six words in the five words Peter speaks to Jesus at the Transfiguration—"Lord, it is well that we are here" (*Bonum est nos hic esse*)—in an effort to particularize even further his interpretation of church history.[103] Vieira had long shown a talent for unleashing the sheer physical drama of evangelization to teach and encourage the young. Here he transforms the apostolic resolve contained in the *hic* spoken by Peter into a call to the Jesuits to affirm the permanence of their presence in the New World.

In a final extension of the logic of his 1662 *Sermão da Epiphania*, Vieira explicitly asks the Jesuit missionaries to break with both the Magi and the shepherds by remaining fixed in the New World. The Magi and the shepherds all returned home; only the star traveled to Bethlehem and did not return.

> And no one knows what happened to it, because it unmade itself there. He who does not unmake himself at the sight of the Word made flesh does not do what he must. . . . Let us compare the *Transeamus usque ad Bethlehem* [Let us go over to Bethlehem] of the Shepherds with the *Usque dum veniens staret* [till it came to rest] of the Star. The destination and the *Usque* were the

[101] Calling for works of conversion rather than works that glorify the religious themselves, Vieira attacks the expansion of the urban churches of the colony even more forcefully than he did in his Lisbon letter of 1680: "The Son of God has nowhere to lay his head, and stays in a den of beasts; and you build magnificent palaces" (*Sermões*, 16: 67). Vieira's 1680 letter concerning the church of Nossa Senhora da Luz in São Luiz is in *Cartas*, 3: 432–33.

[102] The passage represents a gloss on part of the text for the sermon, "Let us go over to Bethlehem" (Lk 2.15; *Sermões*, 16: 69).

[103] Mt 17.4.

same, but the *Transeamus* and the *Staret* very different. The Shepherds traveled and yet did not travel; the Star came to rest, and did not leave that place.[104]

Like the distinction in the *Sermão da sexagésima* between sowers who stay and sowers who go out, the difference between *transeamus* and *staret* expresses the vocation for which the Society of Jesus is named. The future of the missionary enterprise lies with the Jesuit missionaries who will unmake themselves in the New World.

The silence identified in the *Sermão do nacimento* and the *Sermão de Santo Estevão* as one of the highest forms of service to God was embraced by Vieira himself, most notably in the famous letter he sent to the Conde da Castanheira in 1694. The letter was accompanied by a request that it be circulated among the Portuguese nobility. In this letter, Vieira formally takes leave of his correspondents, telling them he is no longer able to write and expressing the wish that they, in turn, stop writing to him. As the opening sentences of the letter suggest, the decision to suspend communication had been a difficult one for Vieira.

> It is such a natural thing to respond that even the jagged cliffs do so, and produce echoes of our voices. In the contrary sense, it is such a great violence not to respond that nature made deaf those who were born mute, for if they were to hear, and be unable to respond, they would break apart in pain.[105]

The idea that silence is unnatural is consistent with Vieira's deep human attachments. A few lines later, though, he once again takes up the themes of the sermons for the novices, in an effort to locate the apostolic uses of silence. Vieira anticipates his friends' objections to his farewell letter; he asks them to consider the infirmity that keeps him from writing as a blessing, both for him and for them.

> If I lack one hand with which to write, I shall have two hands that will be freer to bring themselves to heaven and to pray to God for those to whom I do not write, producing a far greater correspondence in my gratitude to them. For a letter placed on every fleet is a remembrance once each year, while the prayers of every hour are remembrances many times each day.[106]

104 Vieira, *Sermões*, 16: 69.
105 Vieira, *Cartas*, 3: 661.
106 Ibid., 662.

For the next three years, with the help of his friend José Soares, Vieira continued to work on *Clavis Prophetarum*. He died at the Jesuit college in Bahia on July 18, 1697.

Vieira's affirmation of the singular role to be played by the Jesuits in the postprimitive church completed the transformation of his theory and methodology of conversion. This transformation had begun more than 40 years earlier, when he forged the first of a series of strategic compromises with the Portuguese settlers, who had battled the Jesuits since the time of Nóbrega. Vieira spent more than half his life in the Brazilian mission field and never abandoned hope that the responsibilities of apostleship might one day be accepted by all members of Luso-Brazilian society. But in assessing the missionary and imperial projects at the end of his life, he concluded that the Jesuits would do better to separate themselves from the settlers in Brazil than to compromise their missionary vocation in an effort to retain their influence in colonial society.

By summoning the Jesuits to the missionary enterprise with his image of the fire of tongues, Vieira both affirmed the Ignatian ideal and made a muted concession to the constraints under which the Society worked in the colony. The Jesuits would complete, through sheer hard work, the process of restoration that the world had awaited since the destruction of the Tower of Babel. This process began when the first Apostles (preaching after the infusion of the tongues of fire) constructed a second tower; namely, the primitive church. The Jesuits would construct a third and final tower, which would embrace the multiplicity of languages and peoples of the New Worlds of America, Asia, and Africa.

Without calling into question the fundamental principles of imperial expansion, Vieira sought to invert the categories through which Europeans viewed the New World. He called on the Portuguese to recognize in Scripture the one infallible history of the empire, and then to act on that recognition by becoming apostles throughout the world. In issuing this call, Vieira was not trying to temper the expansionist zeal of the Portuguese. Instead, he wished to convert his contemporaries by showing them that the riches of empire and the progress of the church were inseparably linked.

The various histories of Portugal, Eduardo Lourenço has written, "are models of 'Robinsonized' histories: they recount the celestial adventures of an isolated hero in a universe that was previously deserted. Everything happens as if we had no interlocutor."[107] It is fitting that Vieira's most famous texts are the sermons in which he treated his listeners and readers as interlocutors, seeking not only to instruct them but also to provoke them to respond and to act. The crowning achievement of Vieira's interpretation of the postprimitive church was his ability to look ahead to two complementary forms of mission. Traditional catechesis—even catechesis born of the fire of tongues—had to be accompanied by the silence of the missionary who kept his eyes fixed on the example of the newborn Jesus. The Jesuit successors to the Apostles would perfect a new kind of preaching by unmaking themselves in their adopted homelands and disappearing, in the manner of the star that guided the Magi. The lessons of this silent preaching were to be no less permanent for being less easily identifiable in the missionary church on pilgrimage in the New World.

[107] Lourenço, *O labirinto da saudade*, 17–18.

REFERENCE MATTER

Bibliography

Acosta, José de. *Historia natural y moral de las Indias* [1590]. Edited by Edmundo O'Gorman. Mexico City, 1962.
———. *De procuranda indorum salute* [1577]. Edited by Luciano Pereña. 2 vols. Madrid, 1984–87. Vol. 1: books 1–3; vol. 2: books 4–6.
Acuña, Cristóbal de, S.J. *Nuevo descubrimento del gran río de las Amazonas* [1641]. 2d ed. Madrid, 1891.
Aldama, Antonio de, S.J. *The Formula of the Institute: Notes for a Commentary.* Translated by Ignacion Echániz. Rome: Centrum Ignatianum Spiritualitatis; St. Louis: Institute of Jesuit Sources, 1990.
Alden, Dauril. *Royal Government in Colonial Brazil.* Berkeley: University of California Press, 1968.
———. "Black Robes versus White Settlers: The Struggle for 'Freedom of the Indians' in Colonial Brazil." In *Attitudes of Colonial Powers Toward the American Indian,* edited by Howard Peckham and Charles Gibson, 19–45. Salt Lake City: University of Utah Press, 1969.
———. "Sugar Planters by Necessity, Not Choice: The Role of the Jesuits in the Cane Sugar Industry of Colonial Brazil, 1601–1759." In *The Church and Society in Latin America,* edited by Jeffrey A. Cole, 139–70. New Orleans: Tulane University Center for Latin American Studies, 1984.
———. "Indian versus Black Slavery in the State of Maranhão During the Seventeenth and Eighteenth Centuries." In *Iberian Colonies, New World Societies: Essays in Memory of Charles Gibson,* edited by Richard L. Garner and William B. Taylor, 71–102. University Park: Pennsylvania State University Press, 1986.
———. "Changing Jesuit Perceptions of the Brasis During the Sixteenth Century." *Journal of World History* 3, no. 2 (1992): 205–18.
———. *The Making of an Enterprise: The Society of Jesus in Portugal, Its Empire, and Beyond, 1540–1750.* Stanford: Stanford University Press, 1996.
Almeida, Fortunato de. *História da igreja em Portugal.* 2d ed. 4 vols. Edited by Damião Peres. Porto: Portucalense Editora, 1967–71.
Almeida, Gregorio de [João de Vasconcelos]. *Restauração de Portugal prodigiosa*

[1643]. Edited by Damião Peres. 4 vols. Barcelos: Companhia Editora do Minho, 1939–40.

Alter, Robert, and Frank Kermode, eds. *The Literary Guide to the Bible*. Cambridge: Harvard University Press, 1987.

Anchieta, José de. *Cartas, informações, fragmentos históricos e Sermões*. Rio de Janeiro: Civilização Brasileira, 1933.

Andrade e Silva, José Justino de. *Collecção chronologica da legislação portuguesa*. 10 vols. Lisbon: Imprenta de J. J. A. Silva, 1854–59.

Antonil, André João [João António Andreoni]. *Cultura e opulencia do Brasil por suas drogas e minas* [1711]. Edited by Andrée Mansuy. Paris: Institut des Hautes Etudes de l'Amérique Latine, 1968.

Augustine of Hippo. *On Baptism, Against the Donatists*, in *St. Augustine: The Writings Against the Manichaeans and Against the Donatists* (The Nicene and Post-Nicene Fathers of the Christian Church, vol. 4), edited by Philip Schaff. Grand Rapids, Mich.: Wm. B. Eerdmans Publishing, repr. 1979.

———. *City of God*. Translated by Henry Bettenson. Harmondsworth: Penguin, 1972.

Axtell, James. *The Invasion Within: The Contest of Cultures in Colonial North America*. Oxford: Oxford University Press, 1985.

Azevedo, João Lúcio de. *História de António Vieira* [*HAV*]. 2 vols. Lisbon: Livraria Clássica Editora, 1918–20.

———. "Noticia bibliográfica sobre a *Clavis Prophetarum* do Padre António Vieira." *Boletim da Classe de Letras da Academia das Sciências* 13 (1919): 539–60.

———. "Os processos da Inquisição como documentos da história." *Boletim da Classe de Letras da Academia das Sciências* 13 (1921): 1004–28.

———. "O Padre António Vieira julgado em documentos franceses: diplomacia da Restauração." *Arquivo de História e Bibliografia* 1923–1926: 1 (1925), 437–62. Lisbon: Imprensa Nacional—Casa da Moeda, 1976.

———. *Os jesuítas no Grão Pará*. 2d ed. Coimbra: Imprensa da Universidade, 1930.

———. *A evolução do sebastianismo*. 2d ed. Lisbon: Livraria Clássica Editora, 1947.

———. *História dos cristãos novos portugueses*. 2d ed. Lisbon: Livraria Clássica Editora, 1975.

Baêta Neves Flores, Luiz Felipe. *O combate dos soldados de Christo na terra dos papagaios: colonialismo e repressão cultural*. Rio de Janeiro: Forense-Universitária, 1978.

———. *Imaginação social jesuítica e instituição pedagógica: Maranhão e Grão Pará, século XVII*. 3 vols. Ph.D. dissertation, Museu Nacional/Universidade Federal do Rio de Janeiro, 1984.

———. "Palavra, mito e história no *Sermão dos sermões* do Padre António Vieira." In *Narrativa: ficção e história*, organized by Dirce Côrtes Riedel, 170–90. Rio de Janeiro: Imago Editora, 1988.

Baião, António. *Episódios dramaticos da Inquisição portuguesa*. 2d ed. Vol. 3. Lisbon: Seara Nova, 1936.

Bandarra, Gonçalo. *Trovas do Bandarra* [1644]. Porto: Imprensa Popular de J. L. de Sousa, 1866.

Bangert, William V., S.J. *A History of the Society of Jesus*. Rev. ed. St. Louis: Institute of Jesuit Sources, 1986.

Barros, André de, S.J. *Vida do padre António Vieira*. 2d ed. Lisbon: Editores J. M. C. de Seabra e T. Q. Antunes, 1858.

Bataillon, Marcel. "Le Brésil dans une vision d'Isaie selon le père António Vieira." *Bulletin des Etudes Portugaises* 25 (1964): 11–21.

Bayley, Peter. *French Pulpit Oratory, 1598–1650*. Cambridge: Cambridge University Press, 1980.

Belchior Pontes, Maria de Lourdes. *Fr. António das Chagas: um homem e um estilo do séc. XVII*. Lisbon: Instituo de Alta Cultura, 1953.

Benci, Jorge. *Economia cristã dos senhores no governo dos escravos* [1705]. Edited by Serafim Leite. Porto: Livraria Apostolado da Imprensa, 1954.

Berger, Peter L. *The Sacred Canopy: Elements of a Sociological Theory of Religion*. New York: Anchor Books, 1969.

Berredo, B. Pereira de. *Annaes históricos do estado do Maranhão*. 3d ed. 2 vols. Florence: Typographia Barbèra, 1905.

Besselaar, José van den. "António Vieira e o nascimento da filosofia da história." *Coloquio* 53 (April 1969): 51–53; 55 (October 1969): 54–56.

———. "António Vieira e a Holanda." *Revista da Faculdade de Letras de Lisboa*, 3d ser., no. 14 (1971), 5–35.

———. "Achegas para o estudo lexicológico da obra vieiriana." *Aufsätze zur Portugiesischen Kulturgeschichte* 13 (1974/75): 222–46.

———. "Erudição, espírito crítico e acribia na *História do futuro* de António Vieira." *Revista da Faculdade de Filosofia, Ciencias e Letras de Marília* (1976): 45–79.

———. "L'histoire du texte de l'*História do futuro* du père António Vieira." *Actes du 13e Congrès Internationale de Linguistique et Philologie Romanes*, 1971. Vol. 2 (Quebec, 1976): 703–8.

———. *António Vieira: o homen, a obra, as ideias*. Lisbon: Instituto de Cultura e Língua Portuguesa, 1981.

———. *Mauricio de Nassau, esse desconhecido*. Rio de Janeiro: Fundação de Amparo à Pesquisa do Estado do Rio de Janeiro, 1982.

———. *O sebastianismo: história sumária*. Lisbon: Instituto de Cultura e Língua Portuguesa, 1987.

Betendorf, João Felipe. *Chronica da missão dos padres da Companhia de Jesus no estado do Maranhão*. In *Revista do Instituto Histórico e Geográphico Brasileiro* 72, part 1, 1909.

Boff, Leonardo. *Jesus Christ Liberator*. Maryknoll, N.Y.: Orbis Books, 1978.

Bosi, Alfredo. *Dialética da colonização*. São Paulo: Companhia das Letras, 1992.

Boxer, Charles Ralph. "António Vieira, S.J., and the Institution of the Brazil Company in 1649." *Hispanic American Historical Review* 29:4 (November 1949): 474–97.

———. *Salvador de Sá and the Struggle for Brazil and Angola, 1602–1686*. London: Athlone Press, 1952.

————. *A Great Luso-Brazilian Figure: Pe. António Vieira.* London: Hispanic and Luso-Brazilian Councils, 1957.

————. *The Portuguese Seaborn Empire.* London: Hutchinson, 1969.

————. *The Dutch in Brazil, 1624–54.* 2d ed. Hamden, CT: Archon Books, 1973.

————. *The Church Militant and Iberian Expansion, 1440–1770.* Baltimore: Johns Hopkins University Press, 1978.

Braga, Theophilo. *História de Camões.* 2 vols. Porto: Imprensa Portugueza, 1873–74.

[Brandão, Ambrósio Fernandes]. *Diálogos das grandezas do Brasil.* Edited by Rodolfo Garcia. São Paulo: Melhoramentos, 1977.

Brown, Peter. "St. Augustine's Attitude to Religious Coercion." *Journal of Roman Studies* 54 (1964): 107–16.

Cantel, Raymond. "Ouvide et les sermons du père António Vieira." *Bulletin des Etudes Portugaises* 18 (1954): 84–92.

————. *Les sermons de Vieira: étude du style.* Paris: Ediciones Hispano-Americanas, 1959.

————. *Prophétisme et messianisme dans l'oeuvre d'António Vieira.* Paris: Ediciones Hispano-Americanas, 1960.

————. "*L'História do futuro* du père António Vieira: réflexions sur la genèse de l'oeuvre et les différents moments de sa composition." *Bulletin des Etudes Portugaises* 25 (1964): 23–49.

Cardoso, George. *Agiologio lusitano dos sanctos, e varões illustres do reino de Portugal e suas conquistas.* 4 vols. Vol. 4 compiled by D. António Caetano de Sousa. Lisbon: na Officina Craesbeekiana, 1652–1744.

Caxa, Quirício. "Breve relação da vida e morte do Pe. José de Anchieta." Edited by Serafim Leite. *Brotéria* 18 (1934): 165–74, 253–65. Reprinted in Leite, *Novas páginas,* 147–84.

Chrysostom, John. *De Anna sermones 1-5.* In *Patrologia Graeca,* edited by J. P. Migne, vol. 55, cols. 631–76. Paris: J. P. Migne, 1862.

Cidade, Hernani, ed. *Padre António Vieira.* 4 vols. Lisbon: Agência Geral das Colónias, 1940.

Cintra, Luís Filipe Lindley. "Sobre a formação e evolução da lenda de Ourique (até a Crónica de 1419)." In *Miscelanea de estudos em honra do professor H. Cidade,* 168–215. Lisbon: Universidade de Lisboa, Faculdade de Letras, 1957.

Coffin, William Sloane. *Sermons from Riverside, November 6, 1977–November 29, 1987.* New York: Publications Office, Riverside Church, 1977–87.

Collins, John J. "The Court-Tales in Daniel and the Development of Apocalyptic." *Journal of Biblical Literature* 94 (1975): 218–34.

Corpo diplomatico português. Vols. 12–15. Lisbon: Typographia da Academia Real das Sciências, 1902–59.

Couto, Diogo do. *O soldado prático.* 3d ed. Edited by M. Rodrigues Lapa. Lisbon: Livraria Sá da Costa Editora, 1980.

Cruz, Sor Juana Inés de la. *Carta atenagórica. Carta de la Madre Juana Inés de la Cruz, religiosa del convento de San Jerónimo de la ciudad de Méjico, en que hace juicio de un sermón del Mandato que predicó el Reverendísimo P. António de Viey-

ra, de la Compañía de Jesus, en el Colegio de Lisboa. In *Obras completas,* 2d ed. Vol. 4. Edited by Alberto G. Salceda, 412–39. Mexico City: Fondo de Cultura Económica, 1976.

Davies, P. R. "Daniel, Chapter Two." *Journal of Theological Studies,* new ser., 27 (1976): 302–401.

Drury, John. *Luke.* New York: Macmillan, 1973.

Dussel, Enrique. "Theologies of the 'Periphery' and the 'Centre': Encounter or Confrontation?" In *Different Theologies, Common Responsibility: Babel or Pentecost?* Edited by Virgil Elizondo, Claude Geffré, and Gustavo Gutierrez, 87–97. Edinburgh: T. and T. Clark, 1984.

Edmundson, George, Rev. "The Voyage of Pedro Teixeira on the Amazon from Pará to Quito and Back, 1637–39." *Transactions of the Royal Historical Society,* 4th ser., no. 3 (London, 1920): 52–71.

Evennett, H. Outram. *The Spirit of the Counter-Reformation.* Notre Dame: University of Notre Dame Press, 1970.

França, Eduardo d'Oliveira. *Portugal na época da Restauração.* São Paulo: n.p., 1951.

Franco, António. *Imagem da virtude em o noviciado da Companhia de Jesus no Real Collegio de Jesus de Coimbra.* Vol. 1, Evora: na Officina da Universidade, 1719. Vol. 2, Coimbra: no Real Collegio das Artes da Companhia de Jesus, 1719.

Freyre, Gilberto. *The Masters and the Slaves: Casa-Grande and Senzala.* Translated by Samuel Putnam. New York: Alfred A. Knopf, 1956.

Fritz, Samuel. *Journal of the Travels and Labours of Father Samuel Fritz in the River of the Amazons between 1686 and 1723.* Edited by George Edmundson. London: Hakluyt Society, 1922.

Funkenstein, Amos. *Theology and the Scientific Imagination from the Middle Ages to the Seventeenth Century.* Princeton: Princeton University Press, 1986.

Gammie, John G. "The Classification, Stages of Growth, and Changing Intentions in the Book of Daniel." *Journal of Biblical Literature* 95/2 (1976): 191–204.

———. "On the Intention and Sources of Daniel 1–6." *Vetus Testamentum* 31, no. 3 (1981): 282–92.

Gracián, Baltasar. *Agudeza y arte de ingenio* [1648]. 2d ed. Buenos Aires: Espasa-Calpe, 1944.

Graham, Richard. *The Jesuit António Vieira and His Plans for the Economic Rehabilitation of Seventeenth-Century Portugal.* São Paulo: Arquivo do Estado de São Paulo, 1978.

Guibert, Joseph de. *The Jesuits: Their Spiritual Doctrine and Practice.* St. Louis: Institute of Jesuit Sources, 1972.

Guy, Jean-Claude. *Unité et structure logique de la Cité de Dieu de Saint Augustin.* Paris: Etudes Augustiniennes, 1961.

Haubert, Maxime. *L'Eglise et la défense des sauvages: le père Antoine Vieira au Brésil.* Brussels: Académie Royale des Sciences d'Outre-Mer, 1964.

Hemming, John. *Red Gold: The Conquest of the Brazilian Indians, 1500–1760.* Cambridge: Harvard University Press, 1978.

————. *Amazon Frontier: The Defeat of the Brazilian Indians.* Cambridge: Harvard University Press, 1987.

————. "Indians and the Frontier in Colonial Brazil." In *The Cambridge History of Latin America*, vol. 2, *Colonial Latin America*, edited by Leslie Bethell, 501–45. Cambridge: Cambridge University Press, 1984.

Hespanha, António Manuel. *As vésperas do Leviathan: instituições e poder político. Portugal—séc. XVII.* Coimbra: Livraria Almedina, 1994.

Holanda, Sérgio Buarque de. *Visão do paraíso: os motivos edênicos no descobrimento e colonização do Brasil.* 3d ed. São Paulo: Companhia Editora Nacional, 1977.

————. *Raízes do Brasil.* 14th ed. Rio de Janeiro: Livraria José Olympio, 1981.

————. *História geral da civilização brasileira.* Vol. 1, *A época colonial.* 7th ed. São Paulo: Difel, 1985.

Ignatius of Loyola. *Monumenta Ignatiana. Sancti Ignatii de Loyola Societatis Jesu fundatoris epistolae et instructones.* 12 vols. Madrid: Typis G. Lopez del Horno, 1903–11.

————. *Monumenta Ignatiana. Sancti Ignatii de Loyola Constitutiones Societatis Jesu.* 3 vols. Rome: Monumenta Historica Societatis Iesu, 1934–38.

————. *Monumenta Ignatiana. Exercitia spiritualia S. Ignatii de Loyola et eorum directoria.* 2d ed., rev. 2 vols. Rome: Institutum Historicum Societatis Iesu, 1969.

————. *The Constitutions of the Society of Jesus.* Edited by George E. Ganss. St. Louis: Institute of Jesuit Sources, 1970.

————. *Ignatius of Loyola: The Spiritual Exercises and Selected Works.* Edited by George E. Ganss. New York: Paulist Press, 1991.

Joly, Robert. "S. Augustin et l'intolérance religieuse." *Revue Belge de Philologie et d'Histoire* 23 (1955): 263–94.

Kayserling, Meyer. *História dos judeus em Portugal.* Translated by Anita Novinsky. São Paulo: Livraria Pioneira, 1971.

Kiemen, Mathias. *The Indian Policy of Portugal in the Amazon Region, 1614–1693.* Washington, D.C.: The Catholic University of America Press, 1954.

Lacocque, André. *The Book of Daniel.* Atlanta: John Knox Press, 1979.

Leite, Serafim. *História da Companhia de Jesus no Brasil [HCJB].* 10 vols. Lisbon: Livraria Portugal; Rio de Janeiro: Civilização Brasileira, 1938–43.

————. *Luiz Figueira: a sua vida heróica e a sua obra literária.* Lisbon: Agência Geral das Colónias, 1940.

————. *Novas cartas jesuíticas: de Nóbrega a Vieira.* São Paulo: Companhia Editora Nacional, 1940.

————. "O Pe. António Vieira e as ciências sacras no Brasil." *Verbum* 1, no. 3 (1944): 257–59.

————. *Artes e ofícios dos jesuítas no Brasil (1549–1760).* Lisbon: Edições Brotéria; Rio de Janeiro: Livros de Portugal, 1953.

————. *Nóbrega e a fundação de São Paulo.* Lisbon: Instituto de Intercâmbio Luso-Brasileiro, 1953.

————. *Breve itinerário para uma biografia do P. Manuel da Nóbrega.* Lisbon: Edições Brotéria; Rio de Janeiro: Livros de Portugal, 1955.

————. *Novas paginas de história do Brasil.* São Paulo: Companhia Editora Nacional, 1965.

Léry, Jean de. *History of a Voyage to the Land of Brazil, Otherwise Called America* [1578]. Edited and translated by Janet Whatley. Berkeley: University of California Press, 1990.

Liberman, Maria. *O levante do Maranhão: "judeu cabeça do motim."* São Paulo: FFLCH/USP, Centro de Estudos Judaicos, 1983.

Lins, Ivan. *Aspectos do padre António Vieira.* Rio de Janeiro: Livraria São José, 1962.

Lisboa, João Francisco [1858]. *Jornal de Timon e vida do padre António Vieira.* Rio de Janeiro: Editora de Ouro, 1968.

Lobo, D. Francisco Alexandre. *Memoria histórica e crítica acerca do padre António Vieira e das suas obras.* Vizeu: Imprensa da Revista Católica, 1897.

Lourenço, Eduardo. *O labirinto da saudade.* 3d ed. Lisbon: Publicações Dom Quixote, 1988.

MacCormack, Sabine. "António de la Calancha: un agustino del siglo XVII en el Nuevo Mundo." *Bulletin Hispanique* 84, nos. 1–2 (1982): 60–94.

————. "Christ and Empire, Time and Ceremonial in Sixth-Century Byzantium and Beyond." *Byzantion* 52 (Brussels, 1982): 287–309.

————. "'The Heart Has Its Reasons': Predicaments of Missionary Christianity in Early Colonial Peru." *Hispanic American Historical Review* 65, no. 3 (August 1985): 443–66.

————. "Pachacuti: Miracles, Punishments, and Last Judgment: Visionary Past and Prophetic Future in Early Colonial Peru." *American Historical Review* 93, no. 4 (October 1988): 960–1006.

————. *Religion in the Andes: Vision and Imagination in Early Colonial Peru.* Princeton: Princeton University Press, 1991.

Markus, R. A. *Saeculum: History and Society in the Theology of St. Augustine.* Cambridge: Cambridge University Press, 1970.

Marques, João Francisco. *A parenética portuguesa e a dominação filipina.* Porto: Instituto Nacional de Investigação Científica, 1986.

————. *A parenética portuguesa e a Restauração, 1640–1668: a revolta e a mentalidade.* 2 vols. Porto: Instituto Nacional de Investigação Científica, 1989.

Méchoulan, Henri. "Révélation, rationalité et prophétie: quelques remarques sur le livre de Daniel." *Revue des Sciences Philosophiques et Théologiques* 64, no. 1 (1980): 363–71.

Mello Moraes, Alexandre J. de. *Corografia histórica, cronografica, genealogica, nobiliaria e política do Império do Brasil.* 4 vols. Rio de Janeiro: Typographia Americana de J. Soares de Pinho, 1858–63.

Menasseh ben Israel. *The Hope of Israel* [1650]. Edited by H. Méchoulan and G. Nahon. New York: Oxford University Press, 1987.

Mendieta, Gerónimo de. *História ecclesiastica indiana.* 3d ed. Edited by Joaquín García Icazbalceta. Mexico City: Porrúa, 1980.

Meneses, Luis de [Conde da Ericeira]. *História de Portugal restaurado*. Edited by A. Alvaro Dória. 4 vols. Porto: Livraria Civilização, 1946.

Merquior, José Guilherme. *De Anchieta a Euclides: breve história da literatura brasileira—1*. 2d ed. Rio de Janeiro: Livraria José Olympio, 1979.

Momigliano, Arnaldo. *Pagans, Christians, and Jews*. Middletown, CT: Wesleyan University Press, 1987.

Monumenta brasiliae. 5 vols. Rome: Monumenta Historica Societatis Iesu, 1956–58.

Moraes, P. José de, S.J. *História da Companhia de Jesus na vice-provincia do Maranhão e Pará*. Edited by Candido Mendes de Almeida. In *Memorias para a história do extincto estado do Maranhão*, vol. 1. Rio de Janeiro: Typographia do Commercio, de Brito e Braga, 1860.

Morse, Richard M. *The Bandeirantes: The Historical Role of the Brazilian Pathfinders*. New York: Alfred A. Knopf, 1965.

———. *El espejo de Próspero: un estudio de la dialéctica del Nuevo Mundo*. Mexico City: Siglo Veintiuno Editores, 1982.

Muhana, Adma. *Os autos do processo de Vieira na Inquisição*. São Paulo: Editora da Universidade Estadual Paulista; Salvador, Bahia: Fundação Cultural do Estado da Bahia, 1995.

Murdoch, Iris. *The Black Prince*. Harmondsworth: Penguin, 1975.

Nemesio, Vitorino. *O campo de São Paulo: A Companhia de Jesus e o plano português do Brasil (1528–1563)*. Lisbon: Comissão do IV Centenário da Fundação de São Paulo, 1954.

Nóbrega, P. Manuel da. *Cartas do Brasil e mais escritos do P. Manuel da Nóbrega*. Edited by Serafim Leite. Coimbra: Universidade de Coimbra, 1955.

———. *Diálogo sobre a conversão do gentio*. Edited by Serafim Leite. Lisbon, 1954. First published in *Revista do Instituto Histórico e Geográfico Brasileiro*, 1880, 43, pt. 1, pp. 133–152.

Oliveira, António de. *Poder e oposição política em Portugal no período filipino (1580–1640)*. Lisbon: Difel, 1990.

O'Malley, John W. *The First Jesuits*. Cambridge: Harvard University Press, 1993.

———. "Preaching." In *Encyclopedia of Jesuit History*, ed. Joaquín Domínguez, S.J. Rome: Institutum Historicum Societatis Iesu. Forthcoming.

Pagden, Anthony. *The Fall of Natural Man: The American Indian and the Origins of Comparative Ethnology*. Cambridge: Cambridge University Press, 1982.

Palacin, Luís. *Vieira e a visão trágica do barroco: quatro estudos sobre a consciência possível*. São Paulo: Editora Hucitecs, 1986.

Paz, Octavio. *Sor Juana Inés de la Cruz o las trampas de la fé*. 3d ed. Barcelona: Seix Barral, 1989.

Pécora, António Alcir Bernárdez. *Teatro do sacramento: a unidade teológico-retórico-política dos sermões de António Vieira*. São Paulo: Edusp; Campinas: Editora da da Unicamp, 1994.

Porteous, Norman. *Daniel: A Commentary*. London: Westminster Press, 1969.

Reis, Artur Cézar Ferreira. *História do Amazonas*. Manaus: Officinas Typographicas de A. Reis, 1931.

————, ed. *Livro grosso do Maranhão*. In *Anais da Biblioteca Nacional*, 66, pt. 1. Rio de Janeiro, 1948.

Ricard, Robert. "Les jésuites au Brésil pendant la seconde moitié du XVIe siècle." *Revue d'histoire des missions* 3 (Sept. 1937): 321–66; 4 (Dec. 1937): 435–70.

————. "Prophecy and Messianism in the Works of António Vieira." *The Americas* 37 (1960): 357–68.

————. "António Vieira et Sor Juana Inés de la Cruz." *Bulletin des Etudes Portugaises*, t. 12 (1948): 1–34.

Rodrigues, Francisco. "O P. António Vieira: contradicções e applausos (à luz de documentação inédita)." *Revista de História* 11 (1922): 80–115.

————. *História da Companhia de Jesus na assistencia de Portugal*. 4 vols. in 7. Porto: Apostolado da Imprensa, 1931–50.

Rodrigues, José Honorio. "António Vieira, doutrinador do imperialismo português." *Kriterion: Revista da Faculdade de Filosofia de Minas Gerais*, no. 61–62 (1962): 628–51.

Russell-Wood, A. J. R. "United States Scholarly Contributions to the Historiography of Colonial Brazil." *Hispanic American Historical Review* 65, no. 4 (Nov. 1985): 683–723.

Saraiva, António José. "António Vieira, Menasseh ben Israel, et le cinquième empire." *Studia Rosenthaliana* 6, no. 1 (1972): 25–57.

————. *O discurso engenhoso*. São Paulo: Editora Perspectiva, 1980.

Schwartz, Stuart B. "Luso-Spanish Relations in Habsburg Brazil, 1580–1640." *The Americas* 25 (1968): 33–48.

————. *Sugar Plantations and the Formation of Brazilian Society: Bahia, 1550–1835*. Cambridge: Cambridge University Press, 1985.

————. "The Formation of a Colonial Identity in Brazil." In *Colonial Identity in the Atlantic World, 1500–1800*, edited by Anthony Pagden and Nicholas Canny, 15–50. Princeton: Princeton University Press, 1987.

————. "The Voyage of the Vassals: Royal Power, Noble Obligations, and Merchant Capital Before the Portuguese Restoration of Independence, 1624–1640." *American Historical Review* 96, no. 3 (June 1991): 735–62.

Silva Dias, J. S. da. *Correntes do sentimento religioso em Portugal*. Coimbra: Universidade de Coimbra, 1960.

————. *Os descobrimentos e a problematica cultural do século XVI*. Coimbra: Universidade de Coimbra, 1973.

Smith, David Grant. *The Mercantile Class of Portugal and Brazil in the Seventeenth Century: A Socioeconomic Study of the Merchants of Lisbon and Bahia*. Ph.D. dissertation, University of Texas, Austin, 1975.

Smith, Hilary Dansey. *Preaching in the Spanish Golden Age: A Study of Some Preachers of the Reign of Philip III*. New York: Oxford University Press, 1978.

Spence, Jonathan. *The Memory Palace of Matteo Ricci*. New York: Viking Penguin, 1985.

Studart, Barão de, ed. *Documentos para a história do Brasil e especialmente a do Ceará*. 4 vols. Fortaleza: Typographia Minerva, 1904–21.

Sturm, Fred Gillette. "'Estes têm alma como nós?' Manuel da Nóbrega's View of the Brazilian Indians." In *Empire in Transition: The Portuguese World in the Time of Camões*, edited by Alfred Hower and Richard A. Preto-Rodas, 72–82. Gainesville: University of Florida Press, 1985.

Sweet, David Graham. "A Rich Realm of Nature Destroyed: The Middle Amazon Valley, 1640–1750." Ph.D. dissertation, University of Wisconsin, Madison, 1974.

Taunay, Affonso de E. *História das bandeiras paulistas*. 2d ed. 3 vols. São Paulo: Melhoramentos, 1961.

Tenenbaum, Barbara, ed. *Scribner's Encyclopedia of Latin American History*. 5 vols. New York: Macmillan, 1995.

Thompson, Colin. *The Strife of Tongues: Fray Luís de Leon and the Golden Age of Spain*. Cambridge: Cambridge University Press, 1988.

Torgal, Luis Reis. *Ideología política e teoria do estado na Restauração*. 2 vols. Coimbra: Biblioteca Geral da Universidade, 1981–82.

Turner, Victor. "Betwixt and Between: The Liminal Period in Rites of Passage." *Proceedings of the Annual Spring Meeting of the American Ethnological Society for 1964* (Seattle: University of Washington Press, 1964): 4–20.

Valente, Vasco Pulido. "A sociedade, o estado e a história na obra de António Vieira (para a história da filosofia política em Portugal no século XVII." In *Estudos sobre a crise nacional* (Lisbon: Imprensa Nacional—Casa da Moeda, 1980), 95–240.

Varnhagen, Francisco Adolfo de. *História geral do Brasil*. 10th ed. 5 vols. in 3. Belo Horizonte: Editora Itatiaia; São Paulo: Universidade de São Paulo, 1981.

Vasconcelos, Simão de. *Crônica da Companhia de Jesus* [1663]. 4th ed. 2 vols. Petrópolis: Editora Vozes, 1977.

———. *Vida do veneravel Padre José de Anchieta*. Lisbon, na Officina de Ioam da Costa, 1672.

Vieira, António. *História do futuro*. Edited by João Lúcio de Azevedo. In *Boletim da Segunda Clase da Academia das Sciências de Lisboa* 12:1 (1917–18), 110–247.

———. *Cartas do padre António Vieira*. Edited by João Lúcio de Azevedo. 3 vols. Coimbra: Imprensa da Universidade, 1925–28.

———. *Sermões*. 16 vols. São Paulo: Editora Anchieta, 1943–45. Facsimile of first edition.

———. *Obras escolhidas*. Edited by Hernani Cidade and António Sérgio. 12 vols. Lisbon: Livraria Sá da Costa Editora, 1951–54.

———. *Defesa perante o tribunal do santo ofício*. Edited by Hernani Cidade. 2 vols. Salvador, Bahia: Publicações da Universidade da Bahia, 1957.

———. *Livro anteprimeiro da história do futuro*. Edited by José van den Besselaar. 2 vols. Munster: Aschendorffsche Verlagsbuchhandlung, 1976.

———. *História do futuro*. Edited by Maria Leonor Carvalhão Buescu. Lisbon: Imprensa Nacional—Casa da Moeda, 1982.

———. *Apologia das coisas profetizadas*. Edited by Adma Muhana. Lisbon: Edições Cotovia, 1994.

————. A *arte de morrer: os sermões de quarta-feira de cinza de António Vieira*. Edited by Alcir Pécora. São Paulo: Nova Alexandria, 1994.

Vieira Mendes, Margarida. *A oratória barroca de António Vieira*. Lisbon: Editorial Caminho, 1989.

————. "Vieira no Cabo de Não: os descobrimentos no *Livro Anteprimeiro da história do futuro*." *Claro-Escuro* 6–7 (1991), 9–20.

————. "Comportamento profético e comportamento retórico em Vieira." In *Actas do I Congresso Internacional do Barroco*, 2: 59–71. 2 vols. Porto: Reitoria da Universidade do Porto; Governo Civil do Porto, 1991.

Xavier, Francis. *Epistolae S. Francisci Xavierii aliaque eius scripta*. Volume 2 (1549–1552). Edited by George Schurhammer, S.J., and Joseph Wicki, S.J. Rome: Monumenta Historica Societatis Iesu, 1945.

Index

In this index an "f" after a number indicates a separate reference on the next page, and an "ff" indicates separate references on the next two pages. A continuous discussion over two or more pages is indicated by a span of page numbers, e.g., "57–59." *Passim* is used for a cluster of references in close but not consecutive sequence.

Library of Congress Cataloging-in-Publication Data

Cohen, Thomas M.
    The fire of tongues : António Vieira and the missionary
church in Brazil and Portugal / Thomas M. Cohen.
        p.   cm.
    Includes bibliographical references and index.
    ISBN 0-8047-2907-7 (alk. paper)
    1. Vieira, António 1608–1697.   2. Missionaries—Brazil—
Biography.   3. Jesuits—Brazil—Biography.   4. Missionaries—
Portugal—Biography.   5. Jesuits—Portugal—Biography.
I. Title.

BV3705.V54C64   1998
266'.2'092—dc21   97-47357
                                                                        CIP

This book is printed on acid-free, recycled paper.

Original printing 1998
Last figure below indicates year of this printing:
07   06   05   04   03   02   01   00   99